RACING RULES OF SAILING 2021-2024

2021—2024
帆船竞赛规则

世界帆船运动联合会　编著
中国帆船帆板运动协会　审定

总编译：曲　春
翻　译：辛　婧　康　鹏　姜作濡
　　　　叶乔林　赵　群　孟淑霞
校　对：辛　婧　陈　琨

中国海洋大学出版社
· 青岛 ·

World Sailing

As the leading authority for the sport, World Sailing promotes and supports the protection of the environment in all sailing competitions and related activities throughout the world.

Contact Details for the World Sailing Executive Office:

World Sailing
20 Eastbourne Terrace
Paddington
London W2 6LG
UK

Telephone: + 44 (0)20 3940 4888
General Email: office@sailing.org
Racing Rules Email: rules@sailing.org

Website: **sailing.org**

Published by World Sailing (UK)Limited, London, UK

June 2020

世界帆船运动联合会

作为帆船运动的领导机构，世界帆联在全球所有帆船比赛和相关活动中推行并支持环境保护。

世界帆联执委会办公室联络信息：

世界帆联
伊斯特本街区 20 号
帕丁顿
伦敦 W2 6LG
英国

电话：+44（0）20 3940 4888
综合邮箱：office@sailing.org
竞赛规则邮箱：rules@sailing.org

网址：sailing.org

英国伦敦世界帆联(英国)有限公司出版

2020 年 6 月

CONTENTS

目 录

RACE SIGNALS

The meanings of visual and sound signals are stated below. An arrow pointing up or down (↑↓) means that a visual signal is displayed or removed. A dot (•) means a sound; five short dashes (-----) mean repetitive sounds; a long dash (—) means a long sound. When a visual signal is displayed over a class flag, fleet flag, event flag or race area flag, the signal applies only to that class, fleet, event or race area.

Postponement Signals

↑•• ↓•

AP Races not started are *postponed*. The warning signal will be made 1 minute after removal unless at that time the race is *postponed* again or *abandoned*.

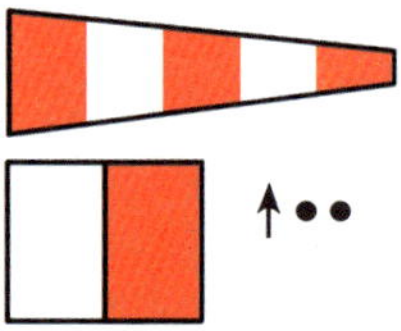

↑••

AP over H
Races not started are *postponed*. Further signals ashore.

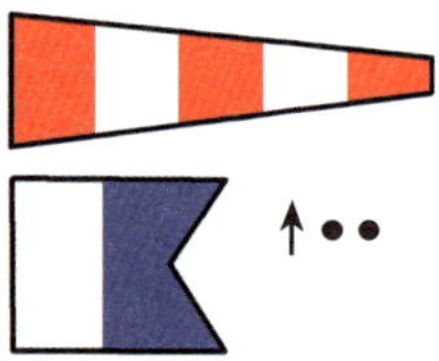

↑••

AP over A Races not started are *postponed*. No more racing today.

AP over a Numeral Pennant 1–9

Pennant 1 ↑•• ↓•

Pennant 2 ↑•• ↓•

Pennant 3 ↑•• ↓•

Pennant 4 ↑•• ↓•

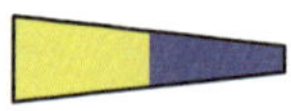

Pennant 5 ↑•• ↓•

Pennant 6 ↑•• ↓•

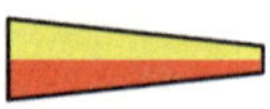

Pennant 7 ↑•• ↓•

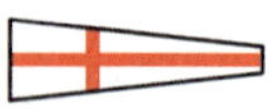

Pennant 8 ↑•• ↓•

Pennant 9 ↑•• ↓•

Postponement of 1–9 hours from the scheduled starting time.

竞赛信号

下面是对视觉和音响信号含义的说明。一个向上或向下指的箭头(↑ ↓)意为一个视觉信号的展示或移除。一个点(•)意为一声音响信号;5 个半字线(-----)意为重复的音响信号;一个一字线(—)意为一声长音响信号。当一个视觉信号在一面级别旗、组别旗、项目旗或竞赛区域旗之上展示时,该信号只适用于那个级别、组别、项目或竞赛区域。

推迟信号

↑•• ↓•

AP 旗:*推迟*未起航的竞赛。移除后 1 分钟发出预告信号,除非那时竞赛再次被*推迟*或*放弃*。

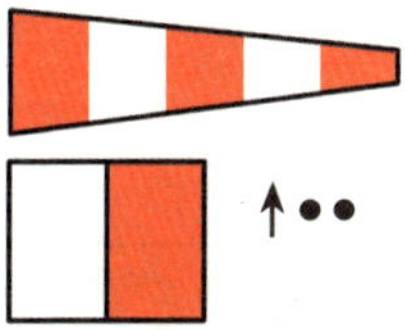

↑••

AP 旗在 H 旗之上:*推迟*未起航的竞赛。岸上等信号。

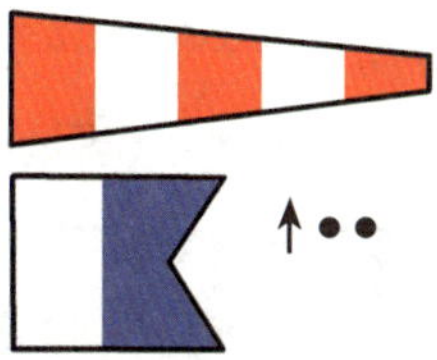

↑••

AP 旗在 A 旗之上:*推迟*未起航的竞赛。今天没有竞赛了。

AP 旗在 1 ~ 9 中一个数字的三角旗之上:

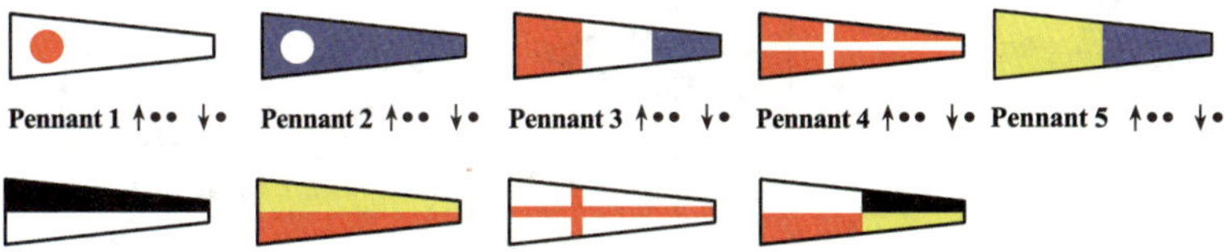

Pennant 1 ↑•• ↓• Pennant 2 ↑•• ↓• Pennant 3 ↑•• ↓• Pennant 4 ↑•• ↓• Pennant 5 ↑•• ↓•

Pennant 6 ↑•• ↓• Pennant 7 ↑•• ↓• Pennant 8 ↑•• ↓• Pennant 9 ↑•• ↓•

比排定的起航时间*推迟* 1 ~ 9 小时。

Abandonment Signals

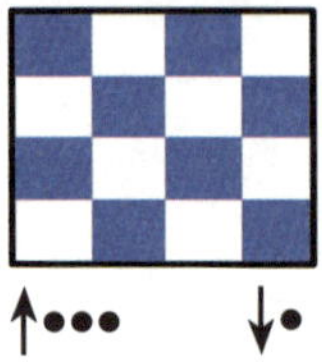

N All races that have started are *abandoned*. Return to the starting area. The warning signal will be made 1 minute after removal unless at that time the race is *abandoned* again or *postponed*.

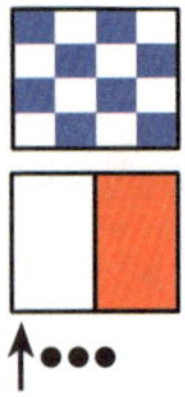

N over H All races are *abandoned*. Further signals ashore.

N over A All races are *abandoned*. No more racing today.

Safety

V Monitor communication channel for safety instructions (see rule 37).

Preparatory Signals

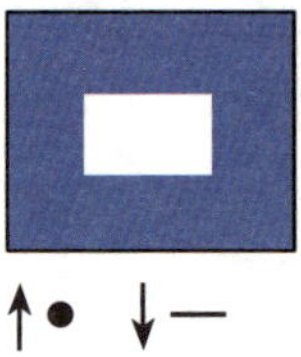

P Preparatory signal.

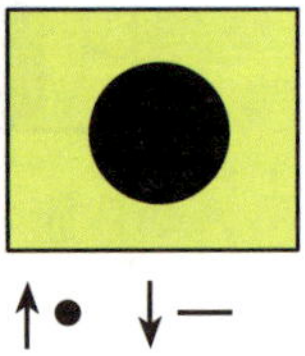

I Rule 30.1 is in effect.

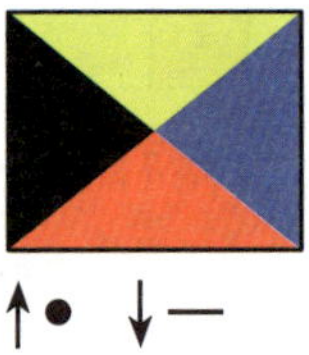

Z Rule 30.2 is in effect.

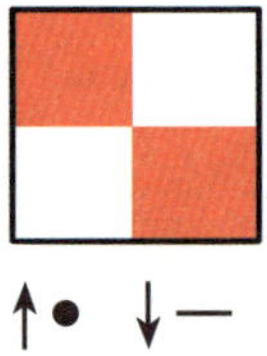

U Rule 30.3 is in effect.

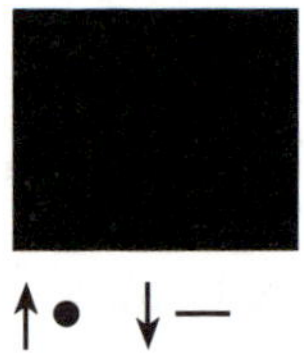

Black flag. Rule 30.4 is in effect.

Recall Signals

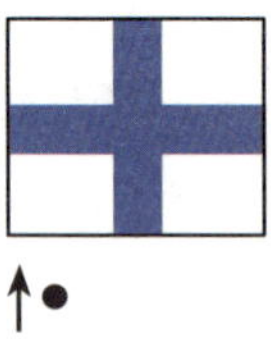

X Individual recall.

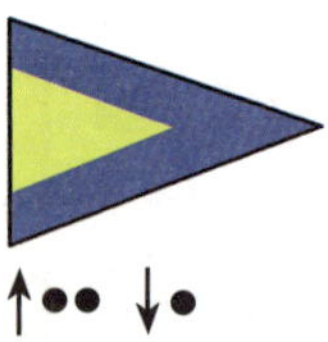

First Substitute General recall. The warning signal will be made 1 minute after removal.

Shortened Course

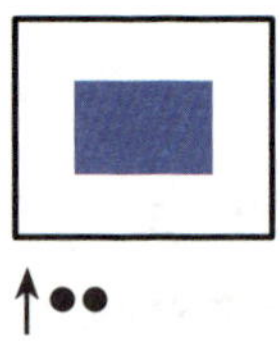

S The course has been shortened. Rule 32.2 is in effect.

放弃信号

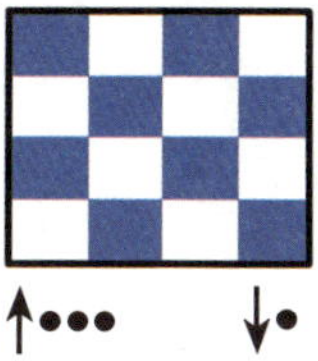

N 旗：*放弃*所有已起航的竞赛。回到起航区。移除后 1 分钟发出预告信号，除非那时竞赛再次被*放弃或推迟*。

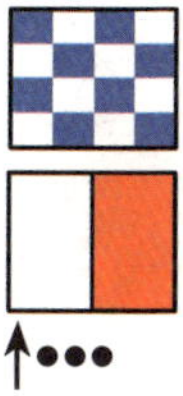

N 旗在 H 旗之上：*放弃*所有的竞赛，岸上等信号。

N 旗在 A 旗之上：*放弃*所有竞赛，今天没有竞赛了。

安全

V 旗：守听安全指令的通信频道（见规则 37）。

准备信号

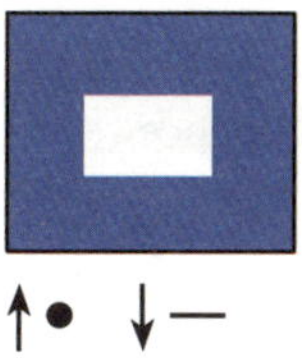

P 旗：准备信号。

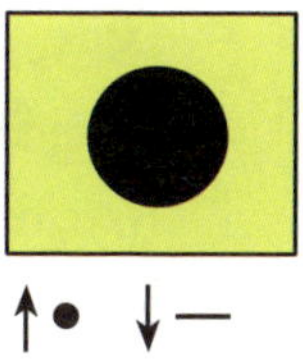

I 旗：规则 30.1 生效。

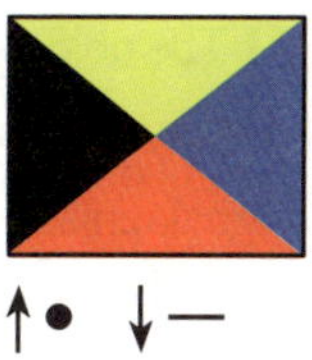

Z 旗：规则 30.2 生效。

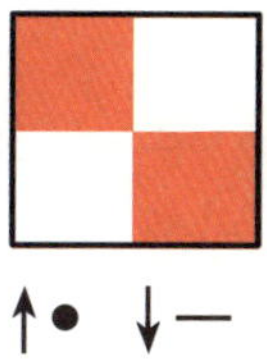

U 旗：规则 30.3 生效。

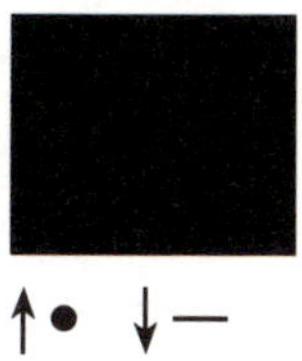

黑旗：规则 30.4 生效。

召回信号

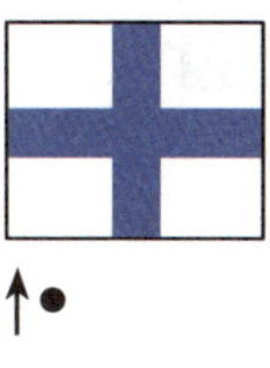

X 旗：个别召回。

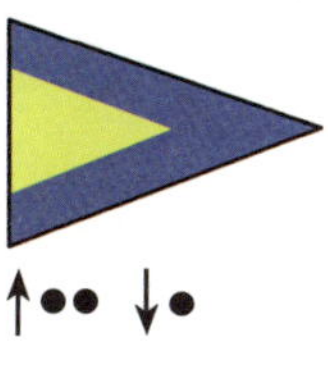

代一旗：全部召回。移除后 1 分钟发出预告信号。

缩短航线

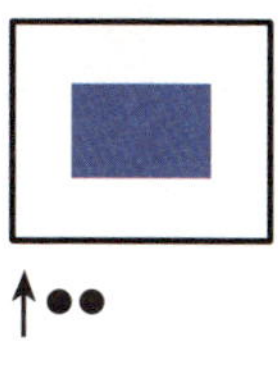

S 旗：缩短航线。规则 32.2 生效。

Changing the Next Leg

C The position of the next *mark* has been changed:

to starboard;

to port;

to decrease the length of the leg;

to increase the length of the leg.

Other Signals

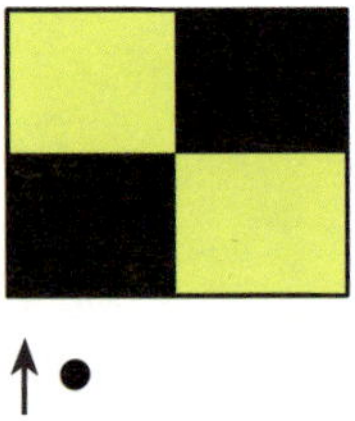

L Ashore: A notice to competitors has been posted. Afloat: Come within hail or follow this vessel.

M The object displaying this signal replaces a missing *mark*.

Y Wear a personal flotation device (see rule 40).

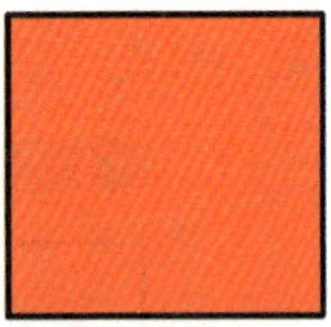

(no sound)

Orange flag. The staff displaying this flag is one end of the starting line.

(no sound)

Blue flag. The staff displaying this flag is one end of the finishing line.

改变下一个航段

C 旗：下一个标志的位置改变了：

向右边改变；

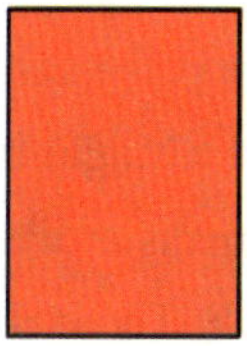

向左边改变；

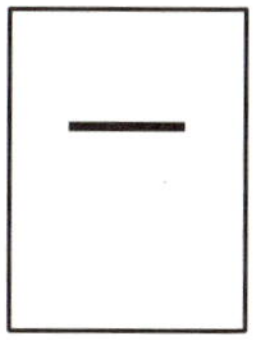

减小航段的长度；

增加航段的长度。

其他信号

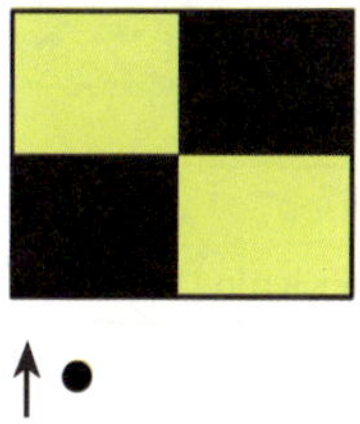

L 旗：在岸上展示：贴出了一个选手通知。在水上展示：靠近或跟随这条船。

M 旗：展示此信号的物体代替了一个丢失的标志。

Y 旗：穿戴个人助浮装备（见规则 40）。

（无音响）

橙旗：展示这面旗的旗杆是起航线的一端。

（无音响）

蓝旗：展示这面旗的旗杆是终点线的一端。

ONLINE RULES DOCUMENTS

World Sailing has established a single internet address at which readers will find links to all the documents available on the World Sailing website that are mentioned in this book. Those documents are listed below. Links to other rules documents will also be provided at that address.

The address is: **sailing.org/racingrules/documents**

Document	*Mentioned in*
Guidelines for discretionary penalties	Introduction
Changes made to these rules after 1 January 2021	Introduction
World Sailing Regulations	Introduction
The Case Book	Introduction
The Call Books for various disciplines	Introduction
World Sailing Regulations with the status of a *rule*	Definition Rule (b)
Interpretations of Rule 42, Propulsion	Rule 42
World Sailing Offshore Special Regulations	Rule 49.2
Equipment Rules of sailing	Rule 55
Appendix TS, Traffic Separation Schemes	Rule 56.2
Hearing Request and Hearing Decision Forms	Part 5 Preamble
Rules for other windsurfing competition formats	Appendix B Preamble
Standard Notice of Race for Match Racing	Appendix C Preamble
Standard Sailing Instructions for Match Racing	Appendix C Preamble
Match Racing Rules for Blind Competitors	Appendix C Preamble
Test Rules for Umpired Radio Sailing	Appendix E Preamble
Rules for other kiteboarding competition formats	Appendix F Preamble
Up-to-date table of national sail letters	Appendix G
Notice of Race Guide	Appendix K Notice
Sailing Instructions Guide	Appendix L Notice
Guidance on conflicts of interest	Appendix M2.3
Guidance on misconduct	Appendix M5.8
World Sailing Judges Manual	Appendix T Preamble

在线规则文件

世界帆联已经发布了独立的网络地址，读者可以在世界帆联的网站查找到这本书所有相关的文件。这些文件如下所列。其他规则的链接也将在此网络地址列出。

网址是：*sailing.org/racingrules/documents*

文件	*涉及章节*
自由裁量的判罚指南	导言
2021 年 1 月 1 日后对规则的更改	导言
世界帆联规章	导言
案例书	导言
各类竞赛项目*判例书*	导言
具有*规则*地位的世界帆联规章	定义规则(b)
规则 42，推进的解释	规则 42
世界帆联离岸赛特别规则	规则 49. 2
帆船器材规则	规则 55
附录 TS，分道通航制	规则 56. 2
审理要求和审理裁决表	第五章前言
其他帆板竞赛模式的规则	附录 B 前言
标准对抗赛竞赛通知	附录 C 前言
标准对抗赛航行细则	附录 C 前言
盲人选手的对抗赛规则	附录 C 前言
现场裁决的无线电遥控帆船竞赛测试版规则	附录 E 前言
其他风筝板竞赛模式的规则	附录 F 前言
最新版本的国家和地区代码表	附录 G
竞赛通知指南	附录 K 通知
航行细则指南	附录 L 通知
利益冲突的指南	附录 M2. 3
品行不端的指南	附录 M5. 8
世界帆联仲裁手册	附录 T 前言

INTRODUCTION

The Racing Rules of Sailing includes two main sections. The first, Parts 1–7, contains rules that affect all competitors. The second, the appendices, provides details of rules, rules that apply to particular kinds of racing, and rules that affect only a small number of competitors or officials.

Terminology A term used in the sense stated in the Definitions is printed in italics or, in preambles, in bold italics (for example, *racing* and ***racing***).

Each of the terms in the table below is used in *The Racing Rules of Sailing* with the meaning given.

Term	*Meaning*
Boat	A sailboat and the crew on board.
Competitor	A person who races or intends to race in the event.
National authority	A World Sailing member national authority.
Race committee	The race committee appointed under rule 89.2(c) and any other person or committee performing a race committee function.
Racing rule	A rule in *The Racing Rules of Sailing*.
Technical committee	The technical committee appointed under rule 89.2(c) and any other person or committee performing a technical committee function.
Vessel	Any boat or ship.

Other words and terms are used in the sense ordinarily understood in nautical or general use.

导　言

*《帆船竞赛规则》*包括两个主要部分。第一部分为1—7章，包含了与所有选手有关的规则。第二部分为附录部分，包含规则的细节、适用于特定竞赛形式的规则，以及只涉及少数选手或官员的规则。

术语：与定义中所述意义相同的术语用斜体印刷，在前言中用***粗斜体***印刷（例如：*竞赛*与***竞赛***）。

下表中的每一个术语都以其对应的含义在*《帆船竞赛规则》*中出现。

术语	*含义*
船	帆船及船上的人员。
选手	在赛事中参加竞赛或者打算参加竞赛的人。
国家和地区管理机构	世界帆联会员国家和地区管理机构。
竞赛委员会	根据规则89.2（c）任命的竞赛委员会以及其他任何履行竞赛委员会职能的个人或委员会。
竞赛规则	*《帆船竞赛规则》*中的规则。
技术委员会	根据规则89.2（c）任命的技术委员会以及其他任何履行技术委员会职能的个人或委员会。
船舶	任意船艇或者轮船。

其他的词语和术语按照其在航海和日常使用情况下的意义使用。

Hails A language other than English may be used for a hail required by the *rules* provided that it is reasonable for it to be understood by all boats affected. However, a hail in English is always acceptable.

Notation The notation '[DP]' in a *rule* means that the penalty for a breach of the *rule* may, at the discretion of the protest committee, be less than disqualification. Guidelines for discretionary penalties are available on the World Sailing website.

Revision The racing rules are revised and published every four years by World Sailing, the international authority for the sport. This edition becomes effective on 1 January 2021 except that for an event beginning in 2020 the date may be postponed by the notice of race or sailing instructions. Marginal markings indicate important changes to Parts 1–7 and the Definitions in the 2017–2020 edition. No changes are contemplated before 2025, but any changes determined to be urgent before then will be announced through national authorities and posted on the World Sailing website.

Appendices When the rules of an appendix apply, they take precedence over any conflicting rules in Parts 1–7 and the Definitions. Each appendix is identified by a letter. A reference to a rule in an appendix will contain the letter and the rule number (for example, 'rule A1'). The letters I, O and Q are not used to designate appendices in this book.

World Sailing Regulations The Regulations are referred to in the definition *Rule* and in rule 6, but they are not included in this book because they can be changed at any time. The most recent versions of the Regulations are published on the World Sailing website; new versions will be announced through national authorities.

Interpretations World Sailing publishes the following authoritative interpretations of the racing rules:

- *The Case Book – Interpretations of the Racing Rules*,

呼喊:*规则*中要求的呼喊可以使用英语以外的其他语言,前提是所有受影响的船都能理解该语言。但是,用英语呼喊总是可以接受的。

注释:*规则*中的注释标记"[DP]"表示抗议委员会对违反*规则*的行为做出的自由裁量的惩罚,可能会轻于取消资格。关于自由裁量的判罚指南可以在世界帆联网站上查询。

修订:本竞赛规则由帆船运动的国际管理机构——世界帆联负责每四年一次的修订和出版。除了 2020 年开始的被竞赛通知或航行细则推迟的赛事外,本版规则于 2021 年 1 月 1 日生效。页边标记表明该处是对 2017—2020 年版规则中 1—7 章和定义的重要修改。2025 年前无意对本规则进行修改,但在此之前被认定需紧急修改的地方将通过国家和地区管理机构公布,并在世界帆联网站发布。

附录:附录中的规则适用时,优先于1—7章和定义中任何与之冲突的规则。每个附录以一个字母为代码来识别。涉及某附录中某一条规则时要包含附录字母和规则号码(如:"规则A1")。字母I、O和Q在本书中不作为指定附录的字母。

世界帆联规章:规章在定义*规则*及规则 6 中被提及,但由于规章可随时更改,因此未包含在本书中。最近版本的规章发布在世界帆联网站上;新版本将通过国家和地区管理机构公布。

解释:世界帆联针对竞赛规则出版了以下权威解释:

- *案例书——竞赛规则的解释,*

- *The Call Books*, for various disciplines,
- Interpretations of Rule 42, Propulsion, and
- Interpretations of the Regulations, for those Regulations that are *rules.*

These publications are available on the World Sailing website. Other interpretations of the racing rules are not authoritative unless approved by World Sailing in accordance with Regulation 28.4.

- *判例书*,适用于各种不同的比赛项目,
- 规则 42,推进的解释,和
- 规章的解释,针对竞赛规则中那些同时是世界帆联规章的*规则*。

这些出版物可在世界帆联网站上查阅。其他对竞赛规则的解释,除非按照规章 28. 4 获得了世界帆联的批准,否则均被视为非权威解释。

DEFINITIONS

A term used as stated below is shown in italic type or, in preambles, in bold italic type. The meaning of several other terms is given in Terminology in the Introduction.

Abandon A race that a race committee or protest committee *abandons* is void but may be resailed.

Clear Astern and Clear Ahead; Overlap One boat is *clear astern* of another when her hull and equipment in normal position are behind a line abeam from the aftermost point of the other boat's hull and equipment in normal position. The other boat is *clear ahead*. They *overlap* when neither is *clear astern*. However, they also *overlap* when a boat between them *overlaps* both. These terms always apply to boats on the same *tack*. They apply to boats on opposite *tacks* only when rule 18 applies between them or when both boats are sailing more than ninety degrees from the true wind.

Conflict of Interest A person has a *conflict of interest* if he

(a) may gain or lose as a result of a decision to which he contributes,

(b) may reasonably appear to have a personal or financial interest which could affect his ability to be impartial, or

(c) has a close personal interest in a decision.

Fetching A boat is *fetching a mark* when she is in a position to pass to windward of it and leave it on the required side without changing *tack*.

Finish A boat *finishes* when, after *starting*, any part of her hull crosses the finishing line from the course side. However, she has not *finished* if after crossing the finishing line she

(a) takes a penalty under rule 44.2,

(b) corrects an error in *sailing the course* made at the line, or

定　义

下列术语将在本书中以斜体字出现或在前言中以粗斜体出现。其他一些术语的释义已经在导言中列举。

放弃　被竞赛委员会或抗议委员会*放弃*的一轮竞赛是无效的，但是可以重赛。

明显在后与明显在前；相联　当一条船的船体和其处于正常位置的器材位于另一条船船体和其处于正常位置的器材的最后一点的正横线之后，该船为*明显在后*。另一条船为*明显在前*。当没有任何一条船为*明显在后*时，她们为*相联*。但是，当她们中间有一条船跟她俩均*相联*时，这两条船也*相联*。这些术语总是适用于相同*舷风*的船。除非规则 18 适用或两船同真风风向的角度均大于 90 度，否则这些术语不适用于相对*舷风*的船。

利益冲突　一个人如果有以下情况，就有*利益冲突*：

(a) 所做的决定可能会导致其获利或损失，

(b) 可能会出现影响其保持公正能力的个人利益或经济利益，或者

(c) 在一个裁决中有密切的个人利益。

飞驰　船处于从一个*标志*上风通过并从规定的一侧离开此*标志*而无需换*舷*的位置时，即该船为正在*飞驰*此*标志*。

到达终点　当一条船在*起航*后，船体的任一部分从航线一侧越过终点线即为*到达终点*。但是，如果在越过终点线后她有如下情况，则为没有*到达终点*：

(a) 根据规则 44. 2 做解脱，

(b) 改正在终点线上犯的*行驶航线*的错误，或者

(c) continues to *sail the course*.

Keep Clear A boat *keeps clear* of a right-of-way boat

(a) if the right-of-way boat can sail her course with no need to take avoiding action and,

(b) when the boats are *overlapped*, if the right-of-way boat can also change course in both directions without immediately making contact.

Leeward and Windward A boat's *leeward* side is the side that is or, when she is head to wind, was away from the wind. However, when sailing by the lee or directly downwind, her *leeward* side is the side on which her mainsail lies. The other side is her *windward* side. When two boats on the same *tack overlap*, the one on the *leeward* side of the other is the *leeward* boat. The other is the *windward* boat.

Mark An object the sailing instructions require a boat to leave on a specified side, a race committee vessel surrounded by navigable water from which the starting or finishing line extends, and an object intentionally attached to the object or vessel. However, an anchor line is not part of the *mark*.

Mark-Room *Room* for a boat to leave a *mark* on the required side. Also,

(a) *room* to sail to the *mark* when her *proper course* is to sail close to it, and

(b) *room* to round or pass the *mark* as necessary to *sail the course* without touching the *mark*.

However, *mark-room* for a boat does not include *room* to tack unless she is *overlapped* inside and to *windward* of the boat required to give *mark-room* and she would be *fetching* the *mark* after her tack.

Obstruction An object that a boat could not pass without changing course substantially, if she were sailing directly towards it and one of her hull lengths from it. An object that can be safely passed on only one side and an object, area or line so designated by the sailing （c）继续*行驶航线*。

避让 如果符合以下条件，一条船就*避让*了一条航行权船：

（a）航行权船不需要采取躲避行动就可以行驶在其航线上，并且

（b）当两条船*相联*时，航行权船在两个方向上都能改变航线而不会立刻造成接触。

下风和上风 船的*下风*边就是离开风的那一边，她到正顶风时，就是此前离开风的那一边。但当背风（by the lee）航行或正顺风航行时，她的*下风*边就是其主帆所在的一边。另外一边为其*上风*边。当两条船同*舷风相联*时，处在一条船的*下风*边的船是*下风*船，这条船是*上风*船。

标志/标 航行细则规定一条船以其特定一侧驶离的物体，由可航行水域包围的、由此延伸出起航线或终点线的竞赛委员会船舶，以及有意附着在此物体或船舶上的物体。但是，锚绳不是*标志*的一部分。

绕标空间 一条船以其规定一侧驶离*标志*时所需的*空间*。也包括：

（a）当她的*正当航线*是需要驶近*标志*时，行驶到*标志*的*空间*，以及

（b）*行驶航线*而不碰*标*时所需要的绕行或通过*标志*的*空间*。

但是，对于一条船来说，*绕标空间*不包括其迎风换舷的*空间*，除非该船在需要给予她*绕标空间*的船的内侧和*上风*与之*相联*，而且在迎风换舷后该船将飞*驰该标志*。

障碍物 船正在直接驶向一个物体并且距其一倍船长时，若她不明显改变航线就不能通过的物体。只能从一侧安全通过的物体和航行细则中特指的物体、区域或线也可作为*障碍物*。但是，正

instructions are also *obstructions*. However, a boat *racing* is not an *obstruction* to other boats unless they are required to *keep clear* of her or, if rule 22 applies, avoid her. A vessel under way, including a boat *racing*, is never a continuing *obstruction*.

Overlap See ***Clear Astern and Clear Ahead; Overlap.***

Party A *party* to a hearing is

(a) for a protest hearing: a protestor, a protestee;

(b) for a redress hearing: a boat requesting redress or for which redress is requested; a boat for which a hearing is called to consider redress under rule 60.3(b); a race committee acting under rule 60.2(b); a technical committee acting under rule 60.4(b);

(c) for a redress hearing under rule 62.1(a): the body alleged to have made an improper action or omission;

(d) a person against whom an allegation of a breach of rule 69.1(a) is made; a person presenting an allegation under rule 69.2(e)(1);

(e) a *support person* subject to a hearing under rule 60.3(d) or 69; any boat that person supports; a person appointed to present an allegation under rule 60.3(d).

However, the protest committee is never a *party*.

Postpone A *postponed* race is delayed before its scheduled start but may be started or *abandoned* later.

Proper Course A course a boat would choose in order to *sail the course* and *finish* as soon as possible in the absence of the other boats referred to in the rule using the term. A boat has no *proper course* before her starting signal.

在*竞赛*的船对其他船不构成*障碍物*，除非这些船需要*避让*她，或规则 22 适用时，躲避她。正在行驶的各种船舶，包括正在*竞赛*的船，永远不是连续*障碍物*。

相联 参见***明显在后和明显在前；相联***。

一方 （译者注：译文中本术语的复数形式以斜体或粗斜体“*各方*”表示）审理的一方，

（a）对于抗议审理，是抗议者，被抗议者；

（b）对于补偿审理，是提出补偿要求或被要求补偿的船；是根据规则 60.3（b）考虑补偿而为其召集审理的船；是按规则 60.2（b）行动的竞赛委员会；是按规则 60.4（b）行动的技术委员会；

（c）对于依规则 62.1（a）的补偿审理，是被指控有不当行为或疏漏的主体；

（d）是被指控违反规则 69.1（a）的人；是根据规则 69.2（e）（1）提出指控的人；

（e）是根据规则 60.3（d）或 69 接受审理的*后援人员*；是受该人员支持的船；是根据规则 60.3（d）被指定去指控违规过程的人。

但抗议委员会从来都不作为一方。

推迟 *推迟*的竞赛是在排定的起航前被延迟，但随后可以开始或*放弃*的竞赛。

正当航线 在使用该术语的规则中提到的其他船只不存在的前提下，选择去*行驶航线*并尽快*到达终点*的那条航线。船在起航信号前没有*正当航线*。

Protest An allegation made under rule 61.2 by a boat, a race committee, a technical committee or a protest committee that a boat has broken a *rule*.

Racing A boat is *racing* from her preparatory signal until she *finishes* and clears the finishing line and *marks* or retires, or until the race committee signals a general recall, *postponement* or *abandonment*.

Room The space a boat needs in the existing conditions, including space to comply with her obligations under the rules of Part 2 and rule 31, while manoeuvring promptly in a seamanlike way.

Rule

(a) The rules in this book, including the Definitions, Race Signals, Introduction, preambles and the rules of relevant appendices, but not titles;

(b) World Sailing Regulations that have been designated by World Sailing as having the status of a *rule* and are published on the World Sailing website;

(c) the prescriptions of the national authority, unless they are changed by the notice of race or sailing instructions in compliance with the national authority's prescription, if any, to rule 88.2;

(d) the class rules (for a boat racing under a handicap or rating system, the rules of that system are 'class rules');

(e) the notice of race;

(f) the sailing instructions; and

(g) any other documents that govern the event.

Sail the Course A boat *sails the course* provided that a string representing her track from the time she begins to approach the starting line from its prestart side to start until she *finishes*, when drawn taut,

抗议 由船、竞赛委员会、技术委员会或抗议委员会根据规则61.2所提出的关于某条船违反*规则*的指控。

竞赛 *竞赛*是指船从其准备信号开始直至她*到达终点*并完全离开终点线和*标志*或退出，或直至竞赛委员会发出全部召回、*推迟*或*放弃信号*。

空间 船在现有条件下以正常的方式快速进行航行操作所需的空间，包括履行规则第二章和规则31的义务所需要的空间。

规则

（a）本书中的规则，包括定义、竞赛信号、导言、各章前言和有关的附录规则，但不包括标题；

（b）被世界帆联指定为具有*规则*地位并发布在世界帆联网站上的世界帆联规章；

（c）国家和地区管理机构的规定，除非竞赛通知或航行细则对其做出了更改，此更改要符合国家和地区管理机构规定中针对规则88.2的规定（如果有的话）；

（d）级别规则（对于以让分或评级办法进行竞赛的船来说，该办法中的规则就是“级别规则”）；

（e）竞赛通知；

（f）航行细则；以及

（g）所有该赛事执行的其他文件。

行驶航线 只要代表船只从准备起航一侧靠近起航线去*起航*直至其*到达终点*的轨迹的那条线被拉紧时，满足以下条件，即为*行驶航线*：

(a) passes each *mark* of the course for the race on the required side and in the correct order,

(b) touches each *mark* designated in the sailing instructions to be a rounding *mark*, and

(c) passes between the *marks* of a gate from the direction of the course from the previous *mark*.

Start A boat *starts* when, her hull having been entirely on the pre-start side of the starting line at or after her starting signal, and having complied with rule 30.1 if it applies, any part of her hull crosses the starting line from the pre-start side to the course side.

Support Person Any person who

(a) provides, or may provide, physical or advisory support to a competitor, including any coach, trainer, manager, team staff, medic, paramedic or any other person working with, treating or assisting a competitor in or preparing for the competition, or

(b) is the parent or guardian of a competitor.

Tack, Starboard or Port A boat is on the *tack, starboard* or *port*, corresponding to her *windward* side.

Windward See ***Leeward and Windward***.

Zone The area around a *mark* within a distance of three hull lengths of the boat nearer to it. A boat is in the *zone* when any part of her hull is in the *zone*.

（a）从规定的一侧按照正确的顺序通过该轮竞赛航线的每个*标志*，

（b）触及航行细则中指定的每个绕行的*标志*，以及

（c）从上一个*标志*来的航线的方向，在两个门*标*之间通过。

起航 在起航信号发出时或发出后，船体完全位于起航线准备区一侧并且遵守了规则30.1（如果采用该规则），其船体的任何部分从起航准备区一侧向航线一侧越过起航线即为*起航*。

后援人员 满足以下条件的任何人：

（a）提供，或可以为选手提供有形的或咨询类的支持，包括教练、陪练、管理人员、后勤人员、医务人员、护理人员，或者其他与选手一起工作、治疗或协助选手做比赛准备工作的人员，或者

（b）选手的父母或者监护人。

舷风、右舷或左舷 船的*舷风边*、*右舷*或*左舷*是与其*上风边*一致的。

上风 参见***上风***和***下风***。

标区 离*标志*最近的船的3倍船长的*标志*周围区域。当船体的任何部分在此*标区*内即为该船在此*标区*内。

BASIC PRINCIPLES

SPORTSMANSHIP AND THE RULES

Competitors in the sport of sailing are governed by a body of *rules* that they are expected to follow and enforce. A fundamental principle of sportsmanship is that when a boat breaks a *rule* and is not exonerated she will promptly take an appropriate penalty or action, which may be to retire.

ENVIRONMENTAL RESPONSIBILITY

Participants are encouraged to minimize any adverse environmental impact of the sport of sailing.

基本原则

体育道德与规则

帆船运动选手要自觉遵守所执行的全部*规则*。体育道德的基本原则是当船违反某条*规则*并未被免责时应尽快接受恰当的惩罚或采取行动,这可能是退出竞赛。

环保责任

鼓励参与者将帆船运动对环境的不利影响最小化。

PART 1–FUNDAMENTAL RULES

1 SAFETY

1.1 Helping Those in Danger

A boat, competitor or *support person* shall give all possible help to any person or vessel in danger.

1.2 Life-Saving Equipment and Personal Flotation Devices

A boat shall carry adequate life-saving equipment for all persons on board, including one item ready for immediate use, unless her class rules make some other provision. Each competitor is individually responsible for wearing a personal flotation device adequate for the conditions.

2 FAIR SAILING

A boat and her owner shall compete in compliance with recognized principles of sportsmanship and fair play. A boat may be penalized under this rule only if it is clearly established that these principles have been violated. The penalty shall be a disqualification that is not excludable.

3 DECISION TO RACE

The responsibility for a boat's decision to participate in a race or to continue *racing* is hers alone.

4 ACCEPTANCE OF THE RULES

4.1

(a) By participating or intending to participate in an event conducted under the *rules*, each competitor and boat owner agrees to accept the *rules*.

(b) A *support person* by providing support, or a parent or guardian by permitting their child to enter an event, agrees to accept the *rules*.

第一章　基本规则

1 安全

1.1　援助处于危险中的船或人员

船、选手或*后援人员*须对处于危险中的任何人员或船舶给予一切尽可能的援助。

1.2　救生器材和个人助浮装备

每条船须为船上所有的人员携带足够的救生器材，包括一件待命应急使用的设备，除非该船级别规则另有规定。穿用符合条件的个人助浮装备是每位选手的个人责任。

2 公平航行

船及其船东须按照公认的体育道德和公平竞赛的原则进行比赛。船只有在被清晰地确定违背了这些原则时方可因本规则受到惩罚。违反本规则的判罚须是不能去掉的取消资格（DNE）。

3 参赛的决定

决定是否参加竞赛或继续*竞赛*是该船自己的责任。

4 接受规则

4.1

（a）参加或准备参加执行*规则*的赛事，每位选手和船东即同意接受*规则*。

（b）*后援人员*提供支持，或父母和监护人允许其子女参加一场赛事，即同意接受*规则*。

4.2 Each competitor and boat owner agrees, on behalf of their *support persons*, that such *support persons* are bound by the *rules*.

4.3 Acceptance of the rules includes agreement

(a) to be governed by the *rules*;

(b) to accept the penalties imposed and other action taken under the *rules*, subject to the appeal and review procedures provided in them, as the final determination of any matter arising under the *rules*;

(c) with respect to any such determination, not to resort to any court of law or tribunal not provided for in the *rules*; and

(d) by each competitor and boat owner to ensure that their *support persons* are aware of the *rules*.

4.4 The person in charge of each boat shall ensure that all competitors in the crew and the boat's owner are aware of their responsibilities under this rule.

4.5 This rule may be changed by a prescription of the national authority of the venue.

5 RULES GOVERNING ORGANIZING AUTHORITIES AND OFFICIALS

The organizing authority, race committee, technical committee, protest commi ttee and other race officials shall be governed by the *rules* in the conduct and judging of the event.

6 WORLD SAILING REGULATIONS

6.1 Each competitor, boat owner and *support person* shall comply with the World Sailing Regulations that have been designated by World Sailing as having the status of a *rule*. These regulations as of 30 June 2020 are the World Sailing:

- Advertising Code
- Anti-Doping Code

4.2 每位选手和船东代表其*后援人员*同意这些*后援人员受规则*的约束。

4.3 接*受规则*包括同意：

(a) *受规则*的约束；

(b) 接受强制的判罚和其他根据*规则*采取的行动，包括其中所规定的上诉和审核程序的约束，作为由*规则*而生的任何问题的最终决议；

(c) 尊重任何诸如此类的决议，不诉诸*规则*中未规定的任何法院或特别法庭；同时

(d) 每位选手和船东要确保其*后援人员*都清楚了解*规则*。

4.4 船只负责人须确保该船的所有选手和船东了解在本条规则下他们要承担的责任。

4.5 本规则可以根据场馆所在地国家和地区管理机构的规定进行更改。

5 约束组织机构和竞赛官员的规则

在赛事的组织和执裁中，组织机构、竞赛委员会、技术委员会、抗议委员会和其他竞赛官员须*受规则*的约束。

6 世界帆联规章

6.1 每名选手、船东和*后援人员*须遵守世界帆联指定的具有*规则*地位的世界帆联规章。截至 2020 年 6 月 30 日，这些世界帆联的规章包括：

- 广告守则
- 反兴奋剂守则

- Betting and Anti-Corruption Code
- Disciplinary Code
- Eligibility Code
- Sailor Categorization Code

6.2 Rule 63.1 does not apply unless *protests* are permitted in the Regulation alleged to have been broken.

• 博彩和反腐败守则

• 纪律守则

• 资格法规

• 选手分类法规

6.2 除非涉嫌违反的规章允许*抗议*，否则规则 63.1 不适用。

PART 2–WHEN BOATS MEET

The rules of Part 2 apply between boats that are sailing in or near the racing area and intend to ***race****, are* ***racing****, or have been* ***racing****. However, a boat not* ***racing*** *shall not be penalized for breaking one of these rules, except rule 14 when the incident resulted in injury or serious damage, or rule 23.1.*

When a boat sailing under these rules meets a vessel that is not, she shall comply with the International Regulations for Preventing Collisions at Sea (IRPCAS) *or government right-of-way rules. If the notice of race so states, the rules of Part 2 are replaced by the right-of-way rules of the* IRPCAS *or by government right-of-way rules.*

SECTION A-RIGHT OF WAY

A boat has right of way over another boat when the other boat is required to ***keep clear*** *of her. However, some rules in Sections B, C and D limit the actions of a right-of-way boat.*

10 ON OPPOSITE TACKS

When boats are on opposite *tacks*, a *port-tack* boat shall *keep clear* of a *starboard-tack* boat.

11 ON THE SAME TACK, OVERLAPPED

When boats are on the same *tack* and *overlapped*, a *windward* boat shall *keep clear* of a *leeward* boat.

12 ON THE SAME TACK, NOT OVERLAPPED

When boats are on the same *tack* and not *overlapped*, a boat *clear astern* shall *keep clear* of a boat *clear ahead*.

13 WHILE TACKING

After a boat passes head to wind, she shall *keep clear* of other boats until she is on a close-hauled course. During that time

第二章　船只相遇时

*第二章的规则适用于在竞赛场地区域内或场地区域附近航行及准备**竞赛**、正在**竞赛**或一直在**竞赛**的船之间。然而，除了事件造成受伤或者严重损坏时的规则14，或除规则23.1外，不参加**竞赛**的船不得因违反这些规则中的某一条而受到惩罚。*

一条按照这些规则航行的船与一艘未按这些规则航行的船舶相遇时，须遵守《国际海上避碰规则（IRPCAS）》或航行权的政府规定。如果竞赛通知中做出了这样的说明，那么，IRPCAS或航行权的政府规定将替代第二章的规则。

A节　航行权

*当另一条船需要**避让**这一条船时，这条船对另一条船拥有航行权。但是，B节、C节和D节中的部分规则对航行权船的行为有所限制。*

10　相对舷风

当船相对*舷风*行驶时，*左舷*船须*避让右舷*船。

11　同舷风、相联

当船同*舷风相联*行驶时，*上风*船须*避让下风*船。

12　同舷风、不相联

当船同*舷风*但不*相联*时，*明显在后*的船须*避让明显在前*的船。

13　迎风换舷时

一条船越过正顶风后，在行驶至近迎风航线上之前，须*避让*其他船。在这期间规则10、11和12不适用。如果两

rules 10, 11 and 12 do not apply. If two boats are subject to this rule at the same time, the one on the other's port side or the one astern shall *keep clear*.

SECTION B – GENERAL LIMITATIONS

14 AVOIDING CONTACT

A boat shall avoid contact with another boat if reasonably possible. However, a right-of-way boat, or one sailing within the *room* or *mark-room* to which she is entitled, need not act to avoid contact until it is clear that the other boat is not *keeping clear* or giving *room* or *mark-room*.

15 ACQUIRING RIGHT OF WAY

When a boat acquires right of way, she shall initially give the other boat *room* to *keep clear*, unless she acquires right of way because of the other boat's actions.

16 CHANGING COURSE

16.1 When a right-of-way boat changes course, she shall give the other boat *room* to *keep clear*.

16.2 In addition, on a beat to windward when a *port-tack* boat is *keeping clear* by sailing to pass to leeward of a *starboard-tack* boat, the *starboard-tack* boat shall not bear away if as a result the *port-tack* boat must change course immediately to continue *keeping clear*.

17 ON THE SAME TACK; PROPER COURSE

If a boat *clear astern* becomes *overlapped* within two of her hull lengths to *leeward* of a boat on the same *tack*, she shall not sail above her *proper course* while they remain on the same *tack* and *overlapped* within that distance, unless in doing so she promptly sails astern of the other boat. This rule does not apply if the *overlap* begins while the *windward* boat is required by rule 13 to *keep clear*.

条船同时受本规则约束，在另一条船的左舷或在后的船须*避让*。

B 节 一般限制

14 避免接触

若合理可行，一条船须避免与另外一条船接触。但是，航行权船、行驶在她享有的*空间*或*绕标空间*内的船，在另外一条船明显地不*避让*或不给予*空间*或*绕标空间*前，无需采取避免接触的行为。

15 获取航行权

当一条船获取航行权时，她须于开始时给予另外一条船*避让*的*空间*，除非该船是因另外那条船的行为而获得航行权。[译者注：此处的获取航行权特指主动获取。]

16 改变航线

16.1 当航行权船改变航线时，她须给予另外一条船*空间*去*避让*。

16.2 另外，在驶向上风的迎风航段上，一条*左舷*船以从*右舷*船下风通过的方式*避让*时，如果*右舷*船顺风偏转会造成*左舷*船必须马上改变航线继续*避让*，那么，*右舷*船就不得顺风偏转。

17 同舷风；正当航线

如果一条*明显在后*的船在其 2 倍船长间距内在一条同*舷风*船的下风变成*相联*关系，当她们在此间距内仍保持同*舷风*和*相联*时，她不得高于其*正当航线*，除非在这样做时她迅即行驶到另一条船的船尾后面。如果*相联*开始建立时，*上风*船被要求根据规则 13 *避让*，此规则就不适用。

SECTION C – AT MARKS AND OBSTRUCTIONS

Section C rules do not apply at a starting ***mark*** *surrounded by navigable water or at its anchor line from the time boats are approaching them to* ***start*** *until they have passed them.*

18 MARK-ROOM

18.1 When Rule 18 Applies

Rule 18 applies between boats when they are required to leave a *mark* on the same side and at least one of them is in the *zone*. However, it does not apply

(a) between boats on opposite *tacks* on a beat to windward,

(b) between boats on opposite *tacks* when the *proper course* at the *mark* for one but not both of them is to tack,

(c) between a boat approaching a *mark* and one leaving it, or

(d) if the *mark* is a continuing *obstruction*, in which case rule 19 applies.

Rule 18 no longer applies between boats when *mark-room* has been given.

18.2 Giving Mark-Room

(a) When boats are *overlapped* the outside boat shall give the inside boat *mark-room*, unless rule 18.2(b) applies.

(b) If boats are *overlapped* when the first of them reaches the *zone*, the outside boat at that moment shall thereafter give the inside boat *mark-room*. If a boat is *clear ahead* when she reaches the *zone*, the boat *clear astern* at that moment shall thereafter give her *mark-room*.

(c) When a boat is required to give *mark-room* by rule 18.2(b),

(1) she shall continue to do so even if later an *overlap* is broken or a new *overlap* begins;

C 节 在标志和障碍物旁

*从船驶近被航行水域环绕的起航***标志***或其锚绳去***起航***，直至通过它们，C 节的规则在上述位置不适用。*

18 绕标空间

18.1 规则 18 适用时

当船被要求以同侧离开*标志*，并且至少其中一条船在*标区*内时，规则 18 在她们之间适用。然而，其不适用于：

(a) 在驶向上风的迎风航段上，相对*舷风*行驶的船之间，

(b) 当其中仅一条船在*标*旁的*正当航线*是去迎风换舷时，相对*舷风*的两船之间，

(c) 在一条正驶近*标志*的船和一条正离开*标志*的船之间，或者

(d) 如果*标志*是一个连续*障碍物*，这种情况下规则 19 适用。

规则 18 不再适用于已经给予了*绕标空间*的两船之间。 |

18.2 给予绕标空间

(a) 当两船*相联*时，外侧船须给予内侧船*绕标空间*，除非规则 18.2 (b)适用。

(b) 如果两船*相联*，其中第一条船到达*标区*时，此时的外侧船此后须给予内侧船*绕标空间*。如果一条船到达*标区*时*明显在前*，此时*明显在后*的船此后须给予*绕标空间*。

(c) 当一条船需要根据规则 18.2 (b)给予*绕标空间*时，

(1) 即使之后*相联*被打破或者新的*相联*建立，她须继续这样做；

(2) if she becomes *overlapped* inside the boat entitled to *mark-room*, she shall also give that boat *room* to sail her *proper course* while they remain *overlapped*.

(d) Rules 18.2(b) and (c) cease to apply if the boat entitled to *mark-room* passes head to wind or leaves the *zone*.

(e) If there is reasonable doubt that a boat obtained or broke an *overlap* in time, it shall be presumed that she did not.

(f) If a boat obtained an inside *overlap* from *clear astern* or by tacking to *windward* of the other boat and, from the time the *overlap* began, the outside boat has been unable to give *mark-room*, she is not required to give it.

18.3 Passing Head to Wind in the Zone

If a boat in the *zone* of a *mark* to be left to port passes head to wind from *port* to *starboard tack* and is then *fetching* the *mark*, she shall not cause a boat that has been on *starboard tack* since entering the *zone* to sail above close-hauled to avoid contact and she shall give *mark-room* if that boat becomes *overlapped* inside her. When this rule applies between boats, rule 18.2 does not apply between them.

18.4 Gybing

When an inside *overlapped* right-of-way boat must gybe at a *mark* to sail her *proper course*, until she gybes she shall sail no farther from the *mark* than needed to sail that course. Rule 18.4 does not apply at a gate *mark*.

19 ROOM TO PASS AN OBSTRUCTION

19.1 When Rule 19 Applies

Rule 19 applies between two boats at an *obstruction* except

(a) when the *obstruction* is a *mark* the boats are required to leave on the same side, or

(b) when rule 18 applies between the boats and the *obstruction* is another boat *overlapped* with each of them.

(2) 如果她在享有*绕标空间*的船内侧变成*相联*，在保持*相联*期间，仍须给予对方行驶*正当航线*的*空间*。

(d) 如果享有*绕标空间*的船越过了正顶风或离开了*标区*，规则 18. 2 (b)和(c)停止适用。

(e) 如果对船是否及时建立或打破了*相联*存有合理的怀疑，须假定其没有。

(f) 如果一条船从*明显在后*或通过迎风换舷至另一条船*上风*的方式建立内侧*相联*，自*相联*开始起，若外侧船已经不能够给予*绕标空间*，她就不必给予*绕标空间*。

18.3 在标区内越过正顶风

如果一条船在以左舷一侧离开的*标志*的*标区*内从*左舷*越过正顶风至*右舷*后飞驰该*标志*，她不得造成进入*标区*时已经是*右舷*的船高于近迎风行驶来避免接触，而且，如果那条船在她内侧变成*相联*，她须给予*绕标空间*。当此规则适用于两船之间时，规则 18. 2 在她们之间就不适用。

18.4 顺风换舷

当一条内侧*相联*的航行权船在*标志旁*必须顺风换舷来行驶她的*正当航线*时，顺风换舷前她离*标志*的距离不得远于行驶那个航线所需的距离。在门*标*时，规则 18. 4 不适用。

19 通过障碍物的空间

19.1 规则 19 适用时

规则 19 适用于在*障碍物旁*的两船之间，以下情况除外：

(a) 当*障碍物*是一个*标志*时，两船被要求以同一侧驶离，或

(b) 当规则 18 适用于两船之间时，该*障碍物*是另一条与她俩分别*相联*的船。

However, at a continuing *obstruction*, rule 19 always applies and rule 18 does not.

19.2 Giving Room at an Obstruction

(a) A right-of-way boat may choose to pass an *obstruction* on either side.

(b) When boats are *overlapped*, the outside boat shall give the inside boat *room* between her and the *obstruction*, unless she has been unable to do so from the time the *overlap* began.

(c) While boats are passing a continuing *obstruction*, if a boat that was *clear astern* and required to *keep clear* becomes *overlapped* between the other boat and the *obstruction* and, at the moment the *overlap* begins, there is not *room* for her to pass between them,

(1) she is not entitled to *room* under rule 19.2(b), and

(2) while the boats remain *overlapped*, she shall *keep clear* and rules 10 and 11 do not apply.

20 ROOM TO TACK AT AN OBSTRUCTION

20.1 Hailing

A boat may hail for *room* to tack and avoid a boat on the same *tack*. However, she shall not hail unless

(a) she is approaching an *obstruction* and will soon need to make a substantial course change to avoid it safely, and

(b) she is sailing close-hauled or above.

In addition, she shall not hail if the *obstruction* is a *mark* and a boat that is *fetching* it would be required to change course as a result of the hail.

20.2 Responding

(a) After a boat hails, she shall give a hailed boat time to respond.

(b) A hailed boat shall respond even if the hail breaks rule 20.1.

然而，在通过连续*障碍物*时，规则 19 总是适用，而规则 18 却不适用。

19.2 在障碍物旁给予空间

（a）航行权船可以选择以任意一侧通过*障碍物*。

（b）当船*相联*时，外侧船须给予内侧船在她和*障碍物*之间的*空间*，除非从*相联*开始的时候她已经做不到这一点。

（c）当船正在通过一个连续*障碍物*时，如果一条*明显在后*需要进行*避让*的船在另一条船和*障碍物*之间变成*相联*，在*相联*开始时刻，若没有她可通过的*空间*，

（1）根据规则 19. 2（b），她无权享有*空间*，并且

（2）当两船保持*相联*时，她须*避让*，规则 10 和 11 不适用。

20 障碍物旁迎风换舷的空间

20.1 呼喊

船可以呼喊要求迎风换舷并躲避另一条同*舷风*船的*空间*。但是，除以下情况外，她不得呼喊：

（a）她正在接近一个*障碍物*而且很快需要明显改变航线来安全地躲避它，和

（b）她正在近迎风或者高于近迎风航行。

此外，如果*障碍物*是一个*标志*，而一条*飞驰*它的船会因为该呼喊而需要改变航线，她就不得呼喊。

20.2 回应

（a）一条船呼喊后，她须给予被呼喊的船时间以回应。

（b）即使呼喊违反了规则20. 1，被呼喊的船也须做出回应。

(c) A hailed boat shall respond either by tacking as soon as possible, or by immediately replying 'You tack' and then giving the hailing boat *room* to tack and avoid her.

(d) When a hailed boat responds, the hailing boat shall tack as soon as possible.

(e) From the time a boat hails until she has tacked and avoided a hailed boat, rule 18.2 does not apply between them.

20.3 Passing On a Hail to an Additional Boat

When a boat has been hailed for *room* to tack and she intends to respond by tacking, she may hail another boat on the same *tack* for *room* to tack and avoid her. She may hail even if her hail does not meet the conditions of rule 20.1. Rule 20.2 applies between her and a boat she hails.

20.4 Additional Requirements for Hails

(a) When conditions are such that a hail may not be heard, the boat shall also make a signal that clearly indicates her need for *room* to tack or her response.

(b) The notice of race may specify an alternative communication for a boat to indicate her need for *room* to tack or her response, and require boats to use it.

SECTION D – OTHER RULES

When rule 21 or 22 applies between two boats, Section A rules do not.

21 STARTING ERRORS; TAKING PENALTIES;BACKING A SAIL

21.1 A boat sailing towards the pre-start side of the starting line or one of its extensions after her starting signal to *start* or to comply with rule 30.1 shall *keep clear* of a boat not doing so until her hull is completely on the pre-start side.

21.2 A boat taking a penalty shall *keep clear* of one that is not.

(c) 被呼喊的船须尽快通过迎风换舷，或立即回答“你迎风换舷”来回应并且给予呼喊的船迎风换舷和躲避她的*空间*。

(d) 当被呼喊的船做出回应，呼喊的船须尽快迎风换舷。

(e) 从船呼喊的那一刻起，直到其完成换舷并躲避了被呼喊的船为止，规则 18.2 在她们之间不适用。

20.3 向另一条船传递呼喊

当一条船被呼喊迎风换舷的*空间*并且她也打算做迎风换舷来回应呼喊时，她可以呼喊另一条与其同*舷风*的船给予迎风换舷并躲避她的*空间*。即使她的呼喊不符合规则 20.1 的条件，她也可以呼喊。规则 20.2 在她和被她呼喊的那条船之间适用。

20.4 呼喊的附加要求

(a) 在可能听不到呼喊的情况下，船还须发出清晰表明其需要迎风换舷*空间*或其回应的信号。

(b) 竞赛通知可以规定一条船表明其需要迎风换舷*空间*或其回应的替代沟通方式，并要求参赛船使用。

D 节 其他规则

当规则 21 或 22 适用于两船之间时，A 节规则不适用。

21 起航失误；解脱；帆反受风

21.1 起航信号发出后向起航线或者其两端延长线的准备区一侧航行去*起航*的船，或执行规则 30.1 的船须*避让*没有这样做的船直至自己的船体完全处于起航准备区一侧。

21.2 正在做解脱的船须*避让*其他没有在做解脱的船。

21.3 A boat moving astern, or sideways to windward, through the water by backing a sail shall *keep clear* of one that is not.

22 CAPSIZED, ANCHORED OR AGROUND; RESCUING

If possible, a boat shall avoid a boat that is capsized or has not regained control after capsizing, is anchored or aground, or is trying to help a person or vessel in danger. A boat is capsized when her masthead is in the water.

23 INTERFERING WITH ANOTHER BOAT

23.1 If reasonably possible, a boat not *racing* shall not interfere with a boat that is *racing*.

23.2 If reasonably possible, a boat shall not interfere with a boat that is taking a penalty, sailing on another leg or subject to rule 21.1. However, after the starting signal this rule does not apply when the boat is sailing her *proper course*.

21.3 通过让帆反受风使船相对于水体向后移动或向上风横移的船须*避让*没有这样做的船。

22 倾覆、抛锚或搁浅；救援

一条船如有可能须躲避倾覆的船或倾覆后未能重新获得操纵能力的船，躲避抛锚或搁浅的船，以及正在帮助处在危险中的人或船舶的船。当船的桅顶在水中时即为倾覆。

23 妨碍另外一条船

23.1 若合理可行的话，不参加*竞赛*的船不得妨碍正在*竞赛*的船。

23.2 若合理可行的话，一条船不得妨碍正在做解脱的船，不得妨碍航行在另外一个航段上的船或规则 21.1 所描述的船。但是，起航信号发出后，该规则不适用于正在行驶*正当航线*的船。

PART 3–CONDUCT OF A RACE

25 NOTICE OF RACE, SAILING INSTRUCTIONS AND SIGNALS

25.1 The notice of race shall be made available to each boat that enters an event before she enters. The sailing instructions shall be made available to each boat before a race begins.

25.2 The meanings of the visual and sound signals stated in Race Signals shall not be changed except under rule 86.1(b). The meanings of any other signals that may be used shall be stated in the notice of race or sailing instructions.

25.3 When the race committee is required to display a flag as a visual signal, it may use a flag or other object of a similar appearance.

26 STARTING RACES

Races shall be started by using the following signals. Times shall be taken from the visual signals; the absence of a sound signal shall be disregarded.

Minutes before starting signal	*Visual signal*	*Sound signal*	*Means*
5*	Class flag	One	Warning signal
4	P, I, Z, Z with I,U, or black flag	One	Preparatory signal
1	Preparatory flag removed	One long	One minute
0	Class flag removed	One	Starting signal

*or as stated in the notice of race or sailing instructions

第三章　竞赛的实施

25 竞赛通知、航行细则和信号

25.1 竞赛通知须在报名前提供给每条报名参赛的船。航行细则须在竞赛开始前提供给每条参赛船。

25.2 除根据规则 86.1（b)外，竞赛信号中所述的视觉和音响信号的含义不得改变。任何其他可能使用的信号含义须在竞赛通知或航行细则中说明。

25.3 当竞赛委员会需要展示一面旗帜作为视觉信号时，可使用一面旗帜或其他近似外观的物体。

26 竞赛起航

竞赛起航须使用下列信号。计时须以视觉信号为准；音响信号的缺失不必理会。

起航信号前时间（分钟）	*视觉信号*	*音响信号*	*含义*
5*	级别旗	一声	预告信号
4	P, I, Z, Z 和 I, U 旗,或黑旗	一声	准备信号
1	移除准备信号	一长声	1 分钟
0	移除级别旗	一声	起航信号

＊或按竞赛通知或航行细则中的规定

The warning signal for each succeeding class shall be made with or after the starting signal of the preceding class.

27 OTHER RACE COMMITTEE ACTIONS BEFORE THE STARTING SIGNAL

27.1 No later than the warning signal, the race committee shall signal or otherwise designate the course to be sailed if the sailing instructions have not stated the course, and it may replace one course signal with another and signal that wearing personal flotation devices is required (display flag Y with one sound).

27.2 No later than the preparatory signal, the race committee may move a starting *mark*.

27.3 Before the starting signal, the race committee may for any reason *postpone* (display flag AP, AP over H, or AP over A, with two sounds) or *abandon* the race (display flag N over H, or N over A, with three sounds).

28 SAILING THE RACE

28.1 A boat shall *start*, *sail the course* and then *finish*. While doing so, she may leave on either side a *mark* that does not begin, bound or end the leg she is sailing. After *finishing* she need not cross the finishing line completely.

28.2 A boat may correct any errors in *sailing the course*, provided she has not crossed the finishing line to *finish*.

29 RECALLS

29.1 Individual Recall

When at a boat's starting signal any part of her hull is on the course side of the starting line or she must comply with rule 30.1, the race committee shall promptly display flag X

后续每个级别竞赛的预告信号须与前一个级别的起航信号同时或在其之后发出。

27 起航信号前竞赛委员会的其他行动

27.1 如果航行细则中未规定航线，竞赛委员会须不晚于预告信号用信号通知或其他方法指明要行驶的航线，可以用一个航线信号代替另外一个，并发出要求穿着个人助浮装备的信号（展示 Y 旗并伴随一声音响）。

27.2 竞赛委员会可以在不晚于准备信号时移动起航*标志*。

27.3 起航信号之前，竞赛委员会可以因任何理由*推迟*竞赛（展示 AP 旗、AP 旗在 H 旗之上或 AP 旗在 A 旗之上，并伴随两声音响）或*放弃*竞赛（展示 N 旗在 H 旗之上或 N 旗在 A 旗之上，并伴随三声音响）。

28 行驶竞赛航线

28.1 船须先*起航*，*行驶航线*，然后*到达终点*。在这个过程中，可以以任意一侧离开不具有标示所行驶航段的起始、边界或结束功能的*标志*。*到达终点*后她不需要完全通过终点线。

28.2 船可以改正*行驶航线*中的任何错误，前提是其没有通过终点线*到达终点*。

29 召回

29.1 **个别召回**

当起航信号发出时，一条船船体的任何一部分处于起航线的航线一侧或她必须遵守规则 30.1 时，竞赛委员会须迅即展示 X 旗并伴随一声音响。该旗须展示至所有这

with one sound. The flag shall be displayed until the hull of each such boat has been completely on the pre-start side of the starting line or one of its extensions, and until all such boats have complied with rule 30.1 if it applies, but no later than four minutes after the starting signal or one minute before any later starting signal, whichever is earlier. If rule 29.2, 30.3 or 30.4 applies this rule does not.

29.2 General Recall

When at the starting signal the race committee is unable to identify boats that are on the course side of the starting line or to which rule 30 applies, or there has been an error in the starting procedure, the race committee may signal a general recall (display the First Substitute with two sounds). The warning signal for a new start for the recalled class shall be made one minute after the First Substitute is removed (one sound), and the starts for any succeeding classes shall follow the new start.

30 STARTING PENALTIES

30.1 I Flag Rule

If flag I has been displayed, and any part of a boat's hull is on the course side of the starting line or one of its extensions during the last minute before her starting signal, she shall sail across an extension so that her hull is completely on the pre-start side before she *starts*.

30.2 Z Flag Rule

If flag Z has been displayed, no part of a boat's hull shall be in the triangle formed by the ends of the starting line and the first *mark* during the last minute before her starting signal. If a boat breaks this rule and is identified, she shall receive, without a hearing, a 20% Scoring Penalty

样的船的船体完全处于起航线或其中一端延长线的起航准备区一侧，当规则 30. 1 适用时，展示至所有这样的船都遵守了此规则时，但展示时间不得晚于起航信号发出后 4 分钟或下一起航信号前 1 分钟，以这两个时刻先到的那个为准。如果规则 29. 2、30. 3 或 30. 4 适用，则本规则不适用。

29.2　全部召回

当起航信号发出时，竞赛委员会无法识别位于起航线的航线一侧的船或规则 30 适用的那些船，或起航程序有误时，竞赛委员会可以发出全部召回信号（展示代一旗并伴随两声音响）。被全部召回的级别的新的起航预告信号须在代一旗移除（一声音响）后 1 分钟发出，后续所有级别的起航须跟随在这个新的起航之后。

30 起航惩罚

30.1　I 旗规则

如果 I 旗已经展示，当一条船在其起航信号发出前的最后 1 分钟内，船体的任何一部分处于起航线或其其中一端延长线的航线一侧，她须驶过一端的延长线，使船体完全返回起航准备区一侧再去*起航*。

30.2　Z 旗规则

如果 Z 旗已经展示，当一条船在其起航信号发出前的最后 1 分钟内，船体的任何部分不得处于起航线两端与第一个*标志*形成的三角区域内。若某船违反了本规则并被识别，无须审理，她须被处以规则 44. 3（c）规定的 20% 的计分惩罚。除非该轮竞赛在起航信号发出前被*推迟*或

calculated as stated in rule 44.3(c). She shall be penalized even if the race is restarted or resailed, but not if it is *postponed* or *abandoned* before the starting signal. If she is similarly identified during a subsequent attempt to start the same race, she shall receive an additional 20% Scoring Penalty.

30.3 U Flag Rule

If flag U has been displayed, no part of a boat's hull shall be in the triangle formed by the ends of the starting line and the first *mark* during the last minute before her starting signal. If a boat breaks this rule and is identified, she shall be disqualified without a hearing, but not if the race is restarted or resailed.

30.4 Black Flag Rule

If a black flag has been displayed, no part of a boat's hull shall be in the triangle formed by the ends of the starting line and the first *mark* during the last minute before her starting signal. If a boat breaks this rule and is identified, she shall be disqualified without a hearing, even if the race is restarted or resailed, but not if it is *postponed* or *abandoned* before the starting signal. If a general recall is signalled or the race is *abandoned* after the starting signal, the race committee shall display her sail number before the next warning signal for that race, and if the race is restarted or resailed she shall not sail in it. If she does so, her disqualification shall not be excluded in calculating her series score.

放弃,否则即使该轮竞赛再次起航或重新竞赛,此惩罚仍有效。如果在同一轮竞赛的再次起航过程中,她同样被识别出有相似行为,她须被再加 20% 的计分惩罚。

30.3 U 旗规则

如果 U 旗已经展示,当一条船在其起航信号发出前的最后 1 分钟内,船体的任何部分不得处于起航线两端和第一个*标志*形成的三角区域内。若某船违反了本规则并被识别,无须审理,她须被记为取消资格,但该轮竞赛再次起航或重新竞赛的情况除外。

30.4 黑旗规则

如果黑旗已经展示,当一条船在其起航信号发出前的最后 1 分钟内,船体的任何部分不得处于起航线两端与第一个*标志*形成的三角区域内。若某船违反了本规则并被识别,无须审理,她须被记为取消资格,除非在起航信号发出前该轮竞赛被*推迟*或*放弃*,否则即使该轮竞赛再次起航或重新竞赛,此判罚仍有效。如在起航信号后发出全部召回或*放弃*竞赛的信号,竞赛委员会须在该轮竞赛的下一个预告信号前展示该船帆号,如果该轮竞赛再次起航或重新竞赛,她不得在其中参与竞赛。如果她参加了,她的取消资格不得从系列赛计分中去掉。

31 TOUCHING A MARK

While *racing*, a boat shall not touch a starting *mark* before *starting*, a *mark* that begins, bounds or ends the leg of the course on which she is sailing, or a finishing *mark* after *finishing*.

32 SHORTENING OR ABANDONING AFTER THE START

32.1 After the starting signal, the race committee may shorten the course (display flag S with two sounds) or *abandon* the race (display flag N, N over H, or N over A, with three sounds),

(a) because of foul weather,

(b) because of insufficient wind making it unlikely that any boat will *finish* within the race time limit,

(c) because a *mark* is missing or out of position, or

(d) for any other reason directly affecting the safety or fairness of the competition.

In addition, the race committee may shorten the course so that other scheduled races can be sailed, or *abandon* the race because of an error in the starting procedure. However, after one boat has *started*, *sailed the course* and *finished* within the race time limit, if any, the race committee shall not *abandon* the race without considering the consequences for all boats in the race or series.

32.2 If the race committee signals a shortened course (displays flag S with two sounds), the finishing line shall be,

(a) at a rounding *mark*, between the *mark* and a staff displaying flag S;

(b) a line the course requires boats to cross; or

(c) at a gate, between the gate *marks*.

31 碰标

*竞赛*时，船在*起航*前不得触碰起点*标志*，以及不得触碰标示她正在行驶的航段的起始、边界和结束的*标志*，并且*到达终点*后也不得触碰终点*标志*。

32 起航后缩短航线或放弃竞赛

32.1 起航信号发出后，竞赛委员会可以因下列情况而缩短航线（展示 S 旗并伴随两声音响）或*放弃*竞赛（展示 N 旗，或 N 旗在 H 或 A 旗之上，并伴随三声音响）：

（a）恶劣天气，

（b）风力不足，使得任何一条船不可能在竞赛时限内*到达终点*，

（c）*标志*丢失或移位，或者

（d）有直接影响比赛安全或公平的任何其他理由。

此外，竞赛委员会可以缩短航线以便日程排定的其他竞赛可以进行，或者因起航流程中的错误而*放弃*本轮竞赛。但是，如果当一条船*起航*，*行驶航线*，并在时限内（如果有的话）*到达终点*后，竞赛委员会不得在未考虑该轮竞赛或系列赛中所有船的结果的前提下*放弃*该轮竞赛。

32.2 如果竞赛委员会发出了缩短航线的信号（展示 S 旗并伴随两声音响），则终点线：

（a）在一个绕行的*标志*处，须在该*标志*与展示 S 旗的旗杆之间；

（b）须为航线要求船通过的一条线；或者

（c）在门标处，须在两个门*标*之间。

The shortened course shall be signalled before the first boat crosses the finishing line.

33 CHANGING THE NEXT LEG OF THE COURSE

While boats are *racing*, the race committee may change a leg of the course that begins at a rounding *mark* or at a gate by changing the position of the next *mark* (or the finishing line) and signalling all boats before they begin the leg. The next *mark* need not be in position at that time.

(a) If the direction of the leg will be changed, the signal shall be the display of flag C with repetitive sounds and one or both of

(1) the new compass bearing,

(2) a green triangle for a change to starboard or a red rectangle for a change to port.

(b) If the length of the leg will be changed, the signal shall be the display of flag C with repetitive sounds and a '–' if the length will be decreased or a '+' if it will be increased.

(c) Subsequent legs may be changed without further signalling to maintain the course shape.

34 MARK MISSING

If a *mark* is missing or out of position while boats are *racing*, the race committee shall, if possible,

(a) replace it in its correct position or substitute a new one of similar appearance, or

(b) substitute an object displaying flag M and make repetitive sound signals.

35 RACE TIME LIMIT AND SCORES

If one boat *starts*, *sails the course* and *finishes* within the time limit for that race, if any, all boats that *finish* shall be scored

缩短航线的信号须在第一条船通过终点线之前发出。

33 改变航线的下一航段

船在*竞赛*时，竞赛委员会可以从一个绕行的*标志*或者门*标*开始改变航线的一个航段，方法是改变下一个*标志*（或终点线）的位置并在所有船开始这个航段前用信号通知她们。下一*标志*无需在那时就位。

（a）如果将改变航段的方向，信号须是展示 C 旗并伴随重复音响，并且用下面的一种或两种方法一起展示：

（1）新的罗径方位，

（2）一个绿色的三角形表示改变至右舷，或是一个红色的长方形表示改变至左舷。

（b）如果将改变航段的长度，信号须是展示 C 旗并伴随重复音响，并且用"—"表示将减少长度，或用"+"表示将增加长度。

（c）为保持整个航线的形状，可以改变后续航段而不用再发信号。

34 标志丢失

船在*竞赛*时，若一个*标志*丢失或移位，如有可能，竞赛委员会须：

（a）把*标志*重新放到正确的位置，或用新的相似外观的*标志*代替，或

（b）由一个展示 M 旗的物体代替并伴随重复音响。

35 竞赛时限和计分

若一条船*起航*，*行驶航线*，并在那一轮竞赛的时间限制内（如果有的话）*到达终点*，除非竞赛被*放弃*，否则所有*到达终点*的船须

according to their finishing places unless the race is *abandoned*. If no boat *finishes* within the race time limit, the race committee shall *abandon* the race.

36 RACES RESTARTED OR RESAILED

If a race is restarted or resailed, a breach of a *rule* in the original race, or in any previous restart or resail of that race, shall not

(a) prohibit a boat from competing unless she has broken rule 30.4; or

(b) cause a boat to be penalized except under rule 2, 30.2, 30.4 or 69 or under rule 14 when she has caused injury or serious damage.

37 SEARCH AND RESCUE INSTRUCTIONS

When the race committee displays flag V with one sound, all boats and official and support vessels shall, if possible, monitor the race committee communication channel for search and rescue instructions.

按到达终点的顺序计分。如果没有船在竞赛时限内*到达终点*，竞赛委员会须*放弃*该轮竞赛。

36 重新起航或重新竞赛

如果一轮竞赛重新起航或重新竞赛，在那一轮原先的竞赛，或之前任何一次的重新起航或重新竞赛中的违反*规则*，都不得

（a）禁止某条船竞赛，除非她违反了规则 30. 4；或

（b）导致一条船被判罚，除非她违反了规则 2、30. 2、30. 4 或 69，或违反规则 14 时造成了损伤或严重损坏。

37 搜救指令

当竞赛委员会展示 V 旗并伴随一声音响时，如有可能，所有参赛船、官员船和后援船艇须守听竞赛委员会通信频道的搜救指令。

PART 4–OTHER REQUIREMENTS WHEN RACING

Part 4 rules apply only to boats ***racing*** *unless the rule states otherwise.*

SECTION A – GENERAL REQUIREMENTS

40 PERSONAL FLOTATION DEVICES

40.1 Basic Rule

When rule 40.1 is made applicable by rule 40.2, each competitor shall wear a personal flotation device except briefly while changing or adjusting clothing or personal equipment. Wet suits and dry suits are not personal flotation devices.

40.2 When Rule 40.1 Applies

Rule 40.1 applies

(a) if flag Y was displayed afloat with one sound before or with the warning signal, while *racing* in that race; or

(b) if flag Y was displayed ashore with one sound, at all times while afloat that day.

However, rule 40.1 applies when so stated in the notice of race or sailing instructions.

41 OUTSIDE HELP

A boat shall not receive help from any outside source, except

(a) help for a crew member who is ill, injured or in danger;

(b) after a collision, help from the crew of the other vessel to get clear;

(c) help in the form of information freely available to all boats;

(d) unsolicited information from a disinterested source, which may be another boat in the same race.

第四章 竞赛时的其他规定

*规则第四章只适用于**竞赛**的船，除非规则另有说明。*

A 节 一般要求

40 个人助浮装备

40.1 基本规则

当通过规则 40.2 适用规则 40.1 时，除了暂时更换、调整衣物或个人器材外，每位选手须穿戴个人助浮装备。干式或湿式保暖服不是个人助浮装备。

40.2 规则 40.1 适用时

规则 40.1，

(a) 如果在预告信号发出之前或同时在水上展示 Y 旗并伴随一声音响，则适用于那一轮*竞赛*；或

(b) 如果在岸上展示 Y 旗并伴随一声音响，则适用于当天所有水上时段。

然而，当竞赛通知或航行细则做出这样的规定时，规则 40.1 才适用。

41 外部援助

一条船不得从任何外部途径接受援助，以下情况例外：

(a) 援助生病、受伤或处于危险中的选手；

(b) 碰撞后，另一条船舶上的船员为摆脱接触而提供的援助；

(c) 所有船都可随意获取的信息形式的帮助；

(d) 非利益方主动提供的信息，可能会来自于同一轮竞赛中的另一条船。

42 PROPULSION

42.1 Basic Rule

Except when permitted in rule 42.3 or 45, a boat shall compete by using only the wind and water to increase, maintain or decrease her speed. Her crew may adjust the trim of sails and hull, and perform other acts of seamanship, but shall not otherwise move their bodies to propel the boat.

42.2 Prohibited Actions

Without limiting the application of rule 42.1, these actions are prohibited:

(a) pumping: repeated fanning of any sail either by pulling in and releasing the sail or by vertical or athwartship body movement;

(b) rocking: repeated rolling of the boat, induced by

(1) body movement,

(2) repeated adjustment of the sails or centreboard, or

(3) steering;

(c) ooching: sudden forward body movement, stopped abruptly;

(d) sculling: repeated movement of the helm that is either forceful or that propels the boat forward or prevents her from moving astern;

(e) repeated tacks or gybes unrelated to changes in the wind or to tactical considerations.

42.3 Exceptions

(a) A boat may be rolled to facilitate steering.

(b) A boat's crew may move their bodies to exaggerate the rolling that facilitates steering the boat through a tack or a gybe, provided that, just after the tack or gybe is completed, the boat's speed is not greater than it would have been in the absence of the tack or gybe.

42 推进

42.1 基本规则

除规则 42. 3 或规则 45 允许的情况外，一条船在比赛中须仅利用风和水来增加、保持或降低船的速度。其船员可以调整帆和船体并采用其他的海上操作动作，但不得以其他方式移动身体去推进船只。

42.2 禁止的行为

在不限制运用规则 42. 1 的情况下，下列行为被禁止：

（a）摇帆：利用收帆并松帆或上下或沿船体横向晃动身体来反复扇动某面帆；

（b）摇船：通过下述动作使船反复横摇：

（1）身体的移动，

（2）对帆或稳向板的反复调节，或

（3）转向；

（c）前冲：身体突然前移、突然停止；

（d）摇舵：用力的或者能推进船体向前或阻止其向后运动的舵的反复运动；

（e）反复进行与风变或战术考虑无关的迎风换舷或顺风换舷。

42.3 例外

（a）可以横摇船只协助转向。

（b）船员可以移动身体加剧横摇，帮助转向去完成迎风换舷或顺风换舷，前提是在刚好完成换舷后，船速不超过未做换舷时应有的速度。

(c) When surfing (rapidly accelerating down the front of a wave), planing or foiling is possible

(1) to initiate surfing or planing, each sail may be pulled in only once for each wave or gust of wind, or

(2) to initiate foiling, each sail may be pulled in any number of times.

(d) When a boat is above a close-hauled course and either stationary or moving slowly, she may scull to turn to a close-hauled course.

(e) If a batten is inverted, the boat's crew may pump the sail until the batten is no longer inverted. This action is not permitted if it clearly propels the boat.

(f) A boat may reduce speed by repeatedly moving her helm.

(g) Any means of propulsion may be used to help a person or another vessel in danger.

(h) To get clear after grounding or colliding with a vessel or object, a boat may use force applied by her crew or the crew of the other vessel and any equipment other than a propulsion engine. However, the use of an engine may be permitted by rule 42.3(i).

(i) Sailing instructions may, in stated circumstances, permit propulsion using an engine or any other method, provided the boat does not gain a significant advantage in the race.

Note: Interpretations of rule 42 are available at the World Sailing website or by mail upon request.

43 EXONERATION

43.1

(a) When as a consequence of breaking a *rule* a boat has compelled another boat to break a *rule*, the other boat is exonerated for her breach.

(c) 在有可能冲浪(在浪的前坡突然加速下滑)、滑行或使用水翼滑行时,

(1) 为了启动冲浪或滑行,可以收拉任意帆,但每面帆每一个涌浪或一次阵风只能拉动一次,或

(2) 为了启动水翼航行,可以拉动任意帆数次。

(d) 当一条船处在高于近迎风航线上不动或移动缓慢时,她可以摇舵转向一条近迎风航线。

(e) 如果帆骨反扣了,船上的船员可以摇帆直至帆骨不再反扣。如果该行为明显推动了该船,就不被允许。

(f) 船可以反复动舵来减速。

(g) 援助处在危险中的个人或其他船舶时,任何推进方式均可采用。

(h) 船在搁浅或与另外一条船或物体碰撞后,可借用本船或另外一条船舶上船员的力量和除发动机之外的任何器材使船脱离困境。然而,可以通过规则 42.3 (i) 来允许使用发动机。

(i) 航行细则可以规定在特定的情况下,允许使用发动机或其他方式提供的推进,前提是该船在该轮竞赛中没有明显获益。

注:规则 42 的解释在世界帆联网站上可以查询或要求函寄。

43 免责

43.1

(a) 当一条船因为违反*规则*而迫使另外一条船违反*规则*时,另外这条船的该项违规被免责。

(b) When a boat is sailing within the *room* or *mark-room* to which she is entitled and, as a consequence of an incident with a boat required to give her that *room* or *mark-room*, she breaks a rule of Section A of Part 2, rule 15, 16, or 31, she is exonerated for her breach.

(c) A right-of-way boat, or one sailing within the *room* or *mark-room* to which she is entitled, is exonerated for breaking rule 14 if the contact does not cause damage or injury.

43.2 A boat exonerated for breaking a *rule* need not take a penalty and shall not be penalized for breaking that *rule*.

44 PENALTIES AT THE TIME OF AN INCIDENT

44.1 Taking a Penalty

A boat may take a Two-Turns Penalty when she may have broken one or more rules of Part 2 in an incident while *racing*. She may take a One-Turn Penalty when she may have broken rule 31. Alternatively, the notice of race or sailing instructions may specify the use of the Scoring Penalty or some other penalty, in which case the specified penalty shall replace the One-Turn and the Two-Turns Penalty. However,

(a) when a boat may have broken a rule of Part 2 and rule 31 in the same incident she need not take the penalty for breaking rule 31;

(b) if the boat caused injury or serious damage or, despite taking a penalty, gained a significant advantage in the race or series by her breach her penalty shall be to retire.

44.2 One-Turn and Two-Turns Penalties

After getting well clear of other boats as soon after the incident as possible, a boat takes a One-Turn or Two-Turns Penalty by promptly making the required number of turns in the same direction, each turn including one tack and one gybe. When a boat takes the penalty at or near the finishing

(b) 当一条船航行在其享有的*空间*或*绕标空间*内时，因与一条需要给她*空间*或*绕标空间*的船发生的事件而导致她违反规则第二章A节，规则15、16或31时，她的这些违规被免责。

(c) 一条航行权船或航行在所享有的*空间*或*绕标空间*内的船违反了规则14，若接触没有造成损坏或受伤，则该违规被免责。

43.2 一条违反*规则*而被免责的船无需做解脱，且不得因违反那条*规则*而被判罚。

44 事件发生时的惩罚

44.1 解脱

船在*竞赛*中可能违反了规则第二章的一条或多条规则时，她可以做一个两圈解脱。当她可能违反规则31时可以做一个一圈解脱。或者，竞赛通知或航行细则可以规定使用分数惩罚或其他惩罚方法，这种情况下，所规定的惩罚方法须替换一圈或者两圈解脱。然而，

(a) 当一条船在同一事件中可能违反了规则第二章和规则31时，她无需因为违反规则31做解脱；

(b) 如果船造成了损伤或严重损坏，或尽管做了解脱，但由于犯规而在该轮竞赛或系列赛中明显获益，对她的惩罚须为退出竞赛。

44.2 一圈和两圈解脱

船在事件发生后尽快完全避让其他船后，做一个一圈或两圈解脱，方式为迅即在同一方向做被要求次数的转圈，每一圈包括一个迎风换舷和一个顺风换舷。在终点线上或

line, her hull shall be completely on the course side of the line before she *finishes*.

44.3 Scoring Penalty

(a) A boat takes a Scoring Penalty by displaying a yellow flag at the first reasonable opportunity after the incident.

(b) When a boat has taken a Scoring Penalty, she shall keep the yellow flag displayed until *finishing* and call the race committee's attention to it at the finishing line. At that time she shall also inform the race committee of the identity of the other boat involved in the incident. If this is impracticable, she shall do so at the first reasonable opportunity and within the protest time limit.

(c) The race score for a boat that takes a Scoring Penalty shall be the score she would have received without that penalty, made worse by the number of places stated in the notice of race or sailing instructions. When the number of places is not stated, the penalty shall be 20% of the score for Did Not *Finish*, rounded to the nearest whole number (0.5 rounded upward). The scores of other boats shall not be changed; therefore, two boats may receive the same score. However, the penalty shall not cause the boat's score to be worse than the score for Did Not *Finish*.

45 HAULING OUT; MAKING FAST; ANCHORING

A boat shall be afloat and off moorings at her preparatory signal. Thereafter, she shall not be hauled out or made fast except to bail out, reef sails or make repairs. She may anchor or the crew may stand on the bottom. She shall recover the anchor before continuing in the race unless she is unable to do so.

46 PERSON IN CHARGE

A boat shall have on board a person in charge designated by the member or organization that entered the boat. See rule 75.

终点线附近做解脱的船，在其*到达终点*前，她的船体须完全位于终点线的航线一侧。

44.3 分数惩罚

（a）接受分数惩罚的船要在事件发生后的第一合理时机展示黄旗。

（b）当一条船已经接受了分数惩罚，她须展示黄旗直至*到达终点*，并且在到达终点线时提醒竞赛委员会关注它。此时，她还须通知竞赛委员会涉及该事件中的另一条船的身份。如不可行，她须在抗议时限内第一合理时机做到。

（c）接受分数惩罚的船的竞赛分数须为其没有收到惩罚前得到的分数加上竞赛通知或航行细则中规定的名次得出的更差分数。当没有规定加罚的名次数时，该罚分须为没有*到达终点*所对应的分数的 20%（四舍五入取整数）。其他船的分数不得被改变；因此，两条船可能有相同的分数。但是，罚分不得导致该船分数差于没有*到达终点*所对应的分数。

45 拖船上岸；系留；抛锚

船须在准备信号发出后浮于水上并解开系泊索。之后她不得被拖上岸或系留，除非是在排空舱底水、缩帆或维修时。她可以抛锚，或者船员可以站在水底。在继续竞赛前她须起锚，除非她办不到。

46 负责人

船上须有一名由给该船报名的成员或组织指定的负责人。参见规则 75。

47 TRASH DISPOSAL

Competitors and *support persons* shall not intentionally put trash in the water. This rule applies at all times while afloat. The penalty for a breach of this rule may be less than disqualification.

SECTION B – EQUIPMENT-RELATED REQUIREMENTS

48 LIMITATIONS ON EQUIPMENT AND CREW

48.1 A boat shall use only the equipment on board at her preparatory signal.

48.2 No person on board shall intentionally leave, except when ill or injured, or to help a person or vessel in danger, or to swim. A person leaving the boat by accident or to swim shall be back in contact with the boat before the crew resumes sailing the boat to the next *mark*.

49 CREW POSITION; LIFELINES

49.1 Competitors shall use no device designed to position their bodies outboard, other than hiking straps and stiffeners worn under the thighs.

49.2 When lifelines are required by the class rules or any other *rule*, competitors shall not position any part of their torsos outside them, except briefly to perform a necessary task. On boats equipped with upper and lower lifelines, a competitor sitting facing outboard with his waist inside the lower lifeline may have the upper part of his body outside the upper lifeline. Unless a class rule or any other *rule* specifies a maximum deflection, lifelines shall be taut. If the class rules do not specify the material or minimum diameter of lifelines, they shall comply with the corresponding specifications in the *World Sailing Offshore Special Regulations*.

Note: Those regulations are available at the World Sailing website.

47 垃圾处理

选手和*后援人员*不得故意往水中丢垃圾。该条规则适用于整个在水上的时段。违反该条规则的判罚可以轻于取消资格。

B节 器材——相关要求

48 器材和船员的限制

48.1 在准备信号发出时，船须只使用船上的器材。

48.2 除因伤病、救援处在危险中的人或船舶或游泳外，船上的人员不得故意离开。因意外或游泳离开船的船员须在船员将船恢复驶往下一个*标志*前返回接触到船。

49 船员位置；安全护栏

49.1 除使用压舷带和大腿下穿着的硬质撑片外，选手不得使用任何使身体置于船舷外的装置。

49.2 当级别规则或其他*规则*要求有安全护栏时，除短时执行一项必要的任务外，选手不得将其躯干的任何部分置于安全护栏之外。在装有上和下安全护栏的船上，选手面向舷外坐着，腰部在下安全护栏内侧时，可以将身体上半部分探出到上安全护栏外。安全护栏须是拉紧的，除非级别规则或其他*规则*规定了护栏索的最大松偏度。如果级别规则没有规定安全护栏的材质和最小直径，其须遵守《世界帆联离岸赛特别规则》中的相应规定。

注：那些规则可以在世界帆联网站上查到。

50 COMPETITOR CLOTHING AND EQUIPMENT

50.1

(a) Competitors shall not wear or carry clothing or equipment for the purpose of increasing their weight.

(b) Furthermore, a competitor's clothing and equipment shall not weigh more than 8 kilograms, excluding a hiking or trapeze harness and clothing (including footwear) worn only below the knee. Class rules or the notice of race may specify a lower weight or a higher weight up to 10 kilograms. Class rules may include footwear and other clothing worn below the knee within that weight. A hiking or trapeze harness shall have positive buoyancy and shall not weigh more than 2 kilograms, except that class rules may specify a higher weight up to 4 kilograms. Weights shall be determined as required by Appendix H.

(c) A trapeze harness worn by a competitor which may be used to support the competitor on a trapeze shall be of the quick release variety complying with ISO 10862 which allows the competitor to detach from the hook or other method of attachment at any time. A class rule may change this rule to permit trapeze harnesses that are not of the quick release variety, but a class rule may not change the requirement that a quick release harness comply with ISO 10862.

Note: Rule 50.1(c) does not take effect until 1 January 2023.

50.2 Rules 50.1(b) and 50.1(c) do not apply to boats required to be equipped with lifelines.

51 MOVABLE BALLAST

All movable ballast, including sails that are not set, shall be properly stowed. Water, dead weight or ballast shall not be moved for the purpose of changing trim or stability. Floorboards, bulkheads, doors, stairs and water tanks shall be left in place and all cabin fixtures kept on board. However, bilge water may be bailed out.

50 选手的服装与器材

50.1

（a）选手不得穿着或携带意在增加自己体重的服装或器材。

（b）此外，一位选手的服装和器材不得超过 8 千克，不包括压舷裤或吊裤，以及仅穿着在膝盖以下的服装（包括鞋袜）。级别规则或竞赛通知可以规定更低的重量或不超过 10 千克的更高重量。级别规则可以把鞋袜和其他穿着在膝盖以下的服装包括在此重量内。压舷裤或吊裤须有正浮力且重量不得超过 2 千克，除非级别规则可以规定高达 4 千克的更大重量。重量须根据附录 H 的要求确定。

（c）选手穿着的可以用吊索来悬挂的吊裤须为符合 ISO 10862 的各种快速释放装置，能够使选手随时从挂钩或其他连接方式上脱开。级别规则可以更改这条规则，以允许吊裤是非快速释放装置，但是级别规则不可以更改快速释放吊裤要符合 ISO 10862 的要求。

注：规则 50. 1（c）自 2023 年 1 月 1 日起生效。

50.2 规则 50. 1（b）和 50. 1（c）不适用于需要配备安全护栏的船。

51 可移动的压舱物

所有可移动的压舱物须合理放置，包括未升起的帆。不得移动压舱水、固定配重或压舱物来达到改变船的平衡或稳定性的目的。船舱底板、隔舱板、门、梯子和水箱须放置到位，并且所有舱室设施都须保留在船上。但是，可以排出舱底积水。

52 MANUAL POWER

A boat's standing rigging, running rigging, spars and movable hull appendages shall be adjusted and operated only by the power provided by the crew.

53 SKIN FRICTION

A boat shall not eject or release a substance, such as a polymer, or have specially textured surfaces that could improve the character of the flow of water inside the boundary layer.

54 FORESTAYS AND HEADSAIL TACKS

Forestays and headsail tacks, except those of spinnaker staysails when the boat is not close-hauled, shall be attached approximately on a boat's centreline.

55 SETTING AND SHEETING SAILS

55.1 Changing Sails

When headsails or spinnakers are being changed, a replacing sail may be fully set and trimmed before the replaced sail is lowered. However, only one mainsail and, except when changing, only one spinnaker shall be carried set at a time.

55.2 Spinnaker Poles; Whisker Poles

Only one spinnaker pole or whisker pole shall be used at a time except when gybing. When in use, it shall be attached to the foremost mast.

55.3 Sheeting Sails

No sail shall be sheeted over or through any device that exerts outward pressure on a sheet or clew of a sail at a point from which, with the boat upright, a vertical line would fall outside the hull or deck, except:

(a) a headsail clew may be connected (as defined in *The Equipment Rules of Sailing*) to a whisker pole, provided that a spinnaker is not set;

52 人力

船的固定索具、活动索具、杆具及可移动的船体附属物须仅依靠船员的人力来调整和操作。

53 船的表面摩擦

船不得排出或释放出某种物质，比如聚合物，也不得有能够改善边界层内水流特性的特殊质地的船体表面。

54 前支索和前帆前角

前支索和前帆前角须大致被固定在船的中心线上，不在近迎风航行时的球帆支索除外。

55 升帆和操帆

55.1 换帆

在更换前帆或球帆时，替换帆在被替换帆降下之前可以全部升起并调好。但是，一次仅能使用一面主帆，并且除了换帆外，一次仅能使用一面球帆。

55.2 球帆杆；球帆底边撑杆

除顺风换舷外，一次仅能使用一根球帆杆或球帆底边撑杆（译者注：此处特指一端与桅杆连接，另一端与球帆后角连接的杆状物）。使用时，它须被固定在最前面的桅杆上。

55.3 操帆

若帆缭越过或穿过在某一点对缭绳或帆后角施加向外张力的装置来操帆，当船处于直立状态时，从该点引出的垂直线落在了船体或甲板的外边，就不允许，除非：

(a) 前帆后角（按照《帆船器材规则》中的定义）可以连接到球帆底边撑杆上，前提是球帆没有升起；

(b) any sail may be sheeted to or led above a boom that is regularly used for a sail and is permanently attached to the mast from which the head of the sail is set;

(c) a headsail may be sheeted to its own boom that requires no adjustment when tacking; and

(d) the boom of a sail may be sheeted to a bumkin.

55.4 Headsails and Spinnakers

For the purposes of rules 54 and 55 and Appendix G, the definitions of 'headsail' and 'spinnaker' in *The Equipment Rules of Sailing* shall be used.

Note: The Equipment Rules of Sailing are available at the World Sailing website.

56 FOG SIGNALS AND LIGHTS; TRAFFIC SEPARATION SCHEMES

56.1 When so equipped, a boat shall sound fog signals and show lights as required by the *International Regulations for Preventing Collisions at Sea (IRPCAS)* or applicable government rules.

56.2 A boat shall comply with rule 10, Traffic Separation Schemes, of the *IRPCAS*.

Note: Appendix TS, Traffic Separation Schemes, is available at the World Sailing website. The notice of race may change rule 56.2 by stating that Section A, Section B or Section C of Appendix TS applies.

（b）任何帆都可以用帆杆或通过帆杆来进行操帆，这个帆杆通常为张帆所用，并永久性地连接在张挂帆顶的桅杆上；

（c）前帆可以用自己的迎风换舷时无需调节的帆杆来操帆；并且

（d）一面帆的帆杆可以连接到船尾撑杆上来操帆。

55.4 前帆和球帆

对于规则54、55和附录G而言，须使用《帆船器材规则》中的“前帆”和“球帆”定义。

注：《帆船器材规则》可在世界帆联网站上查阅。

56 雾中信号与灯光；分道通航制

56.1 当有如此配置时，船须按照《国际海上避碰规则（IRPCAS）》或适用的政府规定发出雾中音响信号和灯光。

56.2 船须遵守IRPCAS中的第10条规则，分道通航制。

注：附录TS，分道通航制，可以在世界帆联网站上查询。竞赛通知可以更改规则56.2，规定附录TS的A节、B节或C节适用。

PART 5–PROTESTS, REDRESS, HEARINGS, MISCONDUCT AND APPEALS

The protest form that was included in previous editions of this book has been replaced by two forms, a hearing request form and a hearing decision form. The new forms, in various formats, are available at the World Sailing website at sailing.org/racingrules/documents. *They may be downloaded and printed.*

Note that The Racing Rules of Sailing *does not require a particular form to be used.*

Suggestions for improving these forms are welcome and should be sent to rules@sailing.org.

SECTION A – PROTESTS; REDRESS; RULE 69 ACTION

60 RIGHT TO PROTEST; RIGHT TO REQUEST REDRESS OR RULE 69 ACTION

60.1 A boat may

(a) protest another boat, but not for an alleged breach of a rule of Part 2 or rule 31 unless she was involved in or saw the incident;

(b) request redress; or

(c) report to the protest committee requesting action under rule 60.3(d) or 69.2(b).

60.2 A race committee may

(a) protest a boat, but not as a result of information arising from a request for redress or an invalid *protest*, or from a report from a person with a *conflict of interest* other than the representative of the boat herself;

(b) request redress for a boat; or

第五章 抗议、补偿、审理、品行不端和上诉

本书之前版本中的抗议表已经被另外两个表所替代，审理要求表和审理裁决表。不同板式的新表格可以在世界帆联网站 sailing.org/racingrules/documents 上查询，可以下载并打印。

注意，RRS 没有要求使用特定的表格。

欢迎有关这些表格的建议与改善，请发送至 rules@sailing. org。

A 节 抗议；补偿；规则 69 的行动

60 抗议的权利；要求补偿的权利或规则 69 的行动

60.1 一条船可以

(a) 抗议另外一条船，但对涉嫌违反规则第二章或规则 31 的抗议只能当其自己是当事船或目睹事件时才能提出；

(b) 要求补偿；或

(c) 向抗议委员会报告，要求按规则 60. 3（d)或 69. 2（b）采取行动。

60.2 竞赛委员会可以

(a) 抗议一条船，但不能因为从一份补偿要求、一份无效的*抗议*或船只代表之外的有*利益冲突*的人的报告中获得的信息而提出抗议；

(b) 要求给予某条船补偿；或

(c) report to the protest committee requesting action under rule 60.3(d) or 69.2(b).

60.3 A protest committee may

(a) protest a boat, but not as a result of information arising from a request for redress or an invalid *protest*, or from a report from a person with a *conflict of interest* other than the representative of the boat herself. However, it may protest a boat

(1) if it learns of an incident involving her that may have resulted in injury or serious damage, or

(2) if during the hearing of a valid *protest* it learns that the boat, although not a *party* to the hearing, was involved in the incident and may have broken a *rule*;

(b) call a hearing to consider redress;

(c) act under rule 69.2(b); or

(d) call a hearing to consider whether a *support person* has broken a *rule*, based on its own observation or information received from any source, including evidence taken during a hearing.

60.4 A technical committee may

(a) protest a boat, but not as a result of information arising from a request for redress or an invalid *protest*, or from a report from a person with a *conflict of interest* other than the representative of the boat herself. However, it shall protest a boat if it decides that a boat or personal equipment does not comply with the class rules or with rule 50;

(b) request redress for a boat; or

（c）向抗议委员会报告，要求按规则 60. 3（d）或 69. 2（b）采取行动。

60.3 抗议委员会可以

（a）抗议一条船，但不能因为从一份补偿要求、一份无效的*抗议*或该船只代表之外的有*利益冲突*的人的报告中获得的信息而抗议该船。但是，可以在下列情况时对一条船提出抗议：

（1）如果了解到涉及她的事件中可能已经导致受伤或严重损坏，或

（2）如果在审理一个有效*抗议*时，了解到该船虽不是审理的一方，但也涉及该事件并有可能违反了*规则*；

（b）召集审理考虑给予补偿；

（c）按规则 69. 2（b）采取行动；或

（d）基于自身的观察或任何渠道获得的信息，包括审理过程中得到的证据，召集审理，考虑*后援人员*是否已经违反*规则*。

60.4 技术委员会可以

（a）抗议一条船，但不能因为从一份补偿要求、一份无效的*抗议*或船只代表之外的有*利益冲突*的人的报告中获得的信息而提出抗议。但是，如果它确认了某条船或个人器材没有遵守级别规则或规则 50，它须抗议这条船；

（b）为一条船要求补偿；或

(c) report to the protest committee requesting action under rule 60.3(d) or 69.2(b).

60.5 However, neither a boat nor a committee may protest for an alleged breach of rule 69 or a Regulation referred to in rule 6, unless permitted by the Regulation concerned.

61 PROTEST REQUIREMENTS

61.1 Informing the Protestee

(a) The protesting boat shall inform the other boat at the first reasonable opportunity. When her *protest* will concern an incident in the racing area, she shall hail 'Protest' and conspicuously display a red flag at the first reasonable opportunity for each. She shall display the flag until she is no longer *racing*. However,

(1) if the other boat is beyond hailing distance, the protesting boat need not hail but she shall inform the other boat at the first reasonable opportunity;

(2) if the hull length of the protesting boat is less than 6 metres, she need not display a red flag;

(3) if the incident was an error by the other boat in *sailing the course*, she need not hail or display a red flag but she shall inform the other boat either before or at the first reasonable opportunity after the other boat *finishes*;

(4) if at the time of the incident it is obvious to the protesting boat that a member of either crew is in danger, or that injury or serious damage resulted, the requirements of this rule do not apply to her, but she shall attempt to inform the other boat within the time limit of rule 61.3.

(c) 向抗议委员会报告,要求按规则 60.3(d)或 69.2(b)采取行动。

60.5 然而,任何船或委员会都不可以就涉嫌违反规则 69 或规则 6 涉及的规章提出抗议,除非规章本身允许。

61 对抗议的要求

61.1 通知被抗议人

(a) 抗议船须在第一合理时机通知另外一条船。当她的*抗议*是涉及在竞赛区域内的事件时,她须呼喊"抗议"并每次在第一合理时机明显地展示一面红旗。她须将这面旗展示到她不再*竞赛*为止。但是,

(1) 如果另外一条船远于可呼喊距离,抗议船无需呼喊,但须在第一合理时机通知那条船;

(2) 如果抗议船的船体长度短于 6 米,则无需展示红旗;

(3) 如果该事件是另一条船所犯的*行驶航线*的错误,她不需要呼喊或展示红旗,但是她须在另外一条船*到达终点*前或在其*到达终点*后的第一合理时机告知该船;

(4) 如果在事件发生时,对于抗议船而言,明显地任何一方的船员处于危险中,或事件造成了损伤或严重损坏,此条规则的要求对她不适用,但是她须尽力在规则 61.3 规定的时限内通知另外那条船。

(b) If the race committee, technical committee or protest committee intends to protest a boat concerning an incident the committee observed in the racing area, it shall inform her after the race within the time limit of rule 61.3. In other cases the committee shall inform the boat of its intention to protest as soon as reasonably possible. A notice posted on the official notice board within the appropriate time limit satisfies this requirement.

(c) If the protest committee decides to protest a boat under rule 60.3(a)(2), it shall inform her as soon as reasonably possible, close the current hearing, proceed as required by rules 61.2 and 63, and hear the original and the new *protests* together.

61.2 Protest Contents

A *protest* shall be in writing and identify

(a) the protestor and protestee;

(b) the incident;

(c) where and when the incident occurred;

(d) any *rule* the protestor believes was broken; and

(e) the name of the protestor's representative.

However, if requirement (b) is met, requirement (a) may be met at any time before the hearing, and requirements (d) and (e) may be met before or during the hearing. Requirement (c) may also be met before or during the hearing, provided the protestee is allowed reasonable time to prepare for the hearing.

61.3 Protest Time Limit

A *protest* by a boat, or by the race committee, technical committee or protest committee about an incident observed in the racing area, shall be delivered to the race office within the protest time limit stated in the sailing instructions. If none is stated, the time limit is two hours after the last boat in the

(b) 如果竞赛委员会、技术委员会或抗议委员会有意抗议一条与该委员会在竞赛区域观察到的事件有关的船，须在该轮赛后，在规则 61. 3 所规定的抗议时限内通知该船。其他情况下，委员会须尽可能早的告知该船其将被抗议。在恰当的时限内张贴在官方公告栏上的通知是符合此要求的。

(c) 如果抗议委员会决定根据规则 60. 3 (a)(2)向一条船提出抗议，须尽可能早地通知该船，关停当下的审理，按照规则 61. 2 和 63 的要求进行，并将原*抗议*和新*抗议*一同审理。

61.2 抗议内容

*抗议*须以书面形式提出并指明:

(a) 抗议者和被抗议者;

(b) 事件;

(c) 事件发生的时间和地点;

(d) 抗议者认为违反的*规则*;和

(e) 抗议者代表的姓名。

但是，如已满足(b)项要求，可在审理前任何时间满足(a)项要求，在审理前或审理中满足(d)项和(e)项要求。也可以在审理前或者审理中满足(c)项要求，前提是给予了被抗议者合理的时间来为审理做准备。

61.3 抗议时限

一个由船或竞赛委员会、技术委员会或抗议委员会提出的关于其在竞赛水域观察到的事件的*抗议*，须在航行细则规定的抗议时限内递交到竞赛办公室。如未注明时限，该时

race *finishes*. Other *protests* shall be delivered to the race office no later than two hours after the protestor receives the relevant information. The protest committee shall extend the time if there is good reason to do so.

62 REDRESS

62.1 A request for redress or a protest committee's decision to consider redress shall be based on a claim or possibility that a boat's score or place in a race or series has been or may be, through no fault of her own, made significantly worse by

(a) an improper action or omission of the race committee, protest committee, organizing authority or technical committee for the event, but not by a protest committee decision when the boat was a *party* to the hearing;

(b) injury or physical damage because of the action of a boat that was breaking a rule of Part 2 and took an appropriate penalty or was penalized, or of a vessel not *racing* that was required to keep clear or is determined to be at fault under the *IRPCAS* or a government right-of-way rule;

(c) giving help (except to herself or her crew) in compliance with rule 1.1; or

(d) an action of another boat, or a crew member or *support person* of that boat, that resulted in a penalty under rule 2 or a penalty or warning under rule 69.

62.2 A request shall be in writing and identify the reason for making it. If the request is based on an incident in the racing area, it shall be delivered to the race office within the protest time limit or two hours after the incident, whichever is later. Other requests shall be delivered as soon as reasonably possible after learning of the reasons for making the request. The protest committee shall extend the time if there is good reason to do so. No red flag is required.

限为该轮竞赛最后一条船*到达终点*后 2 个小时。其他*抗议*须不晚于抗议者收到相关信息后 2 小时内递交到竞赛办公室。若理由充足，抗议委员会须延长此时间。

62 补偿

62.1 补偿的要求或抗议委员会考虑补偿的决定须基于如下要求或可能，即一船因非自身失误，在一轮竞赛或系列赛中的得分或名次已经或可能因以下原因明显变差：

(a) 赛事的竞赛委员会、抗议委员会、组织机构或技术委员会有不当行为或疏忽，但不是船作为审理一方时由抗议委员会做出的裁决；

(b) 另外一条违反规则第二章并接受了适当的惩罚或被判罚的船的行为，或一条需要避让的不参加*竞赛*或根据 IRPCAS 或政府航行权规则确定为有过错的船舶的行为造成了受伤或有形损坏；

(c) 根据规则 1.1 提供帮助（对自己或对自己的船员除外）；或

(d) 另一条船或那条船的船员或*后援人员*的行为导致根据规则 2 被判罚或根据 69 被判罚或警告。

62.2 补偿要求须以书面形式提出并写明要求补偿的原因。如果要求是基于在竞赛区域发生的事件，补偿要求须在不晚于抗议时限或在事件发生后的 2 小时内提交到竞赛办公室，以后到的时间为准。其他的补偿要求须在得知要求补偿的原因后尽可能快地提交。若理由充足，抗议委员会须延长此时间。不要求展示红旗。

(a) However, on the last scheduled day of racing a request for redress based on a protest committee decision shall be delivered no later than 30 minutes after the decision was posted.

SECTION B – HEARINGS AND DECISIONS

63 HEARINGS

63.1 Requirement for a Hearing

A boat or competitor shall not be penalized without a protest hearing, except as provided in rules 30.2, 30.3, 30.4, 64.4(d), 64.5(b), 64.6, 69, 78.2, A5.1 and P2. A decision on redress shall not be made without a hearing. The protest committee shall hear all *protests* and requests for redress that have been delivered to the race office unless it allows a *protest* or request to be withdrawn.

63.2 Time and Place of the Hearing; Time for Parties to Prepare

All *parties* to the hearing shall be notified of the time and place of the hearing, the *protest* or redress information or the allegations shall be made available to them, and they shall be allowed reasonable time to prepare for the hearing. When two or more hearings arise from the same incident, or from very closely connected incidents, they may be heard together in one hearing. However, a hearing conducted under rule 69 shall not be combined with any other type of hearing.

63.3 Right to Be Present

(a) A representative of each *party* to the hearing has the right to be present throughout the hearing of all the evidence. When a *protest* claims a breach of a rule of Part 2, 3 or 4, the representatives of boats shall have been on board at the time of the incident, unless there is good reason for the protest committee to rule otherwise. Any witness, other than a member of the protest committee, shall be excluded except when giving evidence.

（a）但是，在日程排定的最后一个竞赛日，基于抗议委员会裁决的补偿要求须不晚于裁决张贴后 30 分钟递交。

B 节 审理和裁决

63 审理

63.1 审理的要求

船或选手不得在没有抗议审理的情况下被判罚，规则 30. 2、30. 3、30. 4、64. 4（d）、64. 5（b）、64. 6、69、78. 2、A5. 1 和 P2 的情况例外。在没有审理的情况下不得对补偿做出裁决。抗议委员会须审理所有已经递交到竞赛办公室的*抗议*和补偿的要求，除非其允许撤销某个*抗议*或要求。

63.2 审理的时间和地点；各方准备的时间

审理的时间和地点须通知到参加审理的*各方*，并且他们须能拿到*抗议*或补偿的信息或指控，还须给予他们合理的时间为审理做好准备。当两个或多个审理出自同一事件或联系非常紧密的事件时，可以合并审理。但是，根据规则 69 进行的审理不得与任何其他类型的审理合并。

63.3 出席的权利

（a）*各方*的代表都有权出席对所有证据的审理过程。当*抗议*声称有违反第二、第三或第四章中某条规则时，事件发生时船的代表须在船上，除非抗议委员会有适当的理由另行决定。除抗议委员会的成员外，所有证人除在提供证据时，不得在场。

(b) If a *party* to a hearing does not come to the hearing, the protest committee may nevertheless proceed with the hearing. If the *party* was unavoidably absent, the committee may reopen the hearing.

63.4 Conflict of Interest

(a) A protest committee member shall declare any possible *conflict of interest* as soon as he is aware of it. A *party* to the hearing who believes a member of the protest committee has a *conflict of interest* shall object as soon as possible. A *conflict of interest* declared by a protest committee member shall be included in the written information provided under rule 65.2.

(b) A member of a protest committee with a *conflict of interest* shall not be a member of the committee for the hearing, unless

(1) all *parties* consent, or

(2) the protest committee decides that the *conflict of interest* is not significant.

(c) When deciding whether a *conflict of interest* is significant, the protest committee shall consider the views of the *parties*, the level of the conflict, the level of the event, the importance to each *party*, and the overall perception of fairness.

(d) However, for World Sailing major events, or for other events as prescribed by the national authority of the venue, rule 63.4(b) does not apply and a person who has a *conflict of interest* shall not be a member of the protest committee.

63.5 Validity of the Protest or Request for Redress

At the beginning of the hearing the protest committee shall take any evidence it considers necessary to decide whether all requirements for the *protest* or request for redress have been met. If they have been met, the *protest* or request is （b）如果审理的一方未参加审理，抗议委员会仍然可以开始审理。如果有一方不可避免地缺席审理，委员会可以重新审理。

63.4 利益冲突

（a）抗议委员会成员一旦意识到存在*利益冲突*，须尽快声明。认为一名抗议委员会成员存在*利益冲突*的审理的一方须尽快提出反对意见。抗议委员会的成员所做的*利益冲突*声明须包含在规则 65. 2 规定的书面信息中。

（b）有*利益冲突*的抗议委员会成员不得作为该审理委员会的一员，除非

（1）*各方*都同意，或

（2）抗议委员会认定这个*利益冲突*并不突出。

（c）在判断*利益冲突*是否突出时，抗议委员会须考虑*各方*的意见、冲突的程度、赛事的等级、对*各方*的重要性以及整体公平性。

（d）但是，对于世界帆联的主要赛事，或者赛事举办地国家和地区管理机构规定的其他赛事，规则 63. 4（b）不适用，同时，有*利益冲突*的人不得作为抗议委员会的成员。

63.5 抗议或补偿要求的有效性

审理开始时，抗议委员会须核实其认为必要的一切证据来决定其是否符合*抗议*或者补偿的所有要求。如果符合，则*抗议*或补偿要求有效，须继续审理。如果不符合，抗议委员会须宣布*抗议*或补偿要求无效并关停审理。如果*抗议*

valid and the hearing shall be continued. If not, the committee shall declare the *protest* or request invalid and close the hearing. If the *protest* has been made under rule 60.3(a)(1), the committee shall also determine whether or not injury or serious damage resulted from the incident in question. If not, the hearing shall be closed.

63.6 Taking Evidence and Finding Facts

(a) The protest committee shall take the evidence, including hearsay evidence, of the *parties* present at the hearing and of their witnesses and other evidence it considers necessary. However, the committee may exclude evidence which it considers to be irrelevant or unduly repetitive.

(b) A member of the protest committee who saw the incident shall, while the *parties* are present, state that fact and may give evidence.

(c) A *party* present at the hearing may question any person who gives evidence.

(d) The committee shall then give the weight it considers appropriate to the evidence presented, find the facts and base its decision on them.

63.7 Conflict Between Rules

If there is a conflict between two or more *rules* that must be resolved before the protest committee makes a decision, the committee shall apply the *rule* that it believes will provide the fairest result for all boats affected. Rule 63.7 applies only if the conflict is between rules in the notice of race, the sailing instructions, or any of the other documents that govern the event under item (g) of the definition *Rule*.

63.8 Hearings Involving Parties in Different Events

A hearing involving *parties* in different events conducted by different organizing authorities shall be heard by a protest committee acceptable to those authorities.

是根据规则 60.3（a)(1)提出的，抗议委员会也须决定有问题的事件是否造成了受伤或严重损坏。如果没有，须关停此审理。

63.6 取证和认定事实

(a) 抗议委员会须从出席审理的*各方*和他们的证人处获取证据，包括传闻证据，以及获取其认为必要的其他证据。然而，委员会可以排除其认为不相关或过度重复的证据。

(b) 目睹了事件的抗议委员会成员须在*各方*在场时说明事实并提供证据。

(c) 出席审理的一*方*可向任何提供证据的人提问。

(d) 然后，委员会须对其获取的认为适当的证据进行权重分配，认定事实并据此做出裁决。

63.7 规则间的冲突

如果两条或多条*规则*之间发生冲突，则必须在抗议委员会做出裁决之前解决，委员会须采纳其认为能给所有受影响的船提供公平结果的*规则*。只有在竞赛通知、航行细则或*规则*的定义(g)所说的约束赛事的其他文件中的规则之间发生冲突时，规则 63.7 才适用。

63.8 涉及不同赛事中各方的审理

涉及不同组织机构组织的不同赛事中*各方*的审理，须由这些组织机构能接受的一个抗议委员会来审理。

63.9 Hearings under Rule 60.3(d) — Support Persons

If the protest committee decides to call a hearing under rule 60.3(d), it shall promptly follow the procedures in rules 63.2, 63.3, 63.4 and 63.6, except that the information given to the *parties* shall be details of the alleged breach and a person may be appointed by the protest committee to present the allegation.

64 DECISIONS

64.1 Standard of Proof, Majority Decisions and Reclassifying Requests

(a) A protest committee shall make its decision based on a balance of probabilities, unless provided for otherwise in the rule alleged to have been broken.

(b) Decisions of the protest committee shall be by simple majority vote of all members. When there is equal division of votes cast, the chairman may cast an additional vote.

(c) The protest committee shall proceed with each case, as a *protest*, request for redress or other type of request, based on the information in the written request or allegation and testimony during the hearing. This permits the type of case to be changed if appropriate.

64.2 Penalties

When the protest committee decides that a boat that is a *party* to a protest hearing has broken a *rule* and is not exonerated, it shall disqualify her unless some other penalty applies. A penalty shall be imposed whether or not the applicable *rule* was mentioned in the *protest*. If a boat has broken a *rule* when not *racing*, her penalty shall apply to the race sailed nearest in time to that of the incident. However,

(a) if a boat has taken an applicable penalty, she shall not be further penalized under this rule unless the penalty for a *rule* she broke is a disqualification that is not excludable from her series score;

63.9 根据规则 60.3（d)的审理——后援人员

如果抗议委员会决定根据规则 60.3（d)召集审理，它须迅即根据规则 63.2、63.3、63.4 和 63.6 的程序进行，但向一方提供的信息须包括涉嫌违规的细节，抗议委员会可以指定一人出面做指控陈述。

64 裁决

64.1 证据的标准，多数人的决定和请求的重新分类

(a) 抗议委员会须基于盖然性权衡做出裁决，除非涉嫌违反了的规则另有规定。

(b) 抗议委员会的裁决须以简单的所有成员多数票通过。当投出平票时，主席可以多投一票。

(c) 抗议委员会须根据书面申请中的信息或审理期间的指控和证词，将每个案件按照*抗议*、补偿要求或其他类型的要求进行分类处理。在适当时，允许改变案件的类型。

64.2 惩罚

当抗议委员会裁决作为一个*抗议*审理一方的一条船违反了*规则*并不被免责时，须取消其资格，除非有其他适用的惩罚。不管*抗议*中是否提及所适用的*规则*，惩罚都须被执行。如果一条船不是在*竞赛*时违反了*规则*，对其的惩罚须在距离违反*规则*的事件发生时间最近的已航行轮次执行。但是，

(a) 如果一条船已经接受了适用的惩罚，根据规则不得对其做出进一步惩罚，除非其违反*规则*的取消资格的惩罚是不能从系列赛积分中去掉的。

(b) if the race is restarted or resailed, rule 36 applies.

64.3 Decisions on Redress

When the protest committee decides that a boat is entitled to redress under rule 62, it shall make as fair an arrangement as possible for all boats affected, whether or not they asked for redress. This may be to adjust the scoring (see rule A9 for some examples) or finishing times of boats, to *abandon* the race, to let the results stand or to make some other arrangement. When in doubt about the facts or probable results of any arrangement for the race or series, especially before *abandoning* the race, the protest committee shall take evidence from appropriate sources.

64.4 Decisions on Protests Concerning Class Rules

(a) When the protest committee finds that deviations in excess of tolerances specified in the class rules were caused by damage or normal wear and do not improve the performance of the boat, it shall not penalize her. However, the boat shall not *race* again until the deviations have been corrected, except when the protest committee decides there is or has been no reasonable opportunity to do so.

(b) When the protest committee is in doubt about the meaning of a class rule, it shall refer its questions, together with the relevant facts, to an authority responsible for interpreting the rule. In making its decision, the committee shall be bound by the reply of the authority.

(c) When a boat is penalized under a class rule and the protest committee decides that the boat also broke the same rule in earlier races in the same event, the penalty may be imposed for all such races. No further *protest* is necessary.

(d) When a boat penalized under a class rule states in writing that she intends to appeal, she may compete in subsequent

(b) 如果该轮竞赛再次起航或者重赛，规则 36 适用。

64.3 补偿的决定

当抗议委员会决定某船根据规则 62 享有补偿权时，须尽可能对所有受影响的船做出合理公平的安排，不管其是否提出补偿要求。可通过调整计分（见规则 A9 的例子）或船到达终点的时间、*放弃*竞赛、使成绩有效或做出其他安排。当对事实、竞赛或系列赛成绩的任何安排结果有疑问时，特别是在*放弃*竞赛前，抗议委员会须从适当的来源中找出证据。

64.4 涉及级别规则抗议的裁决

(a) 当抗议委员会发现由于受损或正常磨损而使船的误差超过了级别规则的规定，但并不会提高该船的性能时，不得对其做出惩罚。但是，该船在修正误差之前不得再参加*竞赛*，除非抗议委员会认为该船此时没有或已经没有合理的机会进行修正。

(b) 当抗议委员会对某一级别规则的含义有疑问时，它须将问题连同有关事实一起提交给负责解释规则的一个管理机构。抗议委员会须依据管理机构的回复进行裁决。

(c) 当一条船由于违反级别规则被判罚，且抗议委员会判定该船在该赛事其他已经完成的轮次中也违反了同样的规则时，该判罚可以适用于所有这样的轮次。无需进一步*抗议*。

(d) 当根据级别规则被判罚的船以书面形式声明她准备提出上诉时，她可在不对船进行改变的情况下继续参

races without changes to the boat. However, if she fails to appeal or the appeal is decided against her, she shall be disqualified without a further hearing from all subsequent races in which she competed.

(e) Measurement costs arising from a *protest* involving a class rule shall be paid by the unsuccessful *party* unless the protest committee decides otherwise.

64.5 Decisions Concerning Support Persons

(a) When the protest committee decides that a *support person* who is a *party* to a hearing under rule 60.3(d) or 69 has broken a *rule*, it may

(1) issue a warning,

(2) exclude the person from the event or venue or remove any privileges or benefits, or

(3) take other action within its jurisdiction as provided by the *rules*.

(b) The protest committee may also penalize a boat that is a *party* to a hearing under rule 60.3(d) or 69 for the breach of a *rule* by a *support person* by changing the boat's score in a single race, up to and including disqualification, when the protest committee decides that

(1) the boat may have gained a competitive advantage as the result of the breach by the *support person*, or

(2) the *support person* committed a further breach after the protest committee warned the boat in writing, following a previous hearing, that a penalty may be imposed.

64.6 Discretionary Penalties

When a boat reports within the protest time limit that she has broken a *rule* subject to a discretionary penalty, the protest committee shall decide the appropriate penalty after taking evidence from the boat and any witnesses it decides are appropriate.

加后面的竞赛。但是，如果她上诉失败或在上诉中被裁决为败诉，那么她后面所有已经参加过的竞赛轮次将被取消的资格，无须进一步审理。

（e）涉及级别规则的*抗议*所产生的丈量费用须由败诉一方支付，除非抗议委员会做出了其他裁决。

64.5 涉及后援人员的裁决

（a）当抗议委员会认定按规则 60.3（d）或 69 作为审理的一方的*后援人员*违反了*规则*，它可以

（1）给予警告，

（2）将其逐出赛事或场馆，或者剥夺其享有的权利或收益，或

（3）在*规则*规定的权限内采取其他行动。

（b）抗议委员会还可以由于*后援人员*违反*规则*，对按规则 60.3（d）或 69 进行审理的一方的船进行惩罚，改变该船单轮计分，判罚最高可至并包括 DSQ，条件是当抗议委员会裁定

（1）该船可能因*后援人员*的犯规而获得竞赛优势，或

（2）在抗议委员会上一次审理后书面警告某船可能对她进行判罚后，其*后援人员*继续犯规。

64.6 自由裁量的判罚

当一条船在抗议时限内报告她违反了自由裁量的*规则*，抗议委员会须在向它认为合适的船和其他证人取证后做出适当的判罚。

65 INFORMING THE PARTIES AND OTHERS

65.1 After making its decision, the protest committee shall promptly inform the *parties* to the hearing of the facts found, the applicable *rules*, the decision, the reasons for it, and any penalties imposed or redress given.

65.2 A *party* to the hearing is entitled to receive the above information in writing, provided she asks for it in writing from the protest committee no later than seven days after being informed of the decision. The committee shall then promptly provide the information, including, when relevant, a diagram of the incident prepared or endorsed by the committee.

65.3 Unless there is good reason not to do so, after any hearing, including a hearing under rule 69, the protest committee may publish the information set out in rule 65.1. The protest committee may direct that the information is to be confidential to the *parties*.

65.4 When the protest committee penalizes a boat under a class rule, it shall send the above information to the relevant class rule authorities.

66 REOPENING A HEARING

66.1 The protest committee may reopen a hearing when it decides that it may have made a significant error, or when significant new evidence becomes available within a reasonable time. It shall reopen a hearing when required by the national authority under rule 71.2 or R5.

66.2 A *party* to the hearing may request a reopening in writing no later than 24 hours after being informed of the decision.

(a) However, on the last scheduled day of racing the request shall be delivered

65 通知各方和其他人

65.1 做出裁决后，抗议委员会须迅即通知参加审理的*各方*所认定的事实、适用的*规则*、裁决及其理由和所给予的惩罚或补偿。

65.2 审理的一方只要在得到裁决通知后 7 天内书面要求抗议委员会提供有关上述裁决的书面材料，她就有权获取该材料。抗议委员会须迅即提供该信息，包括委员会准备或认可的相关的事件图示。

65.3 任何审理之后，包括根据规则 69 进行的审理，抗议委员会可以张贴规则 65. 1 所列出的信息，除非有不这样做的充分理由。抗议委员会可以指出该信息对*各方*是保密的。

65.4 当抗议委员会依据级别规则对某船进行惩罚时，它须将上述信息递交给相关级别规则管理机构。

66 重新审理

66.1 当抗议委员会认为自己可能有明显的错误或在合理的时间内又获得了值得关注的新证据时，可重新召集审理。当国家和地区管理机构根据规则 71. 2 和 R5 要求重审时，抗议委员会须重新审理。

66.2 在得到裁决通知后的 24 小时内，审理的一方可以书面方式要求重新审理。

(a) 但是，在竞赛日程排定的最后一天，须按如下要求递交请求：

(1) within the protest time limit if the requesting *party* was informed of the decision on the previous day;

(2) no later than 30 minutes after the *party* was informed of the decision on that day.

66.3 The protest committee shall consider all requests to reopen. When a request to reopen is being considered or the hearing is reopened,

(a) when based only on new evidence, a majority of the members of the protest committee shall, if practicable, be members of the original committee;

(b) when based on a significant error, the protest committee shall, if practicable, have at least one new member.

67 DAMAGES

The question of damages arising from a breach of any *rule* shall be governed by the prescriptions, if any, of the national authority.

Note: There is no rule 68.

SECTION C – MISCONDUCT

69 MISCONDUCT

69.1 Obligation not to Commit Misconduct; Resolution

(a) A competitor, boat owner or *support person* shall not commit an act of misconduct.

(b) Misconduct is:

(1) conduct that is a breach of good manners, a breach of good sportsmanship, or unethical behaviour; or

(2) conduct that may bring, or has brought, the sport into disrepute.

(c) An allegation of a breach of rule 69.1(a) shall be resolved in accordance with the provisions of rule 69. It shall not be grounds for a *protest* and rule 63.1 does not apply.

（1）如果提出请求的一方是在前一天被告知裁决的，在抗议时限内；

（2）如果一方在当天被告知裁决的，在被告知后 30 分钟内。

66.3 抗议委员会须考虑所有重新审理的请求。当重新审理的请求被考虑或者重新审理时，

（a）如果仅基于新证据，若可行，重新审理的抗议委员会大多数成员须是原抗议委员会的成员；

（b）如果基于明显的错误，若可行，重新审理的抗议委员会须至少有一名新成员。

67 损坏

因违反任一*规则*而引起的损坏问题，如果国家和地区管理机构有此方面的规定，须以此进行处理。

注：此处没有规则 68。

C 节 品行不端

69 品行不端

69.1 不做品行不端的事的义务；解决方法

（a）选手、船东或*后援人员*不得做出品行不端的行为。

（b）品行不端指的是：

（1）不文明礼貌，破坏体育精神的举止或不道德的行为；或

（2）可能或已经给体育运动抹黑的行为。

（c）关于违反规则 69. 1（a）的指控须依据规则 69 的条款解决。它不得作为*抗议*的依据，且规则 63. 1 不适用。

69.2 Action by a Protest Committee

(a) A protest committee acting under this rule shall have at least three members.

(b) When a protest committee, from its own observation or from information received from any source, including evidence taken during a hearing, believes a person may have broken rule 69.1(a), it shall decide whether or not to call a hearing.

(c) When the protest committee needs more information to make the decision to call a hearing, it shall consider appointing a person or persons to conduct an investigation. These investigators shall not be members of the protest committee that will decide the matter.

(d) When an investigator is appointed, all relevant information he gathers, favourable or unfavourable, shall be disclosed to the protest committee, and if the protest committee decides to call a hearing, to the *parties*.

(e) If the protest committee decides to call a hearing, it shall promptly inform the person in writing of the alleged breach and of the time and place of the hearing and follow the procedures in rules 63.2, 63.3(a), 63.4, 63.6, 65.1, 65.2, 65.3 and 66, except that:

(1) unless a person has been appointed by World Sailing, a person may be appointed by the protest committee to present the allegation.

(2) a person against whom an allegation has been made under this rule shall be entitled to have an advisor and a representative with him who may act on his behalf.

(f) If the person

(1) provides good reason why he is unable to come to the hearing at the scheduled time, the protest committee shall reschedule it; or

69.2 抗议委员会的行动

(a) 根据本条规则行事的抗议委员会至少须有 3 名成员。

(b) 当抗议委员会根据自己的观察或从其他任何渠道得来的信息，包括审理中得到的证据，认为某人可能已经违反了规则 69.1(a)，委员会须决定是否要召集审理。

(c) 当抗议委员会需要更多的信息来决定召集审理时，须考虑任命一名或多名人员来进行调查。这些调查员不得为对此事有决定作用的抗议委员会成员。

(d) 调查人员被任命之后，他所搜集的所有相关信息，不管是有利的还是不利的，都须对抗议委员会公开，如果抗议委员会决定召集审理，这些信息须对各方公开。

(e) 如果抗议委员会决定召集审理，委员会须迅即以书面形式通知此人其被控违反规则的行为，以及审理的时间和地点，并遵守规则 63.2、63.3(a)、63.4、63.6、65.1、65.2、65.3 和 66 中的程序，以下情况除外：

(1) 除非世界帆联已任命一位人员来提出指控，否则抗议委员会可以指定一名人员提出指控。

(2) 在此规则下，指控所针对的那个人须有权拥有一名顾问及一名能代表其言行的代表。

(f) 如果此人

(1) 提供了其不能在排定的时间出席审理的充足的理由，抗议委员会须重新安排审理时间；或

(2) does not provide good reason and does not come to the hearing, the protest committee may conduct it without the person present.

(g) The standard of proof to be applied is the test of the comfortable satisfaction of the protest committee, bearing in mind the seriousness of the alleged misconduct. However, if the standard of proof in this rule conflicts with the laws of a country, the national authority may, with the approval of World Sailing, change it with a prescription to this rule.

(h) When the protest committee decides that a competitor or boat owner has broken rule 69.1(a), it may take one or more of the following actions

(1) issue a warning;

(2) change their boat's score in one or more races, including disqualification(s) that may or may not be excluded from her series score;

(3) exclude the person from the event or venue or remove any privileges or benefits; and

(4) take any other action within its jurisdiction as provided by the *rules*.

(i) When the protest committee decides that a *support person* has broken rule 69.1(a), rule 64.5 applies.

(j) If the protest committee

(1) imposes a penalty greater than one DNE;

(2) excludes the person from the event or venue; or

(3) in any other case if it considers it appropriate,

it shall report its findings, including the facts found, its conclusions and decision to the national authority of the person or, for specific international events listed in the World Sailing Regulations, to World Sailing. If the protest committee has acted under rule 69.2(f)(2), the report shall

（2）不能提供充足的理由也没有出席审理，抗议委员会可以进行缺席审理。

（g）所运用的证据标准是测试抗议委员会是否完全满意，同时要考虑到被控品行不端的严重性。然而，如果此规则中的证据标准与某个国家和地区的法律和有关规定相冲突，那么国家和地区管理机构在征得世界帆联同意的前提下，可以通过针对本规则的国家和地区管理机构规定来进行更改。

（h）当抗议委员会认定选手或船东已经违反了规则 69.1（a），可以采取以下一个或多个行动：

（1）发布警告；

（2）更改他们的船在一轮或多轮竞赛中的计分，包括可以和不可以从系列赛计分中去掉的取消资格；

（3）将其逐出赛事或场馆，或者剥夺其享有的权限或利益，以及

（4）在*规则*提供的管辖权内采取其他行动。

（i）当抗议委员会认定某*后援人员*已经违反了规则 69.1（a）时，规则 64.5 适用。

（j）如果抗议委员会

（1）给予一个比 DNE 更严重的判罚；

（2）将此人从赛事或场馆中逐出；或

（3）考虑到其认为合理的其他情况，

委员会须将发现的内容，包括认定的事实、其结论及裁决报送此人所在的国家和地区管理机构，或对于世界帆联规章中列举出来的一些特定国际赛事，向世界

also include that fact and the reasons for it.

(k) If the protest committee decides not to conduct the hearing without the person present, or if the protest committee has left the event and a report alleging a breach of rule 69.1(a) is received, the race committee or organizing authority may appoint the same or a new protest committee to proceed under this rule. If it is impractical for the protest committee to conduct a hearing, it shall collect all available information and, if the allegation seems justified, make a report to the national authority of the person or, for specific international events listed in the World Sailing Regulations, to World Sailing.

69.3 Action by a National Authority and World Sailing

The disciplinary powers, procedures and responsibilities of national authorities and World Sailing that apply are specified in the World Sailing Disciplinary Code. National authorities and World Sailing may impose further penalties, including suspension of eligibility, under that code.

SECTION D – APPEALS

70 APPEALS AND REQUESTS TO A NATIONAL AUTHORITY

70.1

(a) Provided that the right of appeal has not been denied under rule 70.5, a *party* to a hearing may appeal a protest committee's decision or its procedures, but not the facts found.

(b) A boat may appeal when she is denied a hearing required by rule 63.1.

70.2 A protest committee may request confirmation or correction of its decision.

70.3 An appeal under rule 70.1 or a request by a protest committee under rule 70.2 shall be sent to the national authority with

帆联报送。如果抗议委员会依据规则 69. 2 (f)(2)行事,该报告也须包括那项事实及其原因。

(k) 如果抗议委员会决定在当事人缺席的情况下不召集审理,或者如果抗议委员会在离开了赛事的情况下收到了违反规则 69. 1 (a)的指控,竞赛委员会或组织机构可以任命相同或新的抗议委员会依据本条规则处理。如果抗议委员会决定无法组织审理,则须收集所有可用的信息,如果指控看起来是合理的,报送当事人所在的国家和地区管理机构,对于世界帆联规章中列举的一些特定国际赛事,须向世界帆联汇报。

69.3 国家和地区管理机构与世界帆联的行动

国家和地区管理机构和世界帆联适用的纪律处分权力、程序及责任在《世界帆联纪律守则》中有详细的说明。国家和地区管理机构和世界帆联有可能会追加处罚,包括依据守则暂停参赛资格。

D 节 上诉

70 上诉和对国家和地区管理机构的请求

70.1

(a) 只要没有依据规则 70. 5 被驳回上诉权,审理的一方可对抗议委员会的裁决或程序提出上诉,但不能对认定的事实提出上诉。

(b) 当一条船依规则 63. 1 所要求的审理被驳回时,可以上诉。

70.2 抗议委员会可请求对其裁决进行确认和修正。

70.3 根据规则 70. 1 提出的上诉或抗议委员会根据规则 70. 2

which the organizing authority is associated under rule 89.1. However, if boats will pass through the waters of more than one national authority while *racing*, an appeal or request shall be sent to the national authority where the finishing line is located, unless the sailing instructions identify another national authority.

70.4 A club or other organization affiliated to a national authority may request an interpretation of the *rules*, provided that no *protest* or request for redress that may be appealed is involved. The interpretation shall not be used for changing a previous protest committee decision.

70.5 There shall be no appeal from the decisions of an international jury constituted in compliance with Appendix N. Furthermore, if the notice of race or the sailing instructions so state, the right of appeal may be denied provided that

(a) it is essential to determine promptly the result of a race that will qualify a boat to compete in a later stage of an event or a subsequent event (a national authority may prescribe that its approval is required for such a procedure);

(b) a national authority so approves for a particular event open only to boats entered by an organization affiliated to that national authority, a member of an organization affiliated to that national authority, or a personal member of that national authority; or

(c) a national authority after consultation with World Sailing so approves for a particular event, provided the protest committee is constituted as required by Appendix N, except that only two members of the protest committee need be International Judges.

70.6 Appeals and requests shall conform to Appendix R.

提出的要求须被送至按规则 89. 1 与组织机构相关联的国家和地区管理机构。然而，当船在*竞赛*中将通过不止一个国家和地区管理机构的水域时，上诉或请求须送至终点线所在的国家和地区管理机构，除非航行细则明确规定了另一个国家和地区管理机构。

70.4 只要不涉及有可能上诉的*抗议*或补偿要求，隶属某一个国家和地区管理机构的俱乐部或其他组织可要求对*规则*进行解释。解释不得被用来改变抗议委员会之前做出的裁决。

70.5 不得对按附录 N 要求建制的国际仲裁委员会的裁决提出上诉。而且，如竞赛通知或航行细则中有如此规定，上诉权可被驳回，前提是

(a) 必须迅即确定竞赛的结果，以使船有资格参加该赛事后阶段的比赛或后续的赛事（国家和地区管理机构可以规定这样的程序需得到它的批准）；

(b) 在只允许由隶属于国家和地区管理机构的组织、隶属于国家和地区管理机构的组织会员，或是那个国家和地区管理机构的个人会员报名的特定赛事上，国家和地区管理机构批准这样做时；或

(c) 经国家和地区管理机构与世界帆联协商后批准的某一特定赛事中，前提是抗议委员会是按附录 N 的要求建制，其例外是该抗议委员会只需要 2 名成员为国际仲裁。

70.6 上诉和请求须符合附录 R 的规定。

71 NATIONAL AUTHORITY DECISIONS

71.1 A person who has a *conflict of interest* or was a member of the protest committee shall not take any part in the discussion or decision on an appeal or a request for confirmation or correction.

71.2 The national authority may uphold, change or reverse a protest committee's decision including a decision on validity or a decision under rule 69. Alternatively, the national authority may order that a hearing be reopened, or that a new hearing be held by the same or a different protest committee. When the national authority decides that there shall be a new hearing, it may appoint the protest committee.

71.3 When from the facts found by the protest committee the national authority decides that a boat that was a *party* to a protest hearing broke a *rule* and is not exonerated, it shall penalize her, whether or not that boat or that *rule* was mentioned in the protest committee's decision.

71.4 The decision of the national authority shall be final. The national authority shall send its decision in writing to all *parties* to the hearing and the protest committee, who shall be bound by the decision.

71 国家和地区管理机构的裁决

71.1 有*利益冲突*或曾是抗议委员会成员的人不得参加对上诉及确认或修正请求的讨论和裁决。

71.2 国家和地区管理机构可维持、更改或推翻抗议委员会的裁决，包括有效性的裁决或者根据规则 69 做出的裁决。或者，国家和地区管理机构可以要求重新进行审理，或者由相同或不同的抗议委员会进行新的审理。当国家和地区管理机构决定须进行新的审理时，它可以任命该抗议委员会。

71.3 当从抗议委员会认定的事实中，国家和地区管理机构认定作为抗议审理一*方*的某船违反了*规则*且没有被免责，须对其进行惩罚，不管之前的抗议委员会裁决中是否提到该船或那条*规则*。

71.4 国家和地区管理机构的裁决须为最终裁决。国家和地区管理机构须将其裁决以书面形式发至审理的*各方*及抗议委员会，他们须遵守该裁决。

PART 6–ENTRY AND QUALIFICATION

75 ENTERING AN EVENT

To enter an event, a boat shall comply with the requirements of the organizing authority of the event. She shall be entered by

(a) a member of a club or other organization affiliated to a World Sailing member national authority,

(b) such a club or organization, or

(c) a member of a World Sailing member national authority.

76 EXCLUSION OF BOATS OR COMPETITORS

76.1 The organizing authority or the race committee may reject or cancel the entry of a boat or exclude a competitor, subject to rule 76.3, provided it does so before the start of the first race and states the reason for doing so. On request the boat shall promptly be given the reason in writing. The boat may request redress if she considers that the rejection or exclusion is improper.

76.2 The organizing authority or the race committee shall not reject or cancel the entry of a boat or exclude a competitor because of advertising, provided the boat or competitor complies with the World Sailing Advertising Code.

76.3 At world and continental championships no entry within stated quotas shall be rejected or cancelled without first obtaining the approval of the relevant World Sailing Class Association (or the Offshore Racing Congress) or World Sailing.

77 IDENTIFICATION ON SAILS

A boat shall comply with the requirements of Appendix G governing class insignia, national letters and numbers on sails.

第六章　报名与资格

75 赛事报名

船在报名参加一场赛事时，须符合赛事组织机构的要求。她须以下列名义报名：

（a）隶属世界帆联会员管理机构的俱乐部或其他组织的会员，

（b）这样的俱乐部或组织，或

（c）世界帆联会员管理机构的会员。

76 船或选手的禁赛

76.1 在遵从规则 76. 3 的前提下，组织机构或竞赛委员会可以拒绝或取消某条船或选手的报名，但要在第一轮竞赛开始之前并声明此做法的理由。理由须迅即以书面形式应要求告知该船。如果该船认为该拒绝或取消报名是错误的，她可以要求补偿。

76.2 组织机构或者竞赛委员会不得因广告拒绝或者取消一条船或选手的报名，或者拒绝选手参赛，前提是该船或选手符合《世界帆联广告守则》。

76.3 在世界和洲际锦标赛中，如未先获得有关世界帆联级别协会（或离岸赛代表大会）或世界帆联的批准，不得拒绝或取消规定限额内的报名。

77 帆上识别标志

船须遵守附录 G 有关帆上的级别标识、国家和地区代码和帆号的规定。

78 COMPLIANCE WITH CLASS RULES; CERTIFICATES

78.1 While a boat is *racing*, her owner and any other person in charge shall ensure that the boat is maintained to comply with her class rules and that her measurement or rating certificate, if any, remains valid. Inaddition, the boat shall also comply at other times specified in the class rules, the notice of race or the sailing instructions.

78.2 When a *rule* requires a valid certificate to be produced or its existence verified before a boat *races*, and this cannot be done, the boat may *race* provided that the race committee receives a statement signed by the person in charge that a valid certificate exists. The boat shall produce the certificate or arrange for its existence to be verified by the race committee before the start of the last day of the event, or of the first series, whichever is earlier. The penalty for breaking this rule is disqualification without a hearing from all races of the event.

79 CATEGORIZATION

If the notice of race or class rules state that some or all competitors must satisfy categorization requirements, the categorization shall be carried out as described in the World Sailing Sailor Categorization Code.

80 RESCHEDULED EVENT

When an event is rescheduled to dates different from the dates stated in the notice of race, all boats entered shall be notified. The race committee may accept new entries that meet all the entry requirements except the original deadline for entries.

78 遵守级别规则;证书

78.1 当一条船参加*竞赛*,船东和其他负责人须保证该船符合其级别规则,如果有证书的话,须保持其丈量和评级证书有效。此外,在其他时间,该船也须符合级别规则、竞赛通知或航行细则的规定。

78.2 当*规则*要求船在*竞赛*前出示有效的证书或证明证书存在,而未能这样做时,在竞赛委员会收到有船只负责人签字证明的关于有效证书确实存在的声明后,该船可以参加*竞赛*。该船须在赛事或第一个系列赛的最后一个竞赛日(以较早的为准)起航前出示证书或者安排由竞赛委员会验证其证书确实存在。违反本规则的判罚是取消该船在本赛事中所有轮次的资格而无须审理。

79 分类

如果竞赛通知或者级别规则声明一些或者全部的选手必须符合分类的要求,就须根据《世界帆联选手分类法则》所规定的要求来进行分类。

80 日程重新排定的赛事

当一场赛事被重新排定到与竞赛通知所规定的不同时间时,须通知所有已报名的船。竞赛委员会可接受符合除原报名截止日期外的所有报名条件的新报名。

PART 7–RACE ORGANIZATION

85 CHANGES TO RULES

85.1 A change to a *rule* shall refer specifically to the *rule* and state the change. A change to a *rule* includes an addition to it or deletion of all or part of it.

85.2 A change to one of the following types of *rules* may be made only as shown below.

Type of rule	*Change only if permitted by*
Racing rule	Rule 86
Rule in a World Sailing code	A rule in the code
National authority prescription	Rule 88.2
Class rule	Rule 87
Rule in the notice of race	Rule 89.2(b)
Rule in the sailing instructions	Rule 90.2(c)
Rule in any other document governing the event	A rule in the document itself

86 CHANGES TO THE RACING RULES

86.1 A racing rule shall not be changed unless permitted in the rule itself or as follows:

(a) Prescriptions of a national authority may change a racing rule, but not the Definitions; the Basic Principles; a rule in the Introduction; Part 1, 2 or 7; rule 42, 43, 47, 50, 63.4, 69, 70, 71, 75, 76.3 or 79; a rule of an appendix that changes one of these rules; Appendix H or N; or a rule in a World Sailing Code listed in rule 6.1.

第七章　竞赛组织

85 规则的更改

85.1 对*规则*的更改须特别指明哪条*规则*并描述该更改。对*规则*的更改包括对其进行增补或对其全部或部分的删除。

85.2 对以下类型的*规则*的更改只能按照下表所列的情况做出：

规则类型	*只能按以下规则所允许的进行更改*
竞赛规则	规则 86
世界帆联守则中的规则	守则中的规则
国家和地区管理机构的规定	规则 88.2
级别规则	规则 87
竞赛通知中的规则	规则 89.2（b）
航行细则中的规则	规则 90.2（c）
赛事执行的其他文件中的规则	本文件中的规则

86 竞赛规则的更改

86.1 不得更改竞赛规则，除非规则本身允许或有下列情况：

（a）国家和地区管理机构的规定可以更改竞赛规则，但不能更改：定义；基本原则；导言中某条规则；第一、二或七章；规则 42、43、47、50、63.4、69、70、71、75、76.3 和 79；附录中更改这些规则的某条规则；附录 H 和 N；规则 6.1 所列的世界帆联守则中的某条规则。

(b) The notice of race or sailing instructions may change a racing rule, but not rule 76.1 or 76.2, Appendix R, or a rule listed in rule 86.1(a).

(c) Class rules may change only racing rules 42, 49, 51, 52, 53, 54, and 55.

86.2 In exception to rule 86.1, World Sailing may in limited circumstances (see World Sailing Regulation 28.1.3) authorize changes to the racing rules for a specific international event. The authorization shall be stated in a letter of approval to the organizing authority and in the notice of race or sailing instructions, and the letter shall be posted on the official notice board.

86.3 If a national authority so prescribes, the restrictions in rule 86.1 do not apply if rules are changed to develop or test proposed rules. The national authority may prescribe that its approval is required for such changes.

87 CHANGES TO CLASS RULES

The notice of race may change a class rule only when the class rules permit the change, or when written permission of the class association for the change is posted on the official notice board.

88 NATIONAL PRESCRIPTIONS

88.1 Prescriptions that Apply

The prescriptions that apply to an event are the prescriptions of the national authority with which the organizing authority is associated under rule 89.1. However, if boats will pass through the waters of more than one national authority while *racing*, the notice of race shall identify the prescriptions that will apply and when they will apply.

（b）竞赛通知或航行细则可以对竞赛规则进行更改，但不能更改规则 76.1、76.2、附录 R 和规则 86.1（a）中所列的规则。

（c）级别规则只可以对竞赛规则 42、49、51、52、53、54 和 55 进行更改。

86.2 除规则 86.1 的规定外，世界帆联可在有限的条件下（参见世界帆联规章 28.1.3）授权给特定的国际赛事更改规则。该授权须在给赛事组织机构的批准书中以及竞赛通知或航行细则中声明，该批准书须张贴在赛事官方公告栏上。

86.3 若国家和地区管理机构有如此规定，如果规则的更改是为了发展或测试所建议的规则，那么规则 86.1 中的限制不适用。国家和地区管理机构可以在规定中要求此类更改需经其批准。

87 级别规则的更改

只有当级别规则允许更改时，或者当级别协会在官方公告栏发布更改的书面许可时，竞赛通知才可以更改级别规则。

88 国家和地区规定

88.1 适用的国家和地区规定

适用于某赛事的国家和地区规定是按规则 89.1 与组织机构相关联的国家和地区管理机构的规定。然而如果船在*竞赛*中将航越不止一个国家和地区管理机构的水域时，竞赛通知须说明所适用的规定及其适用的时间。

88.2 Changes to Prescriptions

The notice of race or sailing instructions may change a prescription. However, a national authority may restrict changes to its prescriptions with a prescription to this rule, provided World Sailing approves its application to do so. The restricted prescriptions shall not be changed.

89 ORGANIZING AUTHORITY; NOTICE OF RACE; APPOINTMENT OF RACE OFFICIALS

89.1 Organizing Authority

An event shall be organized by an organizing authority, which shall be

(a) World Sailing;

(b) a member national authority of World Sailing;

(c) an affiliated club;

(d) an affiliated organization other than a club and, if so prescribed by the national authority, with the approval of the national authority or in conjunction with an affiliated club;

(e) an unaffiliated class association, either with the approval of the national authority or in conjunction with an affiliated club;

(f) two or more of the above organizations;

(g) an unaffiliated body in conjunction with an affiliated club where the body is owned and controlled by the club. The national authority of the club may prescribe that its approval is required for such an event; or

(h) if approved by World Sailing and the national authority of the club, an unaffiliated body in conjunction with an affiliated club where the body is not owned and controlled by the club.

88.2 国家和地区规定的更改

竞赛通知或航行细则可以更改某一国家和地区规定。然而，国家和地区管理机构可以通过对本条规则做出的规定，限制对其规定的更改，前提是获得世界帆联的批准。受限制的规定不得被更改。

89 组织机构；竞赛通知；竞赛官员的任命

89.1 组织机构

赛事须由下列组织机构来组织：

（a）世界帆船运动联合会；

（b）世界帆船运动联合会的一个会员国家和地区管理机构；

（c）隶属的俱乐部；

（d）如果国家和地区管理机构这样规定的话，获得国家和地区管理机构许可的或者与一个隶属俱乐部联合的一个隶属组织而不是俱乐部；

（e）经国家和地区管理机构批准或与某隶属俱乐部联合的非隶属的级别协会；

（f）2 个或 2 个以上上述组织；

（g）与某隶属俱乐部联合的某非隶属团体，该团体为俱乐部拥有和控制。该俱乐部的国家和地区管理机构可规定此类赛事需得到其批准；或

（h）如果获得了世界帆联和俱乐部的国家和地区管理机构的允许，一个与隶属俱乐部联合，不归此俱乐部拥有和控制的非隶属实体。

In rule 89.1, an organization is affiliated if it is affiliated to the national authority of the venue; otherwise the organization is unaffiliated. However, if boats will pass through the waters of more than one national authority while *racing*, an organization is affiliated if it is affiliated to the national authority of one of the ports of call.

89.2 Notice of Race; Appointment of Race Officials

(a) The organizing authority shall publish a notice of race that conforms to rule J1.

(b) The notice of race may be changed provided adequate notice is given.

(c) The organizing authority shall appoint a race committee and, when appropriate, appoint a protest committee, a technical committee and umpires. However, the race committee, an international jury, a technical committee and umpires may be appointed by World Sailing as provided in its Regulations.

90 RACE COMMITTEE; SAILING INSTRUCTIONS; SCORING

90.1 Race Committee

The race committee shall conduct races as directed by the organizing authority and as required by the *rules*.

90.2 Sailing Instructions

(a) The race committee shall publish written sailing instructions that conform to rule J2.

(b) When appropriate, for an event where entries from other countries are expected, the sailing instructions shall include, in English, the applicable national prescriptions.

在规则 89.1 中，如果一个组织机构隶属于该场馆所在地的国家和地区管理机构，那么该组织机构就是隶属的组织机构，否则就是非隶属的组织机构。但是，如果*竞赛*中船将会航越一个以上国家和地区管理机构的水域，当该组织机构隶属于船只停靠港口之一的国家和地区管理机构时，该组织就是隶属的组织机构。

89.2　竞赛通知；竞赛官员的任命

(a) 组织机构须按照规则 J1 发布竞赛通知。

(b) 只要给予了充分的通知，竞赛通知可以被更改。

(c) 组织机构须任命竞赛委员会并在适当时任命抗议委员会、技术委员会和现场裁判。但是，根据世界帆联规章，世界帆联可任命竞赛委员会、国际仲裁委员会、技术委员会和现场裁判。

90 竞赛委员会；航行细则；计分

90.1　竞赛委员会

竞赛委员会须在组织机构的指导下根据*规则*要求实施竞赛。

90.2　航行细则

(a) 竞赛委员会须发布符合规则 J2 的书面航行细则。

(b) 合适时，当希望有其他国家和地区报名参加赛事的时候，航行细则须包括英文版的所适用的国家和地区规定。

(c) The sailing instructions may be changed provided the change is in writing and posted on the official notice board before the time stated in the sailing instructions or, on the water, communicated to each boat before her warning signal. Oral changes may be given only on the water, and only if the procedure is stated in the sailing instructions.

90.3 Scoring

(a) The race committee shall score a race or series as provided in Appendix A unless the notice of race or sailing instructions specify some other system. A race shall be scored if it is not *abandoned* and if one boat *starts*, *sails the course* and *finishes* within the race time limit, if any, even if she retires after *finishing* or is disqualified.

(b) When a scoring system provides for excluding one or more race scores, any score that is a Disqualification Not Excludable (DNE) shall be included in a boat's series score.

(c) When the race committee determines from its own records or observations that it has scored a boat incorrectly, it shall correct the error and make the corrected scores available to competitors.

(d) The race committee shall implement scoring changes directed by the protest committee or national authority as a result of decisions made in accordance with the *rules*.

(e) When so stated in the notice of race, notwithstanding the provisions of rules 90.3(a), (b), (c) and (d), there shall be no changes to race or series scores resulting from action, including the correction of errors, initiated more than 24 hours after （c）可以更改航行细则，前提是更改要在航行细则规定的时间前以书面形式张贴在官方公告栏上，或当在水上时，于预告信号之前通知到每条船。口头的更改只能在水上进行，并要事先在航行细则中注明口头传达的程序。

90.3 计分

（a）除非竞赛通知或航行细则规定了某些其他方法，否则竞赛委员会须按照附录 A 的规定对一轮竞赛或系列赛进行计分。如果一轮竞赛没有被*放弃*，一条船*起航*、*行驶航线*并在竞赛时限内*到达终点*，即使该船*到达终点*后退出了竞赛或被取消了资格，该轮竞赛也须被计分。

（b）当计分方法规定取消一轮或多轮的分数时，任何被记为不能去掉的取消资格（DNE）的分数都须带入船只系列赛总分。

（c）当竞赛委员会从自己的记录或者观察中确定某条船的计分不正确时，须改正该错误并将改正的得分告知选手。

（d）竞赛委员会须按照抗议委员会或国家和地区管理机构根据*规则*做出的裁决结果进行成绩更改。

（e）尽管规则 90. 3（a）、（b）、（c）和（d）有所规定，但当竞赛通知中规定此条适用时，在下述时间起的 24 小时后，不得因采取的行动而更改竞赛或系列赛的成绩，包括更正错误记分：

(1) the protest time limit for the last race of the series (including a single-race series);

(2) being informed of a protest committee decision after the last race of the series (including a single-race series); or

(3) the results are published.

However, in exception, changes to scores shall be made resulting from a decision under rules 6, 69 or 70. The notice of race may change '24 hours' to a different time.

91 PROTEST COMMITTEE

A protest committee shall be

(a) a committee appointed by the organizing authority or race committee;

(b) an international jury appointed by the organizing authority or as prescribed in the World Sailing Regulations. It shall be composed as required by rule N1 and have the authority and responsibilities stated in rule N2. A national authority may prescribe that its approval is required for the appointment of international juries for races within its jurisdiction, except World Sailing events or when international juries are appointed by World Sailing under rule 89.2(c); or

(c) a committee appointed by the national authority under rule 71.2.

92 TECHNICAL COMMITTEE

92.1 A technical committee shall be a committee of at least one member and be appointed by the organizing authority or the race committee or as prescribed in the World Sailing Regulations.

92.2 The technical committee shall conduct equipment inspection and event measurement as directed by the organizing authority and as required by the *rules*.

(1) 系列赛最后一轮竞赛的抗议时限(包括单一轮次的系列赛);

(2) 系列赛的最后一轮竞赛(包括单一轮次的系列赛)后,得到抗议委员会的裁决通知;或

(3) 发布了成绩。

但例外的是,依规则 6、69、70 做出的裁决结果须更改成绩。竞赛通知可以将"24 小时"改为其他时间。

91 抗议委员会

抗议委员会须是

(a) 由组织机构或竞赛委员会任命的委员会;

(b) 由组织机构或依照世界帆联规章的规定任命的国际仲裁委员会。国际仲裁委员会的建制须遵照规则 N1 的要求,并且享有规则 N2 所规定的权利和义务。国家和地区管理机构对其权限内管辖的竞赛可以做这样的规定:任命的国际仲裁委员会需得到其批准,除非是世界帆联组织的赛事或国际仲裁委员会是按照规则 89.2 (c)由世界帆联任命的;或

(c) 根据规则 71.2 由国家和地区管理机构任命的委员会。

92 技术委员会

92.1 技术委员会须为至少有一名成员的委员会,由国家和地区管理机构或者竞赛委员会,或者按照世界帆联规章的规定任命。

92.2 技术委员会须按照组织机构的指示和*规则*的要求进行器材检查和赛事丈量。

APPENDIX A SCORING

See rule 90.3.

A1 NUMBER OF RACES

The number of races scheduled and the number required to be completed to constitute a series shall be stated in the notice of race or sailing instructions.

A2 SERIES SCORES

A2.1 Each boat's series score shall, subject to rule 90.3(b), be the total of her race scores excluding her worst score. However, the notice of race or sailing instructions may make a different arrangement by providing, for example, that no score will be excluded, that two or more scores will be excluded, or that a specified number of scores will be excluded if a specified number of races are completed. A race is completed if scored; see rule 90.3(a). If a boat has two or more equal worst scores, the score(s) for the race(s) sailed earliest in the series shall be excluded. The boat with the lowest series score wins and others shall be ranked accordingly.

A2.2 If a boat has entered any race in a series, she shall be scored for the whole series.

A3 STARTING TIMES AND FINISHING PLACES

The time of a boat's starting signal shall be her starting time, and the order in which boats *finish* a race shall determine their finishing places. However, when a handicap or rating system is used a boat's corrected time shall determine her finishing place.

附录 A　计分

参见规则 90. 3。

A1 竞赛轮次

在竞赛通知或航行细则中须注明排定的竞赛轮次及构成一场系列赛所要完成的竞赛轮次。

A2 系列赛的计分

A2.1 依据规则 90. 3（b），每条船系列赛的得分须为去掉最差得分的全部竞赛得分的总和。但是，竞赛通知或航行细则可以做出不同的规定，比如不去掉任何得分、去掉两轮或更多的得分，或者完成一定数量轮次的竞赛将去掉一定轮次的分数。如果有计分，该轮竞赛就算完成了；参见规则 90. 3（a）。如果一条船有两个或两个以上的同样最差分数，须去掉在系列赛最前面的竞赛分数。获得最低系列赛分数的船获胜，其他船的排名须依此类推。

A2.2 一旦一条船参加了系列赛中的一轮竞赛，那么其整个系列赛都须被计分。

A3 起航时间和到达终点名次

一条船起航信号的时间须作为其起航时间，须按*到达终点*的顺序决定其终点名次。但如果使用了让分制或评级制的计分法，须按修正后的时间决定其终点名次。

A4 SCORING SYSTEM

This Low Point System will apply unless the notice of race or sailing instructions specify another system; see rule 90.3(a).

Each boat *starting* and *finishing* and not thereafter retiring, being penalized or given redress shall be scored points as follows:

Finishing place	*Points*
First	1
Second	2
Third	3
Fourth	4
Fifth	5
Sixth	6
Seventh	7
Each place thereafter	Add 1 point

A5 SCORES DETERMINED BY THE RACE COMMITTEE

A5.1 A boat that did not *start*, *sail the course* or *finish*, or comply with rule 30.2, 30.3, 30.4 or 78.2, or that retires or takes a penalty under rule 44.3(a), shall be scored accordingly by the race committee without a hearing. Only the protest committee may take other scoring actions that worsen a boat's score.

A5.2 A boat that did not *start,* did not *sail the course*, did not *finish*, retired or was disqualified shall be scored points for the finishing place one more than the number of boats entered in the series. A boat that is penalized under rule 30.2 or that takes a penalty under rule 44.3(a) shall be

A4 计分方法

使用低分计分方法，除非竞赛通知或航行细则中规定了另外的计分方法；参见规则 90.3（a）。

每条船*起航*并*到达终点*，其后没有退出竞赛、没有被惩罚或给予补偿，她们的分数须按如下方法计算：

终点名次	*分数*
第一名	1
第二名	2
第三名	3
第四名	4
第五名	5
第六名	6
第七名	7
此后每名次	加 1 分

A5 竞赛委员会决定的计分

A5.1 一条船没有*起航*，没有*行驶航线*或*到达终点*，或没有遵守规则 30.2、30.3、30.4、78.2，或退出竞赛或按规则 44.3（a）接受惩罚，其分数须由竞赛委员会在无须审理的情况下进行相应计分。只有抗议委员会可以采取其他的计分行动，使一条船的分数更差。

A5.2 一条船没有*起航*，没有*行驶航线*，没有*到达终点*，退出竞赛或被取消资格，其终点名次的计分须为报名参加该系列赛的所有船数加 1。一条船根据规则 30.2 被判罚或根据规则 44.3（a）接受惩罚，其计分须为规则

scored points as provided in rule 44.3(c).

A5.3 If the notice of race or sailing instructions state that rule A5.3 will apply, rule A5.2 is changed so that a boat that came to the starting area but did not *start*, did not *sail the course*, did not *finish*, retired or was disqualified shall be scored points for the finishing place one more than the number of boats that came to the starting area, and a boat that did not come to the starting area shall be scored points for the finishing place one more than the number of boats entered in the series.

A6 CHANGES IN PLACES AND SCORES OF OTHER BOATS

A6.1 If a boat is disqualified from a race or retires after *finishing*, each boat with a worse finishing place shall be moved up one place.

A6.2 If the protest committee decides to give redress by adjusting a boat's score, the scores of other boats shall not be changed unless the protest committee decides otherwise.

A7 RACE TIES

If boats are tied at the finishing line or if a handicap or rating system is used and boats have equal corrected times, the points for the place for which the boats have tied and for the place(s) immediately below shall be added together and divided equally. Boats tied for a race prize shall share it or be given equal prizes.

44.3（c）中所规定的分数。

A5.3 如果竞赛通知或航行细则中规定规则 A5.3 适用，规则 A5.2 则更改为：一条船来到起航区域但没有*起航*，没有*行驶航线*，没有*到达终点*，退出竞赛或被取消资格，其终点名次的计分须为来到起航区域的所有船数加 1，一条船没有来到起航区域，其终点名次的计分须为报名参加该系列赛的所有船数加 1。

A6 其他船的名次和分数的改变

A6.1 如果一条船在一轮竞赛中被取消资格或在*到达终点*后退出竞赛，其后面的每条船须向前移动一个名次。

A6.2 如果抗议委员会为给予一条船补偿而调整分数时，其他船的分数不得改动，除非抗议委员会做出其他决定。

A7 单轮竞赛中的平分

如果在到达终点线后船只出现平分或使用让分或评级制记分方法时船只修正后的时间相同时，平分船的名次得分须与下面紧连的名次得分相加并取其平均分。得分相同的船获得该轮奖励时须共享或获得同等的奖品。

A8 SERIES TIES

A8.1 If there is a series-score tie between two or more boats, each boat's race scores shall be listed in order of best to worst, and at the first point(s) where there is a difference the tie shall be broken in favour of the boat(s) with the best score(s). No excluded scores shall be used.

A8.2 If a tie remains between two or more boats, they shall be ranked in order of their scores in the last race. Any remaining ties shall be broken by using the tied boats' scores in the next-to-last race and so on until all ties are broken. These scores shall be used even if some of them are excluded scores.

A9 GUIDANCE ON REDRESS

If the protest committee decides to give redress by adjusting a boat's score for a race, it is advised to consider scoring her

(a) points equal to the average, to the nearest tenth of a point (0.05 to be rounded upward), of her points in all the races in the series except the race in question;

(b) points equal to the average, to the nearest tenth of a point (0.05 to be rounded upward), of her points in all the races before the race in question; or

(c) points based on the position of the boat in the race at the time of the incident that justified redress.

A10 SCORING ABBREVIATIONS

These scoring abbreviations shall be used for recording the circumstances described:

DNC Did not *start*; did not come to the starting area

DNS Did not *start* (other than DNC and OCS)

A8 系列赛的平分

A8.1 如果在两条船或更多的船之间发生了系列赛的平分，每条船的各轮分数将按从最好到最差的顺序排列，在第一个出现差异的分数处，以分数好者列前来打破平分。不得使用被去掉的分数。

A8.2 如果两条船或更多船的分数仍然相同时，以最后一轮竞赛中船的分数顺序来打破平分。如果有两条以上的船分数仍相同，将根据并列船的倒数第 2 轮的分数来打破并列，以此类推，直到并列被打破。即使是被去掉的分数也须用来打破平分。

A9 补偿指南

如果抗议委员会决定给予一条船补偿而调整一轮分数，建议考虑按如下方式进行计分：

（a）给予的分数等于系列赛中扣除其有问题的一轮竞赛后所有轮次得分的平均数，四舍五入精确到小数点后面一位数；

（b）给予的分数等于有问题的这轮竞赛之前的全部竞赛得分的平均数，四舍五入精确到小数点后面一位数；或

（c）根据给予补偿的事件发生时船所在的位置给予分数。

A10 计分缩写

须使用下列计分缩写记录下述情况：

DNC　未*起航*；未来到起航区

DNS　未*起航*（不同于 DNC 和 OCS）

OCS	Did not *start*; on the course side of the starting line at her starting signal and failed to *start*, or broke rule 30.1
ZFP	20% penalty under rule 30.2
UFD	Disqualification under rule 30.3
BFD	Disqualification under rule 30.4
SCP	Scoring Penalty applied
NSC	Did not *sail the course*
DNF	Did not *finish*
RET	Retired
DSQ	Disqualification
DNE	Disqualification that is not excludable
RDG	Redress given
DPI	Discretionary penalty imposed

OCS 未*起航*；起航信号发出时处于起航线航线一侧并且*起航*失败，或违反规则 30.1

ZFP 根据规则 30.2 执行 20% 惩罚

UFD 根据规则 30.3 被取消资格

BFD 根据规则 30.4 被取消资格

SCP 接受分数惩罚

NSC 未*行驶航线*

DNF 未*到达终点*

RET 退出竞赛

DSQ 取消资格

DNE 不能去掉的取消资格

RDG 给予补偿

DPI 施以自由裁量的惩罚

APPENDIX B WINDSURFING FLEET RACING RULES

Windsurfing fleet races (including marathon races) shall be sailed under The Racing Rules of Sailing *as changed by this appendix. The term 'boat' elsewhere in the racing rules means 'board' or 'boat' as appropriate. A marathon race is a race intended to last more than one hour.*

Note: Rules for Slalom, Expression (including Wave and Freestyle) and Speed disciplines are not included in this appendix. These are available at the World Sailing website.

CHANGES TO THE DEFINITIONS

The definitions *Mark-Room*, and *Tack*, *Starboard* or *Port* are changed to:

Mark-Room *Mark-Room* for a board is room to sail her *proper course* to round or pass the *mark*. However, *mark-room* for a board does not include *room* to tack unless she is *overlapped* inside and to *windward* of the board required to give *mark-room* and she would be *fetching* the *mark* after her tack.

Tack, Starboard or Port A board is on the *tack*, *starboard* or *port*, corresponding to the competitor's hand that would be nearer the mast if the competitor were in normal sailing position with both hands on the wishbone and arms not crossed. A board is on *starboard tack* when the competitor's right hand would be nearer the mast and is on *port tack* when the competitor's left hand would be nearer the mast.

The definition *Zone* is deleted.

Add the following definitions:

Capsized A board is *capsized* when she is not under control because her sail or the competitor is in the water.

附录 B　帆板群发赛规则

帆板群发赛(包括马拉松竞赛)须遵守本附录更改过的《帆船竞赛规则》。在规则其他内容中术语"船"意为"板",或恰当时为"船"。马拉松竞赛是打算航行1小时以上的竞赛。

注:障碍滑项目、表演项目(包括浪上表演和自由滑)、竞速项目规则不包含在本附录中。这些规则可以在世界帆联网站上查阅。

定义的更改

绕标空间、*舷风*、*右舷*或*左舷*的定义更改为:

绕标空间　一条板的*绕标空间*是指行驶她的*正当航线*去绕行或通过*标志*的*空间*。然而,一条板的*绕标空间*不包括其迎风换舷的*空间*,除非该船在需要给予她*绕标空间*的船的内侧和*上风与之相联*,而且在迎风换舷后该船将*飞驰该标志*。

舷风,右舷或左舷　一条板在*右舷风*或*左舷风*是选手处在正常的航行位置,双手握住帆杆,手臂没有交叉时,与选手更接近桅杆的那只手相一致的。一条板在*右舷风*时选手的右手将更接近桅杆,在*左舷风*时选手的左手将更接近桅杆。

标区的定义被删除。

增加以下定义:

倾覆　由于一条板的帆或选手在水中而板失去控制时就是*倾覆*。

Rounding or Passing A board is *rounding or passing* a *mark* from the time her *proper course* is to begin to manoeuvre to round or pass it, until the *mark* has been rounded or passed.

B1 CHANGES TO THE RULES OF PART 1

[No changes.]

B2 CHANGES TO THE RULES OF PART 2

13 WHILE TACKING

Rule 13 is changed to:

After a board passes head to wind, she shall *keep clear* of other boards until her sail has filled. During that time rules 10, 11 and 12 do not apply. If two boards are subject to this rule at the same time, the one on the other's port side or the one astern shall *keep clear*.

17 ON THE SAME TACK BEFORE A REACHING START

Rule 17 is changed to:

When, at the warning signal, the course to the first *mark* is approximately ninety degrees from the true wind, a board *overlapped* to *leeward* of another board on the same *tack* during the last 30 seconds before her starting signal shall not sail above the shortest course to the first *mark* while they remain *overlapped* if as a result the other board would need to take action to avoid contact, unless in doing so she promptly sails astern of the other board.

18 MARK-ROOM

Rule 18 is changed as follows:

The first sentence of rule 18.1 is changed to:

Rule 18 applies between boards when they are required to leave a *mark* on the same side and at least one of them is *rounding or passing* it.

绕行或通过　在*绕过或通过标志*时，一条板的*正当航线*是从她开始准备做动作去绕过或通过*标志*的那一刻开始，直到完全绕过或通过*标志*为止。

B1 第一章规则的更改

[无更改。]

B2 第二章规则的更改

13　迎风换舷时

规则 13 更改为：

一条板越过正顶风后，须*避让*其他的板直至她的帆重新受风。这期间规则 10、11 和 12 不适用。如果两条板同时受本规则约束，在另一条板的左舷或后方的板须*避让*。

17　在横风起航前同舷风

规则 17 更改为：

当预告信号发出，到第一个*标志*的航线大约与真风成 90° 时，在起航信号发出前的最后 30 秒内，与另一条板同*舷风下风相联*的一条板，在*相联*没有打破的情况下，如果会导致另一条板需要采取行动来避免接触，那该板就不得高于其至一*标*的最短航线航行，除非她这样做时能迅即行驶到另一条板的后方。

18　绕标空间

规则 18 更改如下：

规则 18.1 第一句更改为：

当帆板被要求以同一侧离开*标志*，并且至少其中一条帆板正在*绕过或通过标志*时，规则 18 在她们之间适用。

Rule 18.2(b) is changed to:

(b) If boards are *overlapped* when the first of them is *rounding or passing* the *mark*, the outside board at that moment shall thereafter give the inside board *mark-room*. If a board is *clear ahead* when she is *rounding or passing* the *mark*, the board *clear astern* at that moment shall thereafter give her *mark-room*.

Rule 18.2(c) is changed to:

(c) When a board is required to give *mark-room* by rule 18.2(b), she shall continue to do so even if later an *overlap* is broken or a new *overlap* begins.

Rule 18.2(d) is changed to:

(d) Rules 18.2(b) and (c) cease to apply if the board entitled to *mark-room* passes head to wind.

Rule 18.3 is deleted.

18.4 Gybing and Bearing Away

Rule 18.4 is changed to:

When an inside *overlapped* right-of-way board must gybe or bear away at a *mark* to sail her *proper course*, until she gybes or bears away she shall sail no farther from the *mark* than needed to sail that course. Rule 18.4 does not apply at a gate *mark*.

22 CAPSIZED; AGROUND; RESCUING

Rule 22 is changed to:

22.1 If possible, a board shall avoid a board that is *capsized* or has not regained control after *capsizing*, is aground, or is trying to help a person or vessel in danger.

22.2 If possible, a board that is *capsized* or aground shall not interfere with another board.

规则 18.2（b)更改为：

（b）如果板*相联*，当其中的第一条板正在*绕过或通过标志*时，此时处于外侧的板随后须给予内侧板*绕标空间*。如果一条板正在*绕过或通过标志*时*明显在前*，那么此时*明显在后*的板随后须给予*绕标空间*。

规则 18.2（c)更改为：

（c）当一条板根据规则 18.2（b)被要求给予*绕标空间*时，即使稍后*相联*被打破或建立起新的*相联*，她也须继续这么做。

规则 18.2（d)更改为：

（d）如果享有*绕标空间*的板越过了正顶风，规则 18.2（b）和(c)则停止适用。

删除规则 18.3。

18.4 顺风换舷和顺风偏转

规则 18.4 更改为：

如果一条内侧*相联*的航行权板必须在*标志*旁顺风换舷或顺风偏转来行驶其*正当航线*，在顺风换舷或顺风偏转以前，她驶离*标志*的距离不得远于行驶那条航线所需的距离。在门*标*处规则 18.4 不适用。

22 倾覆；搁浅；救援

规则 22 更改为：

22.1 如有可能，一条板须躲避*倾覆*的板或*倾覆*后未能重新获得操纵能力的板，搁浅的板，或正在帮助处在危险中的人员或船舶的板。

22.2 如有可能，一条*倾覆*或搁浅的板不得妨碍其他板。

23 INTERFERING WITH ANOTHER BOARD; SAIL OUT OF WATER

Add new rule 23.3:

23.3 In the last minute before her starting signal, a board shall have her sail out of the water and in a normal position, except when accidentally *capsized*.

B3 CHANGES TO THE RULES OF PART 3

26 STARTING RACES

Rule 26 is changed to:

26.1 System 1 (for Upwind Starts)

Races shall be started by using the following signals. Times shall be taken from the visual signals; the absence of a sound signal shall be disregarded.

Minutes before starting signal	*Visual signal*	*Sound signal*	*Means*
5*	Class flag	One	Warning signal
4	P, I, U, or black flag	One	Preparatory signal
1	Preparatory flag removed	One long	One minute
0	Class flag removed	One	Starting signal

*or as stated in the notice of race or sailing instructions

The warning signal for each succeeding class shall be made with or after the starting signal of the preceding class.

23 妨碍另一条板；帆离开水面

增加新规则 23.3：

23.3 在起航信号发出前的最后 1 分钟，一条板须使帆离开水面并处于正常位置，除非意外*倾覆*。

B3 第三章规则的更改

26 竞赛起航

规则 26 更改为：

26.1 程序 1（迎风起航）

竞赛须使用以下信号来进行起航。时间须以视觉信号为准，不必理会音响信号的缺失。

起航信号前的时间	*视觉信号*	*音响信号*	*含义*
5*	级别旗	一声	预告信号
4	P、I、U 旗或黑旗	一声	准备信号
1	移除准备旗	一长声	1 分钟
0	移除级别旗	一声	起航信号

＊或者遵循竞赛通知或航行细则中的规定

后续每个级别的预告信号须与前一个级别的起航信号同时或在其之后发出。

26.2 System 2 (for Reaching Starts)

Races shall be started by using the following signals. Times shall be taken from the visual signals; the absence of a sound signal shall be disregarded.

Minutes before starting signal	*Visual signal*	*Sound signal*	*Means*
3	Class flag		Attention signal
2	Red flag; attention signal removed	One	Warning signal
1	Yellow flag; red flag removed	One	Preparatory signal
1/2	Yellow flag removed		30 seconds
0	Green flag	One	Starting signal

26.3 System 3 (for Beach Starts)

(a) When the starting line is on the beach, or so close to the beach that the competitor must stand in the water to *start*, the start is a beach start.

(b) The starting stations shall be numbered so that station 1 is the most windward one. Unless the sailing instructions specify some other system, a board's starting station shall be determined

(1) by ranking (the highest ranking board on station 1, the next highest on station 2, and so on), or

(2) by draw.

(c) After boards have been called to take their positions, the race committee shall make the preparatory signal by displaying a red flag with one sound. The starting signal shall be made, at any time after the preparatory signal, by removing the red flag with one sound.

26.2 程序 2（横风起航）

竞赛须使用以下信号来进行起航。时间须以视觉信号为准，不必理会音响信号的缺失。

起航信号前的时间	*视觉信号*	*音响信号*	*含义*
3	级别旗		注意信号
2	红旗；移除注意信号	一声	预告信号
1	黄旗；移除红旗	一声	准备信号
1/2	移除黄旗		30 秒
0	绿旗	一声	起航信号

26.3 程序 3（沙滩起航）

（a）当起航线位于沙滩上，或离沙滩很近使得选手必须站在水中*起航*时，该起航就是沙滩起航。

（b）起航位置须进行编码，1 号位为上风第一个。除非航行细则规定了其他方法，否则一条板的起航位置须按以下方式确定：

（1）按照排名（排名最高的为 1 号位，第二高的为 2 号位，以此类推），或

（2）抽签决定。

（c）当所有板都被召集到起航位置上后，竞赛委员会须发出准备信号，展示红旗并伴随一声音响。在准备信号后的任一时刻，须发出起航信号，移除红旗并伴随一声音响。

(d) After the starting signal each board shall take the shortest route from her starting station to the water and then to her sailing position without interfering with other boards. Part 2 rules will apply when both of the competitor's feet are on the board.

30 STARTING PENALTIES

Rule 30.2 is deleted.

31 TOUCHING A MARK

Rule 31 is changed to:

A board may touch a *mark* but shall not hold on to it.

B4 CHANGES TO THE RULES OF PART 4

42 PROPULSION

Rule 42 is changed to:

A board shall be propelled only by the action of the wind on the sail and by the action of the water on the hull. However, pumping and fanning the sail is permitted. The board shall not be propelled by paddling, swimming or walking.

44 PENALTIES AT THE TIME OF AN INCIDENT

Rule 44 is changed to:

44.1 Taking a Penalty

A board may take a 360°-Turn Penalty when she may have broken one or more rules of Part 2 in an incident while *racing*. The sailing instructions may specify the use of some other penalty. However, if the board caused injury or serious damage or, despite taking a penalty, gained a significant advantage in the race or series by her breach, her penalty shall be to retire.

（d）起航信号后，每条板须在不妨碍其他板的情况下采取自起航位置到水中、而后到航行位置的最短路径。当选手的双脚都位于板上时，规则第二章适用。

30 起航惩罚

删除规则 30.2。

31 碰标

规则 31 更改为：

板可以碰标，但是不得挂住它。

B4 第四章规则的更改

42 推进

规则 42 更改为：

板须仅依靠风对帆的作用、水对板体的作用来推进。但是，允许摇帆和扇动帆。不得通过划水、游泳或是行走使板获得推进。

44 事件发生时的惩罚

规则 44 更改为：

44.1 解脱

在竞赛中，当板违反了规则第二章的一条或多条规则时，她可以进行自转 360° 的解脱。航行细则可以说明其他的惩罚办法。然而，不管做没做解脱，若其造成了受伤或严重损坏，或因其犯规而在竞赛或系列赛中获得明显优势，则对她的惩罚须是退出竞赛。

44.2 360°-Turn Penalty

After getting well clear of other boards as soon after the incident as possible, a board takes a 360°-Turn Penalty by promptly making a 360° turn with no requirement for a tack or a gybe. When a board takes the penalty at or near the finishing line, her hull shall be completely on the course side of the line before she *finishes*.

50 COMPETITOR CLOTHING AND EQUIPMENT

Rule 50.1(a) is changed to:

(a) Competitors shall not wear or carry clothing or equipment for the purpose of increasing their weight. However, a competitor may wear a drinking container that shall have a capacity of no more than 1.5 litres.

PART 4 RULES DELETED

Rules 45, 48.2, 49, 50.1(c), 50.2, 51, 52, 54, 55 and 56.1 are deleted.

B5 CHANGES TO THE RULES OF PART 5

60 RIGHT TO PROTEST; RIGHT TO REQUEST REDRESS OR RULE 69 ACTION

Rule 60.1(a) is changed by deleting 'or saw'.

61 PROTEST REQUIREMENTS

61.1 Informing the Protestee

Rule 61.1(a) is changed to:

(a) The protesting board shall inform the other board at the first reasonable opportunity. When her *protest* will concern an incident in the racing area, she shall hail 'Protest' at the first reasonable opportunity. She shall also inform the race committee of her intention to protest as soon as practicable after she *finishes* or retires. However,

44.2 360° **解脱**

做 360° 解脱的板须在事件发生后尽快完全避开其他板，迅即做出 360° 解脱，不要求做一个迎风换舷和一个顺风换舷。在终点线或终点线附近做解脱的板，其板体须在*到达终点*前完全位于终点线的航线一侧。

50 选手的服装和器材

规则 50. 1（a）更改为：

（a）选手不得穿着或携带专为增加自身体重的服装或器材。但是，选手可以穿戴装有饮料的容器，其容量不得超过 1. 5 升。

第四章删除的规则

删除规则 45、48. 2、49、50. 1（c）、50. 2、51、52、54、55 和 56. 1。

B5 第五章规则的更改

60 抗议的权利；要求补偿的权利或规则 69 **的行动**

规则 60. 1（a）更改部分为删除“或目睹”。

61 对抗议的要求

61.1 通知被抗议人

规则 61. 1（a）更改为：

（a）抗议板须在第一合理时机通知另外一条板。当她的*抗议*是涉及在竞赛区域内的事件时，她须在第一合理时机呼喊“抗议”。她还须在*到达终点*或退出竞赛后尽可能快地通知竞赛委员会其抗议意图。但

(1) if the other board is beyond hailing distance, the protesting board need not hail but she shall inform the other board at the first reasonable opportunity;

(2) no red flag need be displayed;

(3) if the incident was an error by the other board in *sailing the course*, she need not hail but she shall inform the other board either before or at the first reasonable opportunity after the other board *finishes*;

(4) if at the time of the incident it is obvious to the protesting board that either competitor is in danger, or that injury or serious damage resulted, the requirements of this rule do not apply to her, but she shall attempt to inform the other board within the time limit of rule 61.3.

61.2 Protest Contents

Add to rule 61.2:

This rule does not apply to a race in an elimination series that will qualify a board to compete in a later stage of an event.

62 REDRESS

Rule 62.1(b) is changed to:

(b) injury, physical damage or *capsize* because of the action of

(1) a board that broke a rule of Part 2 and took an appropriate penalty or was penalized, or

(2) a vessel not *racing* that was required to keep clear.

（1）如果另外一条板远于可呼喊距离，抗议板无需呼喊，但须在第一合理时机通知另一条板；

（2）无需展示红旗；

（3）如果该事件是另外一条板所犯的*行驶航线*的错误，她不需要呼喊，但是她须在另一条板*到达终点*前或在其*到达终点*后的第一合理时机告知该板；

（4）如果在事件发生时，明显地对于抗议板而言，选手处于危险中，或导致了受伤或严重损坏，那么此条规则的要求对她不适用，但她须尽力在规则 61.3 规定的时限内通知另一条板。

61.2 抗议内容

规则 61.2 增加以下内容：

此条规则不适用于一条板将获得一场赛事后期阶段比赛资格的淘汰系列赛中的竞赛。

62　补偿

规则 62.1（b）更改为：

（b）由于以下行为而导致的受伤、有形损坏或*倾覆*：

（1）一条帆板违反了规则第二章，并做了适当的解脱或被判罚，或

（2）需要避让的不在*竞赛*的船舶。

63 HEARINGS

63.6 Taking Evidence and Finding Facts

Add to rule 63.6:

However, for an elimination series race that will qualify a board to compete in a later stage of an event, *protests* and requests for redress need not be in writing; they shall be made orally to a member of the protest committee as soon as reasonably possible following the race. The protest committee may take evidence in any way it considers appropriate and may communicate its decision orally.

64 DECISIONS

Rule 64.4(b) is changed to:

(b) When the protest committee is in doubt about a matter concerning the measurement of a board, the meaning of a class rule, or damage to a board, it shall refer its questions, together with the relevant facts, to an authority responsible for interpreting the rule. In making its decision, the committee shall be bound by the reply of the authority.

65 INFORMING THE PARTIES AND OTHERS

Add to rule 65.2:

This rule does not apply to a race in an elimination series that will qualify a board to compete in a later stage of an event.

70 APPEALS AND REQUESTS TO A NATIONAL AUTHORITY

Rules 70.5 and 70.5(a) are changed to:

70.5 There shall be no appeal from the decisions of an international jury constituted in compliance with Appendix N, and no appeal from the decisions of the protest committee for a race in an elimination series that will qualify a board to compete in a later stage of an event. Furthermore, if the notice of race or sailing instructions so state, the right of appeal may be denied provided that

63 审理

63.6 取证和认定事实

规则63.6增加以下内容：

但是，对于将使一条板获得赛事后期阶段资格的淘汰系列赛而言，*抗议*和补偿要求不需要以书面形式提出；它们可以在该轮竞赛后的第一合理时机以口头方式向一名抗议委员会成员提出。抗议委员会可以通过其认为适当的任何方式取证，并可以口头传达其裁决。

64 裁决

规则64.4（b）更改为：

（b）当抗议委员会对板的丈量问题、级别规则的含义或板的损坏有疑问时，须将问题连同有关事实一起提交给负责解释规则的一个管理机构。抗议委员会须依据管理机构的回复进行裁决。

65 通知各方和其他人

规则65.2增加以下内容：

此条规则不适用于一条板将获得一场赛事后期阶段比赛资格的淘汰系列赛中的竞赛。

70 上诉及寻求国家和地区管理机构的确认

规则70.5和规则70.5（a）更改为：

70.5 不得对按附录N建制的国际仲裁委员会所做出的裁决提出上诉，也不得对一条板将获得一场赛事后期阶段比赛资格的淘汰系列赛的竞赛的抗议委员会所做出的裁决提出上诉。而且，如竞赛通知或航行细则中有如此规定，上诉权就可被驳回，前提是

(a) it is essential to determine promptly the result of a race that will qualify a board to compete in a subsequent event (a national authority may prescribe that its permission is required for such a procedure);

B6 CHANGES TO THE RULES OF PART 6

78 COMPLIANCE WITH CLASS RULES; CERTIFICATES

Add to rule 78.1: 'When so prescribed by World Sailing, a numbered and dated device on a board and her centreboard, fin and rig shall serve as her measurement certificate.'

B7 CHANGES TO THE RULES OF PART 7

90 RACE COMMITTEE; SAILING INSTRUCTIONS; SCORING

The last sentence of rule 90.2(c) is changed to: 'Oral instructions may be given only if the procedure is stated in the sailing instructions.'

B8 CHANGES TO APPENDIX A

A1 NUMBER OF RACES; OVERALL SCORES

Rule A1 is changed to:

The number of races scheduled and the number required to be completed to constitute a series shall be stated in the notice of race or sailing instructions. If an event includes more than one discipline or format, the notice of race or sailing instructions shall state how the overall scores are to be calculated.

A2 SERIES SCORES

Rule A2.1 is changed to:

Each board's series score shall, subject to rule 90.3(b), be the total of her race scores excluding her

(a) 必须迅即确定竞赛的结果,以使板有资格参加后续的赛事(国家和地区管理机构可以规定这样的程序需得到其批准);

B6 第六章规则的更改

78 遵守级别规则;证书

在规则 78. 1 后添加:"当世界帆联这样规定时,板及其稳向板、尾鳍和索具上被编号和标注日期的装置须作为其丈量证书。"

B7 第七章规则的更改

90 竞赛委员会;航行细则;计分

规则 90. 2 (c)最后一句更改为:"只有航行细则中规定了这个流程,才可以口头传达细则。"

B8 附录 A 的更改

A1 竞赛轮次;总分

规则 A1 更改为:

竞赛通知或航行细则须注明日程排定的竞赛轮次及组成系列赛所需要完成的轮次数目。如果一个赛事包含了不止一种竞赛项目或模式,竞赛通知或航行细则须说明如何计算总分。

A2 系列赛的计分

规则 A2. 1 更改为:

依据规则 90. 3 (b),每条板参加系列赛的得分须为其全部轮次得分的总和,去掉其

(a) worst score when from 5 to 11 races have been completed, or

(b) two worst scores when 12 or more races have been completed.

However, the notice of race or sailing instructions may make a different arrangement. A race is completed if scored; see rule 90.3(a). If a board has two or more equal worst scores, the score(s) for the race(s) sailed earliest in the series shall be excluded. The board with the lowest series score wins and others shall be ranked accordingly.

A5 SCORES DETERMINED BY THE RACE COMMITTEE

Add new rule A5.4:

A5.4 For an elimination series race that will qualify a board to compete in a later stage of an event, a board that did not *start*, did not *sail the course*, did not *finish*, retired or was disqualified shall be scored points equal to the number of boards permitted to sail in that race.

A8 SERIES TIES

Rule A8 is changed to:

A8.1 If there is a series-score tie between two or more boards, each board's excluded race scores shall be listed in order of best to worst, and at the first point(s) where there is a difference the tie shall be broken in favour of the board(s) with the best excluded race score(s).

A8.2 If a tie remains between two or more boards, each board's race scores, including excluded scores, shall be listed in order of best to worst, and at the first point(s) where there is a difference the tie shall be broken in favour of the board(s) with the best score(s). These scores shall be used even if some of them are excluded scores.

(a) 当完成 5 至 11 轮竞赛时，去掉最差的一轮得分，或

(b) 当完成 12 或更多轮次的竞赛时，去掉最差的两轮得分。

然而，竞赛通知或航行细则可以另作安排。如果有计分，该轮竞赛就算完成；参见规则 90. 3（a）。如果一条板有两个或更多相同的最差分数，去掉的须为这条板在系列赛中最靠前的最差分数。系列赛获得总分最低的板获胜，其他板的名次依次排列。

A5 竞赛委员会决定的计分

增加新规则 A5. 4：

A5.4 对于一条板将获得一场赛事后期阶段比赛资格的淘汰系列赛而言，一条板没有*起航*，没有*行驶航线*，没有*到达终点*，退出竞赛或被取消资格，其计分须等于被允许参加这轮竞赛的板数。

A8 系列赛的平分

规则 A8 更改为：

A8.1 如果两条板或多条板之间产生了系列赛的平分，每条板被去掉的轮次分数须按从最好到最差的顺序排列，在第一个出现差异的分数处，须以去掉的分数好者列前来打破平分。

A8.2 如果两条板或多条板中仍有平分，每条板的各轮得分，包括去掉轮次的分数，须按从最好到最差的顺序排列，在第一个出现差异的分数处，以分数最佳者列前来打破平分。被去掉的分数也须用于打破平分。

A8.3 If a tie still remains between two or more boards, they shall be ranked in order of their scores in the last race. Any remaining ties shall be broken by using the tied boards' scores in the nextto- last race and so on until all ties are broken. These scores shall be used even if some of them are excluded scores.

B9 CHANGES TO APPENDIX G

G1 WORLD SAILING CLASS BOARDS

G1.3 Positioning

Rule G1.3 is changed to:

The class insignia shall be displayed once on each side of the sail in the area above a line projected at right angles from a point on the luff of the sail one-third of the distance from the head to the wishbone. The national letters and sail numbers shall be in the central third of that part of the sail above the wishbone, clearly separated from any advertising. They shall be black and applied back to back on an opaque white background. The background shall extend a minimum of 30 mm beyond the characters. There shall be a '–' between the national letters and the sail number, and the spacing between characters shall be adequate for legibility.

A8.3 如果两条板或多条板中依然还有平分，须以最后一轮竞赛中各板的分数顺序来打破平分。此时若还存在平分，须根据存在平分的板的倒数第二轮的分数来打破平分，以此类推，直到所有平分被打破。即使是被去掉的分数也须用于打破平分。

B9 附录 G 的更改

G1　世界帆联级别的帆板

G1.3 位置

规则 G1. 3 更改为：

级别标识须在帆的每一面展示一个，位于从帆杆至帆顶角的上三分之一处前缘做出的直角投影线的上方区域。国家和地区代码和帆号须在帆杆以上帆的中间三分之一处，与广告明显地区别开。它们须为黑色并且背对背粘贴在不透明的白色背景上。背景须至少比字母多出 30mm 的距离。在国家和地区代码和帆号间须有“-”号，字母间须有适当的间距，以便于辨认。

APPENDIX C MATCH RACING RULES

Match races shall be sailed under The Racing Rules of Sailing *as changed by this appendix. Matches shall be umpired unless the notice of race or sailing instructions state otherwise.*

Note: A Standard Notice of Race, Standard Sailing Instructions, and Match Racing Rules for Blind Competitors are available at the World Sailing website.

C1 TERMINOLOGY

'Competitor' means the skipper, team or boat as appropriate for the event. 'Flight' means two or more matches started in the same starting sequence.

C2 CHANGES TO THE DEFINITIONS AND THE RULES OF PARTS 1, 2, 3 AND 4

C2.1 The definition *Finish* is changed to:

Finish A boat *finishes* when any part of her hull crosses the finishing line from the course side after completing any penalties. However, when penalties are cancelled under rule C7.2(d) after one or both boats have *finished* each shall be recorded as *finished* when she crossed the line. A boat has not *finished* if she continues to *sail the course*.

C2.2 The definition *Mark-Room* is changed to:

Mark-Room *Room* for a boat to sail her *proper course* to round or pass the *mark*, and *room* to pass a finishing *mark* after *finishing*.

C2.3 Add to the definition *Proper Course*: 'A boat taking a penalty or manoeuvring to take a penalty is not sailing a *proper course*.'

C2.4 In the definition *Zone* the distance is changed to two hull lengths.

附录 C　对抗赛规则

对抗赛须遵守本附录更改过的《帆船竞赛规则》。除非竞赛通知或航行细则另行规定，否则对抗赛须进行现场裁决。

注意：标准版本的竞赛通知、航行细则，以及盲人选手的对抗赛规则可在世界帆联官网上查看。

C1　术语

"选手"意为适合于本赛事的舵手、参赛队或船。"组"意为排在同一起航序列起航的两个或两个以上的对抗场次。

C2　对定义及第一、第二、第三和第四章规则的更改

C2.1 *到达终点*的定义更改为：

到达终点　船在完成了所有惩罚后，当其船体的任何部分从航线一侧越过终点线时即为*到达终点*。但是，在一条或两条船都*到达终点*后，根据规则 C7. 2(d)惩罚被取消，则每条船越过终点线时须被记为*到达终点*。如果一条船继续*行驶航线*，她则没有*到达终点*。

C2.2 *绕标空间*的定义更改为：

绕标空间　一条船行驶其*正当航线*去绕过或通过*标志*的*空间*，以及*到达终点*后通过终点*标志*的*空间*。

C2.3 在*正当航线*定义中增加："正在做解脱的船或正在操作准备做解脱的船不是在行驶*正当航线*"。

C2.4 定义*标区*中的距离被更改为 2 倍船长。

C2.5 Add new rule 7 to Part 1:

7 LAST POINT OF CERTAINTY

The umpires will assume that the state of a boat, or her relationship to another boat, has not changed, until they are certain that it has changed.

C2.6 Rule 13 is changed to:

13 WHILE TACKING OR GYBING

13.1 After a boat passes head to wind, she shall *keep clear* of other boats until she is on a close-hauled course.

13.2 After the foot of the mainsail of a boat sailing downwind crosses the centreline she shall *keep clear* of other boats until her mainsail has filled or she is no longer sailing downwind.

13.3 While rule 13.1 or 13.2 applies, rules 10, 11 and 12 do not. However, if two boats are subject to rule 13.1 or 13.2 at the same time, the one on the other's port side or the one astern shall *keep clear*.

C2.7 Rule 16.2 is deleted.

C2.8 Rule 17 is deleted.

C2.9 Rule 18 is changed to:

18 MARK-ROOM

18.1 When Rule 18 Applies

Rule 18 applies between boats when they are required to leave a *mark* on the same side and at least one of them is in the *zone*. However, it does not apply between a boat approaching a *mark* and one leaving it. Rule 18 no longer applies between boats when the boat entitled to *mark-room* is on the next leg and the *mark* is astern of her.

C2.5 在第一章中增加新的规则 7：

7　可确定的最后一点

在现场裁判确定某船的状态或她与另一条船之间的关系已经发生了改变之前，他们会假设还没有发生这样的改变。

C2.6 规则 13 更改为：

13　迎风换舷或顺风换舷时

13.1 一条船从越过正顶风后，一直到近迎风航线上，她须*避让*其他船。

13.2 一条顺风航行的船，当其主帆后角越过中线后，须*避让*其他船，直至其主帆受满风或不再顺风航行。

13.3 当规则 13. 1 或 13. 2 适用时，规则 10、11 和 12 不适用。但是，如果两条船同时受规则 13. 1 或 13. 2 约束，在另外一条船左舷一侧的船或在后的船须*避让*。

C2.7 删除规则 16. 2。

C2.8 删除规则 17。

C2.9 规则 18 更改为：

18　绕标空间

18.1 规则 18 适用时

当船被要求以同侧离开*标志*，并且至少其中一条船在*标区*内时，规则 18 在她们之间适用。然而，它并不适用于一条接近*标志*和一条离开*标志*的船之间。当享有*绕标空间*的船处于下一个航段并且该*标志*位于她的船尾时，规则 18 在这些船之间不再适用。

18.2 Giving Mark-Room

(a) When the first boat reaches the *zone*,

(1) if boats are *overlapped*, the outside boat at that moment shall thereafter give the inside boat *mark-room*.

(2) if boats are not *overlapped*, the boat that has not reached the *zone* shall thereafter give *mark-room*.

(b) If the boat entitled to *mark-room* leaves the *zone*, the entitlement to *mark-room* ceases and rule 18.2(a) is applied again if required based on the relationship of the boats at the time rule 18.2(a) is re-applied.

(c) If a boat obtained an inside *overlap* and, from the time the *overlap* began, the outside boat is unable to give *mark-room*, she is not required to give it.

18.3 Tacking or Gybing

(a) If *mark-room* for a boat includes a change of *tack*, such tack or gybe shall be done no faster than a tack or gybe to sail her *proper course*.

(b) When an inside *overlapped* right-of-way boat must change *tack* at a *mark* to sail her *proper course*, until she changes *tack* she shall sail no farther from the *mark* than needed to sail that course. Rule 18.3(b) does not apply at a gate *mark* or a finishing *mark* and a boat shall be exonerated for breaking this rule if the course of another boat was not affected before the boat changed *tack*.

C2.10 Rule 20.4(a) is changed to:

(a) The following arm signals by the helmsman are required in addition to the hails:

18.2 给予绕标空间

（a）当第一条船到达*标区*时，

（1）如果船*相联*，此时外侧船须在此后给予内侧船*绕标空间*。

（2）如果船不*相联*，尚未进入此*标区*的船须在此后给予*绕标空间*。

（b）如果享有*绕标空间*的船离开*标区*，则享有的*绕标空间*权终止，并且在规则 18. 2（a）再次适用时，基于船之间的关系，需要的话，规则 18. 2（a）再次适用。

（c）如果一条船获取了内侧*相联*，从*相联*开始的那一刻起，外侧船无法给予*绕标空间*，外侧船就无需给予*绕标空间*了。

18.3 迎风换舷或顺风换舷

（a）如果一条船的*绕标空间*包含换*舷*，这样的迎风换舷或顺风换舷的动作速度不得快于她迎风换舷或顺风换舷去行驶她的*正当航线*的速度。

（b）如果一条内侧*相联*的航行权船在*标志*旁必须换*舷*来行驶其*正当航线*，直到其换*舷*，她到*标志*的距离不得远于其行驶那条航线所需的距离。规则 18. 3（b）不适用于门*标*或终点*标*处，并且，如果另一条船的航线没有在这条船换*舷*前被影响到，则这条船违反这条规则的行为须被免责。

C2.10 规则 20. 4（a）更改为：

（a）除呼喊外，舵手还被要求使用下列手臂信号：

(1) for *room* to tack, repeatedly and clearly pointing to windward; and

(2) for 'You tack', repeatedly and clearly pointing at the other boat and waving the arm to windward.

C2.11 Rule 21.3 is deleted.

C2.12 Rule 23.1 is changed to:

23.1 If reasonably possible, a boat not *racing* shall not interfere with a boat that is *racing* or an umpire boat.

C2.13 Add new rule 23.3:

23.3 When boats in different matches meet, any change of course by either boat shall be consistent with complying with a *rule* or trying to win her own match.

C2.14 Rule 31 is changed to:

31 TOUCHING A MARK

While *racing*, neither the crew nor any part of a boat's hull shall touch a starting *mark* before *starting*, a *mark* that begins, bounds or ends the leg of the course on which she is sailing, or a finishing *mark* after *finishing*. In addition, while *racing*, a boat shall not touch a race committee vessel that is also a *mark*.

C2.15 Add new rule 41(e):

(e) help to recover from the water and return on board a crew member, provided the return on board is at the approximate location of the recovery.

C2.16 Rule 42 shall also apply between the warning and preparatory signals.

C2.17 Rule 42.2(d) is changed to:

(d) sculling: repeated movement of the helm to propel the boat forward;

（1）要求迎风换舷的*空间*时，反复而清楚地指向上风；和

（2）表示“你迎风换舷”时，反复而明显地指向另外一条船并向上风挥动上臂。

C2.11 删除规则 21. 3。

C2.12 规则 23. 1 更改为：

23.1 如果合理可行，不参加*竞赛*的船不得妨碍正在*竞赛*的船或现场裁判船。

C2.13 增加新的规则 23. 3：

23.3 当不在同一对抗场次的船相遇时，任何一条船在改变航线时须始终遵守*规则*，或其目的是赢得自己的对抗赛。

C2.14 规则 31 更改为：

31　碰标

*竞赛*时，船员及船体的任何一部分不得在*起航*前触碰起航*标志*，不得触碰标示其正在航行的航线上某航段的起点、边界和末端的*标志*，且*到达终点*后也不得触碰终点*标志*。另外，*竞赛*时，船不得触碰作为*标志*的竞赛委员会的船只。

C2.15 增加新的规则 41（e）：

（e）帮助将船员从水中救起并送回船上，前提是在救起的位置附近送回。

C2.16 规则 42 也须适用于预告信号和准备信号之间。

C2.17 规则 42. 2（d）更改为：

（d）摇舵：舵的反复运动推动船向前行驶；

C3 RACE SIGNALS AND CHANGES TO RELATED RULES

C3.1 Starting Signals

The signals for starting a match shall be as follows. Times shall be taken from the visual signals; the failure of a sound signal shall be disregarded. If more than one match will be sailed, the starting signal for one match shall be the warning signal for the next match.

Time in minutes	*Visual signal*	*Sound signal*	*Means*
7	Flag F displayed	One	Attention signal
6	Flag F removed	None	
5	Numeral pennant displayed*	One	Warning signal
4	Flag P displayed	One	Preparatory signal
2	Blue or yellow flag or both displayed**	One**	End of pre-start entry time
1	Flag P removed	One long	
0	Warning signal removed	One	Starting signal

* Within a flight, numeral pennant 1 means Match 1, pennant 2 means Match 2, etc., unless the sailing instructions state otherwise.

** These signals shall be made only if one or both boats fail to comply with rule C4.2. The flag(s) shall be displayed until the umpires have signalled a penalty or for one minute, whichever is earlier.

C3　竞赛信号和相关规则的更改

C3.1 起航信号

一场对抗赛的起航信号须按如下要求发出。时间须以视觉信号为准;音响信号的缺失不必理会。如果将进行一个场次以上的对抗赛,前一场对抗赛的起航信号须为下一场对抗赛的预告信号。

时间	*视觉信号*	*音响信号*	*含义*
7 分钟	展示 F 旗	一声	注意信号
6 分钟	移除 F 旗	无	
5 分钟	展示数字三角旗 *	一声	预告信号
4 分钟	展示 P 旗	一声	准备信号
2 分钟	展示蓝或黄旗,或两面旗都展示 **	一声 **	起航前的入场时间结束
1 分钟	移除 P 旗	一长声	
0 分钟	移除预告信号	一声	起航信号

* 在一组中,数字三角旗 1 意为第一场,数字三角旗 2 意为第二场,以此类推,除非航行细则另有规定。

** 只有在一条船或两条船都没有遵守规则 C4.2 时才须使用这些信号。这些旗须一直展示到现场裁判发出惩罚信号或 1 分钟后,以先到的那个时刻为准。

C3.2 Changes to Related Rules

(a) Rule 29.1 is changed to:

(1) When at a boat's starting signal any part of her hull is on the course side of the starting line or one of its extensions, the race committee shall promptly display a blue or yellow flag identifying the boat with one sound. The flag shall be displayed until the hull of the boat is completely on the pre-start side of the starting line or one of its extensions or until two minutes after her starting signal, whichever is earlier.

(2) When after a boat's starting signal any part of her hull crosses from the pre-start side to the course side of the starting line across an extension without having *started* correctly, the race committee shall promptly display a blue or yellow flag identifying the boat. The flag shall be displayed until the hull of the boat is completely on the pre-start side of the starting line or one of its extensions or until two minutes after her starting signal, whichever is earlier.

(b) In the race signal AP the last sentence is changed to: 'The attention signal will be made 1 minute after removal unless at that time the race is *postponed* again or *abandoned*.'

(c) In the race signal N the last sentence is changed to: 'The attention signal will be made 1 minute after removal unless at that time the race is *abandoned* again or *postponed*.'

C3.3 Finishing Line Signals

The race signal Blue flag or shape shall not be used.

C4 REQUIREMENTS BEFORE THE START

C4.1 At a boat's preparatory signal, her hull shall be completely outside the line that is at a 90° angle to the starting line through

C3.2 相关规则的更改

（a）规则 29. 1 更改为：

（1）一条船在起航信号发出时，其船体的任何部分处在起航线或其一端的延长线的航线一侧时，竞赛委员会须迅即展示一面识别该船的蓝旗或黄旗并伴随一声音响。该旗帜须展示至该船船体完全回到起航线或其一端延长线的准备起航区一侧或起航信号发出后 2 分钟，以先到的那个时刻为准。

（2）一条船在起航信号发出后，其船体的任何部分从准备起航区一侧跨过起航线的一端延长线到航线一侧而未正确*起航*时，竞赛委员会须迅即展示一面识别该船的蓝旗或黄旗。该旗帜须展示至该船船体完全回到起航线或其一端延长线的起航准备区一侧，或起航信号发出后 2 分钟，以先到的那个时刻为准。

（b）竞赛信号 AP 旗的最后一句更改为："在移除后 1 分钟发出注意信号，除非那时竞赛被再次*推迟*或被*放弃*。"

（c）竞赛信号 N 旗的最后一句更改为："在移除后 1 分钟发出注意信号，除非那时竞赛被再次*推迟*或被*放弃*。"

C3.3 终点线信号

不得使用竞赛信号蓝色旗或蓝色物体。

C4　起航前的要求

C4.1 一条船在准备信号发出时，其船体须完全处于自其指定一端的起航*标*引出的与起航线成 90° 角的连线之外。在对阵表

the starting *mark* at her assigned end. In the pairing list, the boat listed on the left-hand side is assigned the port end and shall display a blue flag at her stern while *racing*. The other boat is assigned the starboard end and shall display a yellow flag at her stern while *racing*.

C4.2 Within the two-minute period following a boat's preparatory signal, her hull shall cross and clear the starting line, the first time from the course side to the pre-start side.

C5 SIGNALS BY UMPIRES

C5.1 A green and white flag with one long sound means 'No penalty'.

C5.2 A blue or yellow flag identifying a boat with one long sound means 'The identified boat shall take a penalty by complying with rule C7.'

C5.3 A red flag with or soon after a blue or yellow flag with one long sound means 'The identified boat shall take a penalty by complying with rule C7.3(d).'

C5.4 A black flag with a blue or yellow flag and one long sound means 'The identified boat is disqualified, and the match is terminated and awarded to the other boat.'

C5.5 One short sound means 'A penalty is now completed.'

C5.6 Repetitive short sounds mean 'A boat is no longer taking a penalty and the penalty remains.'

C5.7 A blue or yellow flag or shape displayed from an umpire boat means 'The identified boat has an outstanding penalty.'

C6 PROTESTS AND REQUESTS FOR REDRESS BY BOATS

C6.1 A boat may protest another boat

(a) under a rule of Part 2, except rule 14, by clearly displaying flag Y immediately after an incident in which she was involved;

(b) under any rule not listed in rule C6.1(a) or C6.2 by clearly displaying a red flag as soon as possible after the incident.

中，被列在左边的船须指定在左侧端点，竞赛时须在船尾展示一面蓝旗。另外一条船被指定在右侧端点，竞赛时须在船尾展示一面黄旗。

C4.2 准备信号发出后的 2 分钟之内，一条船的船体须第一次从航线一侧越过并完全离开起航线到达准备起航区一侧。

C5　现场裁判使用的信号

C5.1 一面绿白旗并伴随一声长音响，意为"没有惩罚"。

C5.2 识别一条船的一面蓝旗或黄旗并伴随一声长音响，意为"所识别的船须按规则 C7 做一次解脱"。

C5.3 在展示蓝旗或黄旗同时或紧随其后展示红旗并伴随一声长音响，意为"所识别的船须按规则 C7. 3（d)接受惩罚"。

C5.4 在展示蓝旗或黄旗同时展示黑旗并伴随一声长音响，意为"所识别的船被取消资格，对抗赛终止，另外一条船获胜"。

C5.5 一声短音响意为"惩罚已完成"。

C5.6 重复的短音响意为"某船已不再是做解脱的船，该惩罚保留"。

C5.7 在现场裁判船上展示的蓝旗或黄旗，或同颜色的物体意为"所识别的船有一个未完成的惩罚"。

C6　船的抗议和补偿要求

C6.1 一条船可以抗议另一条船：

(a) 除规则 14 外，依据规则第二章在她涉及其中的事件发生后立即清楚地展示 Y 旗；

(b) 依据未列入规则 C6. 1（a)或 C6. 2 中的任何规则，在事件后尽快清楚地展示红旗。

C6.2 A boat may not protest another boat under

(a) rule 14, unless damage or injury results;

(b) a rule of Part 2, unless she was involved in the incident;

(c) rule 31 or 42; or

(d) rule C4 or C7.

C6.3 A boat requesting redress because of circumstances that arise while she is *racing* or in the finishing area shall clearly display a red flag as soon as possible after she becomes aware of those circumstances, but no later than two minutes after *finishing* or retiring.

C6.4

(a) A boat protesting under rule C6.1(a) shall remove flag Y before or as soon as possible after the umpires' signal.

(b) A boat protesting under rule C6.1(b) or requesting redress under rule C6.3 shall, for her *protest* or request to be valid, keep her red flag displayed until she has so informed the umpires after *finishing* or retiring. No written *protest* or request for redress is required.

C6.5 Umpire Decisions

(a) After flag Y is displayed, the umpires shall decide whether to penalize any boat. They shall signal their decision in compliance with rule C5.1, C5.2 or C5.3. However,

(1) if the umpires decide to penalize a boat, and as a result that boat will have more than two outstanding penalties, the umpires shall signal her disqualification under rule C5.4;

(2) when the umpires penalize a boat under rule C8.2 and in the same incident there is a flag Y from a boat, the umpires may disregard the flag Y.

C6.2 一条船不可以依据下列规则抗议另外一条船：

(a) 规则 14，除非造成了损坏或损伤；

(b) 规则第二章的某一条，除非该船涉及此事件；

(c) 规则 31 或 42；或者

(d) 规则 C4 或 C7。

C6.3 一条船因为在*竞赛*中或终点区域内所发生的情况而要求补偿时，须在其意识到这些情况后尽快清楚地展示红旗，但不得晚于*到达终点*或退出竞赛后的 2 分钟。

C6.4

(a) 按照规则 C6. 1 (a)提出抗议的船须在现场裁判发出信号前或发出后尽快移除 Y 旗。

(b) 为使所提出的*抗议*或要求有效，按照规则 C6. 1 (b)提出抗议或按照规则 C6. 3 提出补偿要求的船，须将红旗展示至*到达终点*或退出竞赛后通知到现场裁判为止。不要求书面的*抗议*或补偿要求。

C6.5 现场裁判的裁决

(a) Y 旗展示后，现场裁判须决定是否判罚某条船。他们须根据规则 C5. 1、C5. 2 或 C5. 3 发出裁决信号。但是，

(1) 如果现场裁判决定判罚一条船，且判罚将导致该船拥有超过 2 个的未完成惩罚，现场裁判须根据规则 C5. 4 发出信号取消其资格；

(2) 当现场裁判按规则 C8. 2 判罚一条船时，即便在同一事件中有船也展示了 Y 旗，现场裁判可无视该 Y 旗。

(b) The red-flag penalty in rule C5.3 shall be used when a boat has gained a controlling position as a result of breaking a *rule*, but the umpires are not certain that the conditions for an additional umpire-initiated penalty have been fulfilled.

C6.6 Protest Committee Decisions

(a) The protest committee may take evidence in any way it considers appropriate and may communicate its decision orally.

(b) If the protest committee decides that a breach of a *rule* has had no significant effect on the outcome of the match, it may

(1) impose a penalty of one point or part of one point;

(2) order a resail; or

(3) make another arrangement it decides is equitable, which may be to impose no penalty.

(c) The penalty for breaking rule 14 when damage or injury results will be at the discretion of the protest committee, and may include exclusion from further races in the event.

C6.7 Add new rule N1.10 to Appendix N:

N1.10 In rule N1.1, one International Umpire may be appointed to the jury, or a panel of it, in place of one International Judge.

C7 PENALTY SYSTEM

C7.1 Deleted Rule

Rule 44 is deleted.

C7.2 All Penalties

(a) A penalized boat may delay taking a penalty within the limitations of rule C7.3 and shall take it as follows:

(1) When on a leg of the course to a windward *mark*, she shall gybe and, as soon as reasonably possible, luff to a closehauled course.

（b）当一条船因违反*规则*而获得了控制船位，但现场裁判又不确定追加一次现场裁判发起的惩罚的条件是否满足时，须使用规则 C5.3 中的红旗惩罚。

C6.6 抗议委员会的裁决

（a）抗议委员会可以按其认为恰当的任何方式取证，并且可以口头传达其裁决结果。

（b）如果抗议委员会认定违反*规则*的行为对该场对抗的结果没有明显影响时，它可以：

（1）施加 1 分或零点几分的惩罚；

（2）命令重新竞赛；或

（3）做出它认为公平的其他安排，这种安排可能是不施加惩罚。

（c）违反规则 14 而造成损坏或受伤的惩罚将由抗议委员会自由裁量，惩罚可以是取消参加后续竞赛的资格。

C6.7 在附录 N 中增加新规则 N1.10：

N1.10 在规则 N1.1 中，一名国际现场裁判可以被任命到仲裁委员会或它的审理小组，以取代一名国际仲裁。

C7　惩罚方法

C7.1 删除规则

删除规则 44。

C7.2 所有惩罚

（a）被惩罚的船可以在规则 C7.3 的限制内延迟做解脱，并须按下列办法进行解脱：

（1）在向上风*标志*行驶的航段上，她须顺风换舷并尽早迎风偏转至近迎风航线上。

(2) When on a leg of the course to a leeward *mark* or the finishing line, she shall tack and, as soon as reasonably possible, bear away to a course that is more than ninety degrees from the true wind.

(b) Add to rule 2: 'When *racing*, a boat need not take a penalty unless signalled to do so by an umpire.'

(c) A boat completes a leg of the course when any part of her hull crosses the extension of the line from the previous *mark* through the *mark* she is rounding, or on the last leg when she *finishes*.

(d) A penalized boat shall not be recorded as having *finished* until she takes her penalty and her hull is completely on the course side of the line and she then *finishes*, unless the penalty is cancelled before or after she crosses the finishing line.

(e) If a boat has one or two outstanding penalties and the other boat in her match is penalized, one penalty for each boat shall be cancelled except that a red-flag penalty shall not cancel or be cancelled by another penalty.

(f) If one boat has *finished* and is no longer *racing*, and the other boat has an outstanding penalty, the umpires may cancel the outstanding penalty.

C7.3 Penalty Limitations

(a) A boat taking a penalty that includes a tack shall have the spinnaker head below the main-boom gooseneck from the time she passes head to wind until she is on a close-hauled course.

(b) No part of a penalty may be taken inside the *zone* of a rounding *mark* that begins, bounds or ends the leg the boat is on.

（2）在向下风*标志*或终点线行驶的航段上，她须迎风换舷并尽早顺风偏转至一个超过真风 90° 的航线上。

（b）在规则 2 后增加：“*竞赛*时，船不需要做解脱，除非现场裁判发出信号要求其这么做。”

（c）当一条船船体的任何部分越过从前一个*标志*至她正在绕行的*标志*连线的延长线时，或在最后一个航段上她*到达终点*时，该船就完成了航线的一个航段。

（d）被判罚的船在做了解脱，船体完全位于终点线的航线一侧，而后*到达终点*之前，不得被记录为*到达终点*，除非她在通过终点线之前或之后惩罚被取消了。

（e）如果一条船有一或两个未完成的惩罚，而本场对抗中的另一条船也被判罚了，则每条船须取消一个惩罚，但红旗惩罚不得取消或因另一条船的惩罚而被取消。

（f）如果一条船已经*到达终点*且不再*竞赛*了，而另一条船有一个未完成的惩罚，现场裁判可以取消这个未完成的惩罚。

C7.3 惩罚限制

（a）一条船做一个包括一次迎风换舷的解脱时，自其越过正顶风直至处于近迎风航线上时，其球帆的帆顶须始终位于主帆杆的鹅颈销之下。

（b）解脱的任何过程不得在标示船所在航段上的起点、边界和结束的需绕行的*标志*的*标区*内进行。

(c) If a boat has one outstanding penalty, she may take the penalty any time after *starting* and before *finishing*. If a boat has two outstanding penalties, she shall take one of them as soon as reasonably possible, but not before *starting*.

(d) When the umpires display a red flag with or soon after a penalty flag, the penalized boat shall take a penalty as soon as reasonably possible, but not before *starting*.

C7.4 Taking and Completing Penalties

(a) When a boat with an outstanding penalty is on a leg to a windward *mark* and gybes, or is on a leg to a leeward *mark* or the finishing line and passes head to wind, she is taking a penalty.

(b) When a boat taking a penalty either does not take the penalty correctly or does not complete the penalty as soon as reasonably possible, she is no longer taking a penalty. The umpires shall signal this as required by rule C5.6.

(c) The umpire boat for each match shall display blue or yellow flags or shapes, each flag or shape indicating one outstanding penalty. When a boat has taken a penalty, or a penalty has been cancelled, one flag or shape shall be removed, with the appropriate sound signal. Failure of the umpires to signal correctly shall not change the number of penalties outstanding.

C8 PENALTIES INITIATED BY UMPIRES

C8.1 Rule Changes

Rules 60.2(a) and 60.3(a) do not apply to *rules* for which penalties may be imposed by umpires.

C8.2 When the umpires decide that a boat has broken rule 31, 42, C4, C7.3(c) or C7.3(d) she shall be penalized by signalling her under rule C5.2 or C5.3. However, if a boat is penalized （c）如果一条船有一个未完成的惩罚，她可在*起航*后和*到达终点*前的任何时间去做解脱。如果一条船有两个未完成的惩罚，她须在合适的机会尽早去完成其中的一个解脱，但不能在*起航*前进行。

（d）当现场裁判在举起惩罚旗同时或随即展示了红旗，被判罚的船须尽早地做解脱，但不能在*起航*前进行。

C7.4 做解脱和完成惩罚

（a）当带有一个未完成惩罚的船在驶向上风*标志*的航段上航行并顺风换舷，或者在向下风*标志*或向终点线航行的航段上航行并越过正顶风时，被视为正在做解脱。

（b）当一条做解脱的船未按正确的方法做解脱或未尽早完成解脱动作时，她不再是做解脱的船。现场裁判须按规则 C5. 6 的要求发出信号。

（c）每一场对抗赛的现场裁判船上须展示蓝色或黄色的旗帜或物体，每面旗或每个物体代表一个未完成的惩罚。当船已做解脱或一个惩罚已被取消时，须移除一面旗或一个物体，伴随适当的音响信号。现场裁判在正确发出信号上的失败不得改变未完成惩罚的次数。

C8　现场裁判发起的判罚

C8.1 规则的更改

规则 60. 2（a)和 60. 3（a)不适用于可能由现场裁判因其而施加判罚的*规则*。

C8.2 当现场裁判认定一条船违反了规则 31、42、C4、C7. 3（c)或 C7. 3（d)时，须按照规则 C5. 2 或 C5. 3 对其发出判罚信号。然而，一条船因为违反规则第二章被判罚时，并且如果她在

for breaking a rule of Part 2 and if she in the same incident breaks rule 31, she shall not be penalized for breaking rule 31. Furthermore, a boat that displays an incorrect flag or does not display the correct flag shall be warned orally and given an opportunity to correct the error before being penalized.

C8.3 When the umpires decide that a boat has

(a) gained an advantage by breaking a *rule* after allowing for a penalty,

(b) deliberately broken a *rule*, or

(c) committed a breach of sportsmanship,

she shall be penalized under rule C5.2, C5.3 or C5.4.

C8.4 If the umpires or protest committee members decide that a boat may have broken a *rule* other than those listed in rules C6.1(a) and C6.2, they shall so inform the protest committee for its action under rule 60.3 and rule C6.6 when appropriate.

C8.5 When, after one boat has *started*, the umpires are satisfied that the other boat will not *start*, they may signal under rule C5.4 that the boat that did not *start* is disqualified and the match is terminated.

C8.6 When the match umpires, together with at least one other umpire, decide that a boat has broken rule 14 and damage resulted, they may impose a points-penalty without a hearing. The competitor shall be informed of the penalty as soon as practicable and, at the time of being so informed, may request a hearing. The protest committee shall then proceed under rule C6.6. Any penalty decided by the protest committee may be more than the penalty imposed by the umpires. When the umpires decide that a penalty greater than one point is appropriate, they shall act under rule C8.4.

同一事件中违反了规则31，她不得因违反规则31而被判罚。此外，如果一条船展示了错误的旗或没有展示正确的旗时须被口头警告，在判罚前可得到改正错误的机会。

C8.3 当现场裁判判定一条船已经

（a）通过违反*规则*虑及惩罚后获得优势时；

（b）故意违反*规则*时，或

（c）违反了体育道德时，

须根据规则 C5. 2、C5. 3 或 C5. 4 受到惩罚。

C8.4 如果现场裁判或抗议委员会成员认定一条船可能已经违反了除规则 C6. 1（a）和 C6. 2 中所列规则以外的*规则*时，他们须在适当时机通知抗议委员会根据规则 60. 3 和 C6. 6 采取行动。

C8.5 一条船已经*起航*后，当现场裁判们认定另外一条船将不会*起航*时，他们可根据规则 C5. 4 发信号通知未*起航*的船被取消资格，竞赛终止。

C8.6 当该场对抗的现场裁判们和至少一名其他的现场裁判同时判定一条船已经违反了规则 14 并且造成了损坏，他们可以不通过审理给予加分惩罚。须在可行的情况下尽快通知选手相关的惩罚，选手在被如此告知时可以要求审理。之后抗议委员会须根据规则 C6. 6 行事。由抗议委员会决定的任何惩罚可以多于现场裁判的罚分。当现场裁判决定多于 1 分的罚分合适时，他们须根据规则 C8. 4 采取行动。

C9 REQUESTS FOR REDRESS OR REOPENING; APPEALS; OTHER PROCEEDINGS

C9.1 There shall be no request for redress or an appeal from a decision made under rule C5, C6, C7 or C8. Rule 66.2 is changed to: 'A *party* to the hearing may not ask for a reopening.'

C9.2 A competitor may not base a request for redress on a claim that an action by an official boat was improper. The protest committee may decide to consider giving redress in such circumstances but only if it believes that an official boat, including an umpire boat, may have seriously interfered with a competing boat.

C9.3 No proceedings of any kind may be taken in relation to any action or non-action by the umpires, except as permitted in rule C9.2.

C10 SCORING

C10.1 The winning competitor of each match scores one point (half a point each for a dead heat); the loser scores no points.

C10.2 When a competitor withdraws from part of an event the scores of all completed races shall stand.

C10.3 When a single round robin is terminated before completion, or a multiple round robin is terminated during the first round robin, a competitor's score shall be the average points scored per match sailed by the competitor. However, if any of the competitors have completed less than one third of the scheduled matches, the entire round robin shall be disregarded and, if necessary, the event declared void. For the purposes of tie-breaking in rule C11.1(a), a competitor's score shall be the average points scored per match between the tied competitors.

C9　要求补偿或重新审理;上诉;其他程序

C9.1 不得对根据规则 C5、C6、C7 或 C8 做出的裁决要求补偿或上诉。规则 66. 2 更改为:“审理的一方不可以要求重新审理。”

C9.2 一条官员船不恰当的行为不能成为选手要求补偿的理由。在这种情况下,抗议委员会可以决定考虑给予补偿,但只能在确信官员船包括现场裁判船可能已严重干扰了参赛船时。

C9.3 除规则 C9. 2 允许的情况外,对现场裁判的行动或不行动不做任何形式的追究。

C10　计分

C10.1 每场对抗赛的胜者记 1 分(平局时每人得半分);负者记零分。

C10.2 当选手退出赛事的一部分时,所有已完成轮次的计分须有效。

C10.3 当单循环在结束前中止,或多循环在第一个单循环期间中止时,选手的成绩须计为她所参加的每场对抗得分的平均分。然而,如果有任何选手完成的对抗场次少于日程中的三分之一时,须忽略整个循环赛,如果需要,该赛事宣布无效。根据规则 C11. 1 (a),为了打破平分,选手的成绩须计为平分的选手之间的每场对抗赛得分的平均分。

C10.4 When a multiple round robin is terminated with an incomplete round robin, only one point shall be available for all the matches sailed between any two competitors, as follows:

Number of matches completed between any two competitors	*Points for each win*
1	One point
2	Half a point
3	A third of a point
(etc.)	

C10.5 In a round-robin series,

(a) competitors shall be placed in order of their total scores, highest score first;

(b) a competitor who has won a match but is disqualified for breaking a *rule* against a competitor in another match shall lose the point for that match (but the losing competitor shall not be awarded the point); and

(c) the overall position between competitors who have sailed in different groups shall be decided by the highest score.

C10.6 In a knockout series the sailing instructions shall state the minimum number of points required to win a series between two competitors. When a knockout series is terminated it shall be decided in favour of the competitor with the higher score.

C10.7 When only one boat in a match fails to *sail the course*, she shall be scored no points (without a hearing).

C11 TIES

C11.1 Round-Robin Series

In a round-robin series competitors are assigned to one or more groups and scheduled to sail against all other

C10.4 当多循环以一个未完成的循环而结束时，对于任何两名选手之间参加的所有对抗赛，须只记 1 分，如下所示：

任何两名选手间完成的对抗赛场次	*每位胜者得分*
1	1 分
2	0.5 分
3	1/3 分
（以此类推）	

C10.5 在一个循环系列赛中，

(a) 选手须根据总分排列名次，总分最高者为第一名；

(b) 一名选手已在一场对抗赛中获胜，但是却因为与另一场对抗赛中的选手相遇违反*规则*而被取消资格，则须失去那场对抗场次的得分（但负者不得获得分数）；和

(c) 在不同组别参加竞赛的两名选手间的总排名须由分数高者确定。

C10.6 淘汰系列赛的航行细则须说明两名选手间赢得系列赛所要求的最小分数值。当淘汰系列赛终止时，获得高分的选手将胜出。

C10.7 当一场对抗中仅有一条船没有*行驶航线*时，她须被记为 0 分（无需审理）。

C11 平分

C11.1 循环系列赛

在循环系列赛中，选手被分配到一个或更多的组中并被安排和其所在组中的所有其他选手进行一次或者多次竞赛。赛事模式中规定的每个独立阶段须为独立的循环系列赛，

competitors in their group one or more times. Each separate stage identified in the event format shall be a separate round-robin series irrespective of the number of times each competitor sails against each other competitor in that stage.

Ties between two or more competitors in a round-robin series shall be broken by the following methods, in order, until all ties are broken. When one or more ties are only partially broken, rules C11.1(a) to C11.1(e) shall be reapplied to them. Ties shall be decided in favour of the competitor(s) who

(a) placed in order, has the highest score in the matches between the tied competitors;

(b) when the tie is between two competitors in a multiple round robin, has won the last match between the two competitors;

(c) has the most points against the competitor placed highest in the round-robin series or, if necessary, second highest, and so on until the tie is broken. When two separate ties have to be resolved but the resolution of each depends upon resolving the other, the following principles shall be used in the rule C11.1(c) procedure:

  (1) the higher-place tie shall be resolved before the lowerplace tie, and

  (2) all the competitors in the lower-place tie shall be treated as a single competitor for the purposes of rule C11.1(c);

(d) after applying rule C10.5(c), has the highest place in the different groups, irrespective of the number of competitors in each group;

(e) has the highest place in the most recent stage of the event (fleet race, round robin, etc.).

不考虑选手之间在那个阶段的相互对抗的次数。

在循环系列赛中，两个或多个选手平分时须使用如下方法打破平分，按照顺序，直到所有平分都打破。当一个或多个平分仅有部分被打破时，须再次运用规则 C11.1（a)至 C11.1（e)。下列选手须在平分中胜出：

(a) 按顺序排列，平分选手间的对抗中的得分最高者；

(b) 在多循环中两个选手平分，两选手间的最后一场对抗中的获胜者；

(c) 在循环系列赛中排名最高者，或如果有必要，排名第二高者，以此类推，直到平分被打破。当不得不解决两个单独的并列，且两个并列的解决相互依赖时，须在规则 C11.1（c)的程序中运用下列原则：

  (1) 排名高的平分者须先于排名低的平分者解决，以及

  (2) 为达到规则 C11.1（c)的目的，所有低排名平分选手须按单个选手对待；

(d) 在运用了规则 C10.5（c)后，在不同组中排名最高者，不考虑每组选手的数量；

(e) 在赛事的最近一个阶段中排名最高者（群发赛、循环赛等）。

C11.2 Knockout Series

Ties (including 0–0) between competitors in a knockout series shall be broken by the following methods, in order, until the tie is broken. The tie shall be decided in favour of the competitor who

(a) has the highest place in the most recent round-robin series, applying rule C11.1 if necessary;

(b) has won the most recent match in the event between the tied competitors.

C11.3 Remaining Ties

When rule C11.1 or C11.2 does not resolve a tie,

(a) if the tie needs to be resolved for a later stage of the event (or another event for which the event is a direct qualifier), the tie shall be broken by a sail-off when practicable. When the race committee decides that a sail-off is not practicable, the tie shall be decided in favour of the competitor who has the highest score in the round-robin series after eliminating the score for the first race for each tied competitor or, should this fail to break the tie, the second race for each tied competitor and so on until the tie is broken. When a tie is partially resolved, the remaining tie shall be broken by reapplying rule C11.1 or C11.2.

(b) to decide the winner of an event that is not a direct qualifier for another event, or the overall position between competitors eliminated in one round of a knockout series, a sail-off may be used (but not a draw).

(c) when a tie is not broken any monetary prizes or ranking points for tied places shall be added together and divided equally among the tied competitors.

C11.2 淘汰系列赛

两个选手在淘汰系列赛中平分(包括 0-0 的平分)须按照下列方法打破平分,按照顺序,直到所有平分都打破。下列选手须在平分中胜出:

(a) 在最近的循环系列赛中排名最高者,如有必要可运用规则 C11. 1;

(b) 平分的选手中在本赛事最近的一场对抗中的获胜者。

C11.3 仍未打破的平分

当规则 C11. 1 或 C11. 2 不能解决平分时,

(a) 如果平分需要在本赛事的后阶段(或另外的赛事,而本赛事是其直接资格赛)解决,可行的话,须由一场加赛来打破平分。当竞赛委员会认定加赛不可行时,在循环系列赛中去掉每个并列选手的第一轮竞赛分数后有最高分数的选手须获胜,或者,如果仍不能打破平分,则去掉每个并列选手的第二轮成绩后来打破平分,以此类推,直到平分被打破。当一个平分部分被解决,仍未打破的平分须通过再次运用规则 C11. 1 或 C11. 2 来打破。

(b) 要决定一个不是另一个赛事的直接资格赛的赛事的胜者,或要决定在一场淘汰系列赛中被淘汰的选手之间的总排名,可以使用一轮加赛(但不使用抽签方式)。

(c) 当平分未能打破时,给予所并列名次的任何奖金或总排名分数须加起来并平均分给平分选手。

APPENDIX D TEAM RACING RULES

Team races shall be sailed under The Racing Rules of Sailing *as changed by this appendix.*

D1 CHANGES TO THE RACING RULES

D1.1 Definitions and the Rules of Parts 2 and 4

(a) In the definition *Finish*, delete the words 'after *starting*'.

(b) In the definition *Zone* the distance is changed to two hull lengths.

(c) Rule 18.2(b) is changed to:

If boats are *overlapped* when the first of them reaches the *zone*, the outside boat at that moment shall thereafter give the inside boat *mark-room*. If a boat is *clear ahead* when she reaches the *zone*, or she later becomes *clear ahead* when another boat passes head to wind, the boat *clear astern* at that moment shall thereafter give her *mark-room*.

(d) Rule 18.4 is deleted.

(e) When stated in the sailing instructions, rule 20 is changed so that the following arm signals are required in addition to the hails:

(1) for *room* to tack, repeatedly and clearly pointing to windward; and

(2) for 'You tack', repeatedly and clearly pointing at the other boat and waving the arm to windward.

(f) Rule 23.1 is changed to: 'If reasonably possible, a boat not *racing* shall not interfere with a boat that is *racing*, and a boat that has *finished* shall not act to interfere with a boat that has not *finished*.'

(g) Add new rule 23.3: 'When boats in different races meet, any change of course by either boat shall be consistent with complying with a *rule* or trying to win her own race.'

附录 D　队赛规则

队赛须遵守本附录更改过的《帆船竞赛规则》。

D1　竞赛规则的更改

D1.1 定义及规则第二章和第四章

(a) 在定义*到达终点*中，删除“*起航*后”。

(b) 在定义*标区*中，距离更改为 2 倍船长。

(c) 规则 18. 2 (b)更改为：

如果两船*相联*，其中的第一条船到达*标区*时，此时的外侧船此后须给予内侧船*绕标空间*。如果一条船到达*标区*时*明显在前*，或是后来，当另外一条船越过正顶风时她变成了*明显在前*，此时*明显在后*的船此后须给予*绕标空间*。

(d) 删除规则 18. 4。

(e) 当航行细则中规定此条适用时，规则 20 更改为，除了呼喊外，还需要做出下列手臂信号：

(1) 要求迎风换舷的*空间*时，反复而明显地指向上风；和

(2) 表示“你迎风换舷”时，反复而明显地指向另外一条船并往上风摆动手臂。

(f) 规则 23. 1 更改为：“若合理可行的话，不参加*竞赛*的船不得妨碍正在*竞赛*的船，已*到达终点*的船不得妨碍未*到达终点*的船。”

(g) 增加新规则 23. 3：“当不同竞赛组别的船相遇时，任何一条船在改变航线时须始终遵守*规则*或其目的是赢得自己的竞赛。”

(h) Add to rule 41:

(e) help from another boat on her team provided electronic communication is not used.

(i) Rule 45 is deleted.

D1.2 Protests and Requests for Redress

(a) Rule 60.1 is changed to:

A boat may

(a) protest another boat, but not for an alleged breach of a rule of Part 2 unless she was involved in the incident or the incident involved contact between members of the other team; or

(b) request redress.

(b) Rule 61.1(a) is changed so that the boat may remove her red flag after it has been conspicuously displayed.

(c) The boat requesting redress for an incident in the racing area shall display a red flag at the first reasonable opportunity after the incident. She shall display the red flag until it is acknowledged by the race committee or by an umpire.

(d) The race committee or protest committee shall not protest a boat for breaking a rule of Part 2 or rule 31 or 42 except

(1) based on evidence in a report from an umpire after a black and white flag has been displayed; or

(2) under rule 14 upon receipt of a report from any source alleging damage or injury.

(e) *Protests* and requests for redress need not be in writing. The protest committee may take evidence in any way it considers appropriate and may communicate its decision orally.

(f) A boat is not entitled to redress based on damage or injury caused by another boat on her team.

(g) When a supplied boat suffers a breakdown, rule D5 applies.

（h）在规则 41 后增加：

（e）来自她同队的另一条船的帮助，前提是不使用电子通信手段。

（i）删除规则 45。

D1.2 抗议和要求补偿

（a）规则 60. 1 更改为：

一条船可以

（a）抗议另外一条船，但对涉嫌违反规则第二章的抗议只能当其自己是当事船或该事件牵涉到其他船队的成员之间的接触时才能提出；或

（b）要求补偿。

（b）规则 61. 1（a）被更改为船已明显地展示红旗后可以将它移除。

（c）因竞赛区域内的事件要求补偿的船须在事件发生后的第一合理时机展示红旗。红旗须展示至被竞赛委员会或现场裁判看到为止。

（d）除下列情况外，竞赛委员会或抗议委员会不得抗议一条船违反规则第二章、规则 31 或规则 42，

（1）基于现场裁判展示黑白旗后报告的证据；或

（2）从任一渠道收到了有关损坏或受伤的报告后，运用规则 14。

（e）*抗议*和补偿要求无需书面提出。抗议委员会可以按自认恰当的任何方式取证，并可以口头传达其裁决结果。

（f）因队友的船导致损坏或受伤的船无权要求补偿。

（g）统一提供的船遭遇故障时，规则 D5 适用。

D1.3 Penalties

(a) Rule 44.1 is changed to:

A boat may take a One-Turn Penalty when she may have broken one or more rules of Part 2, or rule 31 or 42, in an incident while *racing*. However, when she may have broken a rule of Part 2 and rule 31 in the same incident she need not take the penalty for breaking rule 31.

(b) When a boat clearly indicates that she will take a penalty under rule 44.1, she shall take that penalty.

(c) A boat may take a penalty by retiring and informing the race committee or an umpire.

(d) There shall be no penalty for breaking a rule of Part 2 when the incident is between boats on the same team and there is no contact.

D2 UMPIRED RACES

D2.1 When Rule D2 Applies

Rule D2 applies to umpired races. Races to be umpired shall be identified in the notice of race or sailing instructions or by the display of flag J no later than the warning signal.

D2.2 Protests by Boats

When a boat protests under a rule of Part 2 or under rule 31 or 42 for an incident in the racing area, she is not entitled to a hearing and the following applies:

(a) She shall hail 'Protest' and conspicuously display a red flag at the first reasonable opportunity for each.

(b) The boats shall be given time to respond.

(c) If no boat takes a penalty or clearly indicates that she will do so, an umpire shall decide whether to penalize any boat.

D1.3 惩罚

（a）规则 44. 1 更改为：

船在*竞赛*中可能违反了规则第二章的一条或多条、规则 31 或规则 42 时，她可以做一个一圈解脱。但是，当她在同一事件中违反了规则第二章和规则 31 时，无需再为违反规则 31 做解脱。

（b）当一条船明确表示她将根据规则 44. 1 解脱时，她须做出这个解脱。

（c）一条船可以通过退出竞赛并通知竞赛委员会或现场裁判来接受惩罚。

（d）当事件涉及同队的船并没有发生接触时，不必因违反规则第二章被判罚。

D2 现场裁决的竞赛

D2.1 当规则 D2 适用时

规则 D2 适用于现场裁决的竞赛。凡现场裁决的竞赛须在竞赛通知或航行细则中说明或不迟于预告信号发出时展示 J 旗。

D2.2 来自船的抗议

当船因竞赛区域内的一个事件，依据规则第二章的某条、规则 31 或规则 42 提出抗议时，她无权要求审理，以下规定适用：

（a）她须呼喊“抗议”，并每次在第一合理时机清楚地展示红旗。

（b）须给予船只回应的时间。

（c）如果没有船做解脱或没有船明确表示将做解脱，现场裁判须决定是否判罚某船。

(d) If more than one boat breaks a *rule*, an umpire shall decide whether to penalize any boat that did not take a penalty.

(e) An umpire shall signal a decision in compliance with rule D2.4.

D2.3 Penalties Initiated by an Umpire

An umpire may penalize a boat without a *protest* by another boat, or report the incident to the protest committee, or both, when the boat

(a) breaks rule 31 or 42 and does not take a penalty;

(b) breaks a rule of Part 2 and makes contact with another boat on her team or with a boat in another race, and no boat takes a penalty;

(c) breaks a *rule* and her team gains an advantage despite her, or another boat on her team, taking a penalty;

(d) breaks rule 14 and there is damage or injury;

(e) breaks rule D1.3(b);

(f) fails to take a penalty signalled by an umpire;

(g) commits a breach of sportsmanship.

The umpire shall signal a decision in compliance with rule D2.4.

D2.4 Signals by an Umpire

An umpire shall signal a decision with one long sound and the display of a flag as follows:

(a) For no penalty, a green and white flag.

(b) To penalize one or more boats, a red flag. The umpire shall hail or signal to identify each boat penalized.

(c) To report the incident to the protest committee, a black and white flag.

（d）如果一条以上的船违反了*规则*，现场裁判须决定是否判罚没有做解脱的船。

（e）现场裁判须按照规则 D2. 4 发出裁决信号。

D2.3 现场裁判发起的判罚

当船出现下列情况时，现场裁判可以无需另一条船提出*抗议*而判罚某船，或将该事件报告给抗议委员会，或两者都做：

（a）违反了规则 31 或规则 42，且没有做解脱；

（b）违反了第二章中的某条规则，并与其同队的另一条船接触，或与另一个竞赛轮次的船接触，没有船做解脱；

（c）违反了*规则*后，尽管该船或队友的船做了解脱，本队仍然获益；

（d）违反了规则 14 并造成损坏和受伤；

（e）违反了规则 D1. 3（b）；

（f）未按照现场裁判的信号进行解脱；

（g）违反体育精神。

现场裁判须根据规则 D2. 4 发出裁决信号。

D2.4 现场裁判的信号

现场裁判须伴随一声长音响发出裁决信号并展示旗帜如下：

（a）一面绿白旗意为没有判罚。

（b）红旗意为判罚一条或多条船。现场裁判须呼喊或发出信号来指明每条被判罚的船。

（c）黑白旗意为将事件报告给抗议委员会。

D2.5 Penalties Imposed by Umpires

A boat penalized by an umpire shall take a Two-Turns Penalty. However, when a penalty is imposed under rule D2.3 and an umpire hails or signals a number of turns, the boat shall take that number of One-Turn Penalties.

D2.6 Limitations on Other Proceedings

(a) A breach of rule D2.5 shall not be grounds for a protest by a boat.

(b) A decision, action or non-action of an umpire shall not be

(1) grounds for redress,

(2) subject to an appeal under rule 70, or

(3) grounds for *abandoning* a race after it has started.

(c) The protest committee may decide to consider giving redress when it believes that an official boat, including an umpire boat, may have seriously interfered with a competing boat.

D3 SCORING A RACE

D3.1

(a) Each boat *finishing* a race and not retiring thereafter shall be scored points equal to her finishing place. All other boats shall be scored points equal to the number of boats entitled to *race*.

(b) When a boat is scored OCS, 10 points shall be added to her score unless she retired as soon as possible after the starting signal.

(c) When a boat fails to take a penalty imposed by an umpire at or near the finishing line, she shall be scored as retired.

(d) When a boat is scored as retired after *finishing*, each boat with a worse finishing place shall be moved up one place.

(e) When a protest committee decides that a boat that is a *party* to a protest hearing has broken a *rule* and is not exonerated,

D2.5 现场裁判施加的惩罚

被现场裁判判罚的船须进行一个两圈解脱。但是,当根据规则 D2. 3 进行判罚且现场裁判呼喊或出示信号示意了圈数时,该船须进行这个圈数的一圈解脱。

D2.6 其他程序的限制

(a) 一条船不得以违反规则 D2. 5 为由提出抗议。

(b) 现场裁判的裁决、行动或不行动不得

(1) 作为补偿的理由,

(2) 根据规则 70 提出上诉,或

(3) 作为一轮已起航的竞赛*放弃*的理由。

(c) 当抗议委员会认定一条官方船,包括现场裁判船,可能已严重妨碍了一条参赛船时,可以决定考虑给予补偿。

D3 一轮竞赛的计分

D3.1

(a) 一轮竞赛中,每条*到达终点*并且之后没有退出竞赛的船须被记为等于其终点名次的分数。其他所有船的分数须记为等于有权参加竞赛的所有船数。

(b) 当船被记为 OCS 后,须在其成绩上加 10 分,除非她在起航信号后尽快地退出了竞赛。

(c) 当船在终点线上或附近没有按照现场裁判的判罚做解脱时,她须被记为退出竞赛。

(d) 当一条船*到达终点*后被记为退出竞赛时,每条拥有更差终点名次的船须前移一位。

(e) 当抗议委员会认定作为抗议审理一方的一条船已违反*规则*且不能免责时,

(1) if the boat has not taken a penalty, 6 points shall be added to her score;

(2) if the boat's team has gained an advantage despite any penalty taken or imposed, the boat's score may be increased;

(3) when the boat has broken rule 1 or 2, rule 14 when she has caused damage or injury, or a *rule* when not *racing*, half or more race wins may be deducted from her team, or no penalty may be imposed. Race wins deducted shall not be awarded to any other team.

D3.2 When all boats on one team have *finished*, retired or failed to *start*, the other team's boats *racing* at that time shall be scored the points they would have received had they *finished*.

D3.3 The team with the lower total points wins the race. If the totals are equal, the team that does not have first place wins.

D4 SCORING AN EVENT

D4.1 Terminology

(a) The format of an event consists of one or more stages.

(b) In a round-robin stage, teams are divided into one or more groups, and each group is scheduled to sail one or more roundrobins.

(c) A round-robin consists of each team in a group sailing one race against each other team in that group.

(d) A knockout stage consists of one or more rounds in which each team sails one match. A match is one or more races between two teams.

D4.2 Event Format

(a) The sailing instructions shall state the format and stages of the event, and any special scoring rules.

（1）如果该船没有做解脱，须在其成绩上加 6 分；

（2）尽管有任何解脱或施加的惩罚，但其船队仍然获益时，可以给该船增加分数；

（3）当该船违反了规则 1 或 2、违反了规则 14 而导致损坏或受伤，或在非竞赛时违反了某一*规则*时，可以减去该船所在队一半或以上的获胜场次，也可以不施加惩罚。被减去的获胜场次不得奖给其他任何船队。

D3.2 当一个船队的所有船只已经*到达终点*、退出竞赛或没有成功*起航*时，参加*竞赛*的另一船队的船须被记为在那一时刻假设已*到达终点*所应得的分数。

D3.3 获得总分最低的船队在本轮竞赛中获胜。如果总分并列，没有第一名的那支船队胜出。

D4 一场赛事的计分

D4.1 术语

（a）一场赛事的竞赛模式包含一个或多个阶段。

（b）在一个循环赛阶段中，船队被分成一个或多个组别，每个组别被排定进行一场或多场循环赛。

（c）一场循环中包括一个组别中的每支队伍都与该组别中的其他支队伍进行一轮竞赛。

（d）一个淘汰赛阶段包括一个或多个回合，每个回合中每支队伍进行一场对抗。一场对抗为两队之间进行的一轮或多轮竞赛。

D4.2 竞赛模式

（a）航行细则须说明赛事的竞赛模式和阶段，以及任何特殊的计分规则。

(b) In order to conclude an event, the race committee may change or terminate any part of the format at any reasonable time taking into account the entries, weather, time constraints and other relevant factors.

D4.3 Scoring a Round-Robin Stage

(a) Teams in a round-robin group shall be ranked in order of number of race wins, highest first. If the teams have not completed an equal number of races, they shall be ranked in order of the percentage of races won, highest first.

(b) However, if a round-robin is terminated when fewer than 80% of its scheduled races have been completed, its race results shall not be included, but shall be used to break ties between teams in the group who all sailed each other in the terminated roundrobin.

(c) Results from a previous round-robin stage shall only be carried forward if stated in the sailing instructions.

D4.4 Round-Robin Tie Breaks

Ties in a round-robin stage shall be broken using results from that stage only.

(a) If the tied teams have all sailed each other at least once in the stage, the tie shall be broken in the order below.

(1) Percentage of races won in all races between the tied teams, highest first;

(2) Average points per race in all races between the tied teams, lowest first;

(3) If two teams remain tied, the winner of the last race between them;

（b）为了结束一场赛事，竞赛委员会考虑到参赛人员、天气、时间限制和其他相关因素后，可以在任何合理的时间来更改或终止竞赛模式中的任何部分。

D4.3 循环赛阶段的计分

（a）在一场循环赛阶段中，船队须按获胜的场次数量排列名次，获胜场次多者胜。如果船队没有完成同等数量的竞赛场次，则须按获胜场次的百分比排列名次，获胜轮次的百分比高者胜。

（b）但是，如果一场循环在尚未完成 80% 的排定轮次时就被终止，则其竞赛成绩不得被计算在内，但是须用来打破终止的循环赛里的组别中所有相互对抗过的船队间的平分。

（c）只有航行细则中规定此条适用时，才能结转前一个循环赛阶段的成绩。

D4.4 循环赛平分的打破

循环赛阶段的平分须只使用那个阶段的成绩来打破。

（a）如果平分的船队都已在本阶段中至少两两对抗过一次，那么平分须按如下顺序打破。

（1）按平分船队之间竞赛过的所有轮次的获胜百分比，高者胜；

（2）按平分船队之间竞赛过的所有轮次的每轮平均分，低者胜；

（3）如果两队仍然平分，两队之间的最后一轮竞赛赢者胜；

(4) Average points per race in all races against common opponents, lowest first;

(5) A sail-off if possible, otherwise a game of chance.

(b) Otherwise, the tie shall be broken using only steps (4) and (5) above.

(c) When a tie is partially broken by one of the above, the remaining tie shall be broken in accordance with D4.4(a) or (b) as appropriate.

D4.5 Scoring a Knockout Stage

(a) A round shall not be scored unless at least one race has been completed in each match in that round. The final and petit-final are separate rounds.

(b) The winner of a match shall be the first team to score the number of race wins stated in the sailing instructions. If a match is terminated, the winner shall be the team with the higher number of race wins in that match or, if this is a tie, the team that won the last race of the match.

(c) (1) Teams that win in a round shall be ranked ahead of those that lose.

(2) Teams that lose in a round and do not sail again shall be equally ranked.

(3) In a round that is not scored, teams shall be ranked in order of their places in the previous stage of the event, with teams from different groups ranked separately.

D5 BREAKDOWNS WHEN BOATS ARE SUPPLIED BY THE ORGANIZING AUTHORITY

D5.1 Rule D5 applies when boats are supplied by the organizing authority.

(4) 按对抗同一对手的所有轮次的每轮平均分，低者胜；

(5) 如有可能，加赛一场，否则抽签决定。

(b) 除此之外，平分须仅按照上述步骤(4)和(5)进行打破。

(c) 当平分按照上述之一被部分打破时，剩余的平分须酌情按照 D4. 4 (a)或(b)进行打破。

D4.5 淘汰赛阶段的计分

(a) 除非那个回合中每场对抗完成了至少一轮竞赛，否则该回合不得被记分。决赛和半决赛是独立的回合。

(b) 一场对抗的胜者须为第一个获得航行细则中所规定的获胜场次计分的船队。如果对抗被终止，胜者须为该场对抗中获胜轮次数较高的船队，或者，如果这是个平局，胜者为赢得该场对抗最后一轮竞赛的船队。

(c) (1) 赢得一个回合的船队的排名须在输掉的船队之前。

(2) 在一个回合中输掉并没有再赛的船队须排名相等。

(3) 在未计分的回合中，船队须按照赛事前一阶段的名次顺序进行排名，不同组别的船队分开排名。

D5 当组织机构提供的船发生损坏时

D5.1 当组织机构提供参赛船时，规则 D5 适用。

D5.2 When a boat suffers a breakdown in the racing area, she may request a score change by displaying a red flag at the first reasonable opportunity after the breakdown until it is acknowledged by the race committee or by an umpire. If possible, she shall continue *racing*.

D5.3 The race committee shall decide requests for a score change in accordance with rules D5.4 and D5.5. It may take evidence in any way it considers appropriate and may communicate its decision orally.

D5.4 When the race committee decides that the team's finishing position was made significantly worse, that the breakdown was through no fault of the crew, and that in the same circumstances a reasonably competent crew would not have been able to avoid the breakdown, it shall make as equitable a decision as possible. This may be to *abandon* and resail the race or, when the boat's finishing position was predictable, award her points for that position. Any doubt about a boat's position when she broke down shall be resolved against her.

D5.5 A breakdown caused by defective supplied equipment or a breach of a *rule* by an opponent shall not normally be determined to be the fault of the crew, but one caused by careless handling, capsizing or a breach by a boat on the same team shall be. If there is doubt, it shall be presumed that the crew are not at fault.

D5.2 当船在竞赛区域内遭遇损坏，她可以要求分数更改，在损坏后的第一合理时机展示一面红旗直至被竞赛委员会或现场裁判看到。如果可能，她须继续*竞赛*。

D5.3 竞赛委员会须根据规则 D5. 4 和 D5. 5 对更改分数的要求做出裁决。它可以按其认为恰当的任意方式取证，并可以口头传达其裁决结果。

D5.4 当竞赛委员会认定该船队的终点名次明显变差，船的损坏不是船员的过失，而且在这种情况下，任何具备合理能力的船员都无法避免这种损坏时，它须做出尽可能公平的裁决。这一裁决可能是*放弃*该轮竞赛并重赛，或当该船的终点名次可以预见时，给予她该名次相对应的分数。当有损坏发生时，任何对该船的名次的质疑须采纳不利于该船的解决方案。

D5.5 由于所提供器材有缺陷，或由于对手违反某条*规则*造成了损坏，通常不得被认为是该船员的过失，但由于粗心操作、倾覆或同队船犯规造成的损坏须被认为是该船员的过失。如果有怀疑，须假定船员没有过失。

APPENDIX E RADIO SAILING RACING RULES

Radio sailing races shall be sailed under The Racing Rules of Sailing *as changed by this appendix.*

Note: A Test Rule for Umpired Radio Sailing is available at the World Sailing website.

E1 CHANGES TO THE DEFINITIONS, TERMINOLOGY AND THE RULES OF PARTS 1, 2 AND 7

E1.1 Definitions

Add to the definition *Conflict of Interest*:

However, an observer does not have a *conflict of interest* solely by being a competitor.

In the definition *Zone* the distance is changed to four hull lengths.

Add new definition:

Disabled A boat is *disabled* while she is unable to continue in the heat.

E1.2 Terminology

The Terminology paragraph of the Introduction is changed so that:

(a) 'Boat' means a sailboat controlled by radio signals and having no crew. However, in the rules of Part 1 and Part 5, rule E6 and the definitions *Party* and *Protest*, 'boat' includes the competitor controlling her.

(b) 'Competitor' means the person designated to control a boat using radio signals.

(c) In the racing rules, but not in its appendices, replace the noun 'race' with 'heat'. In Appendix E a race consists of one or more heats and is completed when the last heat in the race is completed.

附录 E　无线电遥控帆船竞赛规则

无线电遥控帆船竞赛须遵照本附录更改后的《帆船竞赛规则》执行。

注意:现场裁决的无线电遥控帆船竞赛测试版规则可以在世界帆联官方网站上获取。

E1　对定义、术语以及规则第一章、第二章和第七章的更改

E1.1 定义

*利益冲突*的定义后增加:

但是,观察员不会仅因为本身是选手就有了*利益冲突*。

在*标区*的定义中,距离更改为 4 倍船长。

新增定义:

失能　当船只不能继续当前组别的竞赛时称为*失能*。

E1.2 术语

导言中术语段落的内容被更改,因此:

(a)“船”是指无船员驾驶的由无线电信号操控的帆船。但是,在规则第一章、第五章、规则 E6 以及*一方*和*抗议*的定义中,“船”包括操控她的选手。

(b)“选手”是指特定的通过无线电信号操控船的人。

(c)在竞赛规则而非其附录中,将名词“轮次”替换为“组别”。在附录 E 中,一轮竞赛由一个或多个组别构成,并且当轮次中最后一组竞赛完成时该轮竞赛即为完成。

E1.3 Rules of Parts 1, 2 and 7

(a) Rule 1.2 is deleted.

(b) Hails under rules 20.1 and 20.3 shall include the words 'room' and 'tack' and the sail number of the hailing boat, in any order.

(c) Rule 22 is changed to: 'If possible, a boat shall avoid a boat that is *disabled*.'

(d) Rule 90.2(c) is changed to:

Changes to the sailing instructions may be communicated orally to all affected competitors before the warning signal of the relevant race or heat. When appropriate, changes shall be confirmed in writing.

E2 ADDITIONAL RULES WHEN RACING

*Rule E2 applies only while boats are **racing**.*

E2.1 Hailing Requirements

(a) A hail shall be made and repeated as appropriate so that the competitors to whom the hail is directed might reasonably be expected to hear it.

(b) When a *rule* requires a boat to hail or respond, the hail shall be made by the competitor controlling the boat.

(c) The individual digits of a boat's sail number shall be hailed; for example 'one five', not 'fifteen'.

E2.2 Giving Advice

A competitor shall not give tactical or strategic advice to a competitor controlling a boat that is *racing*.

E2.3 Boat Out of Radio Control

A competitor who loses radio control of his boat shall promptly hail '(The boat's sail number) out of control' and the boat shall retire.

E1.3 规则第一章、第二章和第七章

（a）删除规则 1.2。

（b）在规则 20.1 和规则 20.3 中，呼喊须包含词语“空间”和“迎风换舷”以及发出呼喊的船的帆号，任何顺序皆可。

（c）规则 22 更改为：“如果可能的话，一条船须躲避一条*失能*的船。”

（d）规则 90.2（c）更改为：

对航行细则的更改可在相应轮次或组别的预告信号发出之前，通过口头形式传达到所有受其影响的选手。在合适的时候，更改内容须以书面形式进行确认。

E2 竞赛时的附加规则

*规则 E2 仅在船**竞赛**时适用。*

E2.1 呼喊的要求

（a）发出的呼喊须适当重复，以便使被呼喊的选手合理地被认为可以听到。

（b）当*规则*要求一条船呼喊或回应时，这个呼喊须由控制该船的选手发出。

（c）须呼喊船只帆号的每一位数字；如“一五”，而不是“十五”。

E2.2 给予建议

选手不得给另一名正在操控船只*竞赛*的选手提供战术或战略建议。

E2.3 失控船只

失去对船只无线电操控的选手须立即呼喊“（船只帆号）失控”，且该船须退出竞赛。

E2.4 Transmitter Aerials

If a transmitter aerial is longer than 200mm when extended, the extremity shall be adequately protected.

E2.5 Radio Interference

Transmission of radio signals that cause interference with the control of other boats is prohibited. A competitor that has broken this rule shall not race again until permitted to do so by the *race* committee.

E3 CONDUCT OF A RACE

E3.1 Control Area

Unless the sailing instructions specify a control area, it shall be unrestricted. Competitors shall be in this area when controlling boats that are *racing*, except briefly to handle and then release or relaunch the boat.

E3.2 Launching Area

Unless the sailing instructions specify a launching area and its use, it shall be unrestricted.

E3.3 Course Board

When the sailing instructions require a course board to be displayed, it shall be located in or adjacent to the control area.

E3.4 Starting and Finishing

(a) Rule 26 is changed to:

Heats shall be started using warning, preparatory and starting signals at one-minute intervals. During the minute before the starting signal, additional sound or oral signals shall be made at ten-second intervals, and during the final ten seconds at onesecond intervals. Each signal shall be timed from the beginning of its sound.

(b) The starting and finishing lines shall be between the course sides of the starting and finishing *marks*.

E2.4 发射器天线

如果发射器天线展开长度超过 200 毫米，其末端须有妥善的防护物。

E2.5 无线电干扰

严禁通过发射无线电信号干扰其他船的操控。违反此条规则的选手在得到竞赛委员会许可前不得再次*竞赛*。

E3 竞赛组织

E3.1 操控区

除非航行细则指定操控区，否则不得加以限制。当操控船只*竞赛*时，选手须在此区域中，短暂地拿取然后放开或者让船只重新下水不受此限制。

E3.2 下水区

除非航行细则指定下水区及其用途，否则不得加以限制。

E3.3 航线公告板

当航行细则要求展示航线公告板时，该公告板须位于操控区内或其临近位置。

E3.4 起航和终点

(a) 规则 26 更改为：

组别起航须以 1 分钟作为时间间隔，发出预告、准备以及起航信号。在起航信号发出之前的 1 分钟内，每 10 秒须附加音响或口头信号，在最后 10 秒内，每 1 秒须附加音响或口头信号。每个信号须在音响开始的时刻计时。

(b) 起航线和终点线须位于起航*标志*及终点*标志*航线一侧的两点之间。

E3.5 Individual Recall

Rule 29.1 is changed to:

When at a boat's starting signal any part of her hull is on the course side of the starting line or when she must comply with rule 30.1, the race committee shall promptly hail 'Recall (sail numbers)'. If rule 30.3 or 30.4 applies this rule does not.

E3.6 General Recall

Rule 29.2 is changed to:

When at the starting signal the race committee is unable to identify boats that are on the course side of the starting line or to which rule 30 applies, or there has been an error in the starting procedure, the race committee may hail 'General recall' and make two loud sounds. The warning signal for a new start will normally be made shortly thereafter.

E3.7 U Flag and Black Flag Rules

When the race committee informs a boat that she has broken rule 30.3 or 30.4, the boat shall immediately leave the course area.

E3.8 Other Changes to the Rules of Part 3

(a) Rules 30.2 and 33 are deleted.

(b) All race committee signals shall be made orally or by other sounds. No visual signals are required unless specified in the sailing instructions.

(c) Courses shall not be shortened.

(d) Rule 32.1(a) is changed to: 'because of foul weather or thunderstorms,'.

E3.9 Disabled Competitors

The race committee may make or permit reasonable arrangements to assist disabled competitors to compete on as equal terms as possible. A boat or the competitor controlling her that receives any such assistance, including help from a *support person*, does not break rule 41.

E3.5 个别召回

规则 29. 1 更改为：

一条船的船体的任何部分在起航信号发出时位于起航线的航线一侧，或者当她必须遵守规则30. 1时，竞赛委员会须迅即呼喊“（帆号）召回”。当规则30. 3或30. 4适用时，本条规则不适用。

E3.6 全部召回

规则 29. 2 更改为：

当起航信号发出时，竞赛委员会不能识别位于起航线的航线一侧的船或者规则 30 适用的船时，或者起航过程出现错误时，竞赛委员会可呼喊“全部召回”并发出两声响亮的音响。通常在稍后发出新的起航预告信号。

E3.7 U 旗和黑旗规则

当竞赛委员会通知一条船已经违反了规则 30. 3 或 30. 4 时，这条船须立刻离开航线区域。

E3.8 其他有关规则第三章的更改

(a) 删除规则 30. 2 和 33。

(b) 所有竞赛委员会的信号须口头或者由其他声响发出。除航行细则的规定外，无需视觉信号。

(c) 不得缩短航线。

(d) 规则 32. 1(a)更改为：“由于恶劣天气或雷暴，”。

E3.9 残障选手

为了协助残障选手在尽可能同等的条件下完成竞赛，竞赛委员会可以做出或允许合理的安排。接受以上协助的船或操控她的选手，包含*后援人员*提供的帮助，不违反规则 41。

E4 RULES OF PART 4

E4.1 Deleted Rules in Part 4

Rules 40, 44.3, 45, 48, 49, 50, 52, 54, 55 and 56 are deleted.

E4.2 Outside Help

Rule 41 is changed to:

A boat or the competitor controlling her shall not receive help from any outside source, except

(a) help needed as a direct result of a competitor becoming ill, injured or in danger;

(b) when the boat is entangled with another boat, help from the other competitor;

(c) when the boat is *disabled* or in danger, help from the race committee;

(d) help in the form of information freely available to all competitors;

(e) unsolicited information from a disinterested source. A competitor is not a disinterested source unless acting as an observer.

E4.3 Taking a Penalty

Rule 44.1 is changed to:

A boat may take a One-Turn Penalty when she may have broken one or more rules of Part 2, or rule 31, in an incident while *racing*. However,

(a) when she may have broken a rule of Part 2 and rule 31 in the same incident she need not take the penalty for breaking rule 31;

(b) if the boat gained an advantage in the heat or race by her breach despite taking a penalty, her penalty shall be additional One- Turn Penalties until her advantage is lost;

E4 规则第四章

E4.1 第四章中删除的规则

删除规则40、44.3、45、48、49、50、52、54、55和56。

E4.2 外部援助

规则41更改为：

船或者操控船的选手不得接收任何来自外部资源的帮助，下列情形除外：

（a）选手由于生病、受伤或者处于危险情形而导致直接的必要帮助；

（b）当一条船与另一条船缠绕时，来自另一名选手的帮助；

（c）当船*失能*或身处危险时，来自竞赛委员会的帮助；

（d）所有选手都可随意获取的信息形式的帮助；

（e）非利益方主动提供的信息。选手不是非利益方，除非他是观察员。

E4.3 解脱

规则44.1更改为：

当一条船在*竞赛*的事件中可能已经违反了一条或多条第二章规则，或规则31时，可转一圈进行解脱。但是

（a）当她在同一个事件中违反了第二章的某一条规则以及规则31时，无需再因违反规则31做解脱；

（b）尽管该船已解脱，若仍因违反规则在其组别或轮次中获得优势，她须做追加一圈解脱的惩罚，直到失去优势；

(c) if the boat caused serious damage, or as a result of breaking a rule of Part 2 she caused another boat to become *disabled* and retire, her penalty shall be to retire.

E4.4 Person in Charge

Rule 46 is changed to: 'The member or organization that entered the boat shall designate the competitor. See rule 75.'

E5 RACING WITH OBSERVERS AND UMPIRES

E5.1 Observers

(a) The race committee may appoint observers, who may be competitors.

(b) Observers shall hail the sail numbers of boats that *make contact* with a *mark* or another boat.

(c) At the end of a heat, observers shall report to the race committee all unresolved incidents, and any failure to *sail the course*.

E5.2 Rules for Observers and Umpires

Observers and umpires shall be located in the control area. They shall not use any aid or device that gives them a visual advantage over competitors.

E6 PROTESTS AND REQUESTS FOR REDRESS

E6.1 Right to Protest

Rule 60.1 is changed to:

A boat may

(a) protest another boat, but not for an alleged breach of a rule of Part 2, 3 or 4 unless she was scheduled to sail in that heat; or

(b) request redress.

However, a boat or competitor may not protest for an alleged breach of rules E2 or E3.7.

(c) 若该船导致严重损坏，或因违反规则第二章导致另一条船*失能*并退赛，对她的判罚须为退出竞赛。

E4.4 负责人

规则 46 更改为："为船只报名的成员或组织须指定选手。见规则 75。"

E5　有观察员和现场裁判的竞赛

E5.1 观察员

(a) 竞赛委员会可委派观察员，观察员可以是选手。

(b) 当有船与*标志*或另一条船发生接触时，观察员须呼喊该船的帆号。

(c) 在组别竞赛结束时，观察员须向竞赛委员会报告所有未解决的事件，以及任何未能*行驶航线*的情况。

E5.2 观察员和现场裁判的规则

观察员和现场裁判须位于操控区内。他们不得使用任何辅助工具或设备来获得优于选手的视觉优势。

E6　抗议和要求补偿

E6.1 抗议的权利

规则 60.1 更改为：

一条船可以

(a) 抗议另一条船，但只有她被排定在那一组别时才可提出涉嫌违反规则第二章、第三章或第四章的抗议；或者

(b) 要求补偿。

但是，一条船或选手不可提出涉嫌违反规则 E2 或 E3.7 的抗议。

E6.2 Protest for a Rule Broken by a Competitor

When a race committee, protest committee or technical committee learns that a competitor may have broken a *rule*, it may protest the boat controlled by that competitor.

E6.3 Informing the Protestee

Rule 61.1(a) is changed to:

The protesting boat shall inform the other boat at the first reasonable opportunity. When her *protest* concerns an incident in the racing area, she shall hail '(Her own sail number) protest (the sail number of the other boat)'.

E6.4 Informing the Race Committee

The boat protesting or requesting redress about an incident while *racing* shall inform the race committee as soon as reasonably possible after *finishing* or retiring.

E6.5 Time Limits

A *protest*, request for redress or request for reopening shall be delivered to the race committee no later than ten minutes after the last boat in the heat *finishes* or after the relevant incident, whichever is later.

E6.6 Redress

Add to rule 62.1:

(e) external radio interference acknowledged by the race committee, or

(f) becoming *disabled* because of the action of a boat that was breaking a rule of Part 2 or of a vessel not *racing* that was required to keep clear.

E6.7 Right to Be Present

In rule 63.3(a) 'the representatives of boats shall have been on board' is changed to 'the representative of each boat shall be the competitor designated to control her'.

E6.2 抗议选手违反某条规则

当竞赛委员会、抗议委员会或技术委员会得知有选手可能已经违反了某条*规则*时，它可以抗议该选手操控的船。

E6.3 通知被抗议人

规则 61. 1 (a)更改为：

提出抗议的船须在第一合理时机通知另一条船。当她的*抗议*有关于竞赛区域发生的一个事件时，她须呼喊“（她自己的帆号）抗议（另一条船的帆号）”。

E6.4 通知竞赛委员会

对*竞赛*时发生的事件提出抗议或请求补偿的船须在*到达终点*或退出竞赛后尽可能快地通知竞赛委员会。

E6.5 时限

抗议、补偿请求或重审请求须在同组别最后一条船*到达终点*或者相关事件发生后 10 分钟内提交给竞赛委员会，以较迟的那个时间为准。

E6.6 补偿

规则 62. 1 后增加：

(e) 竞赛委员会认可的外部无线电干扰，或者

(f) 由于一条违反规则第二章的船或者一条不参加*竞赛*而需要避让的船的行为而导致*失能*。

E6.7 出席的权利

规则 63. 3 (a)中“船的代表须在事件发生时在船上”更改为“每一条船的代表须是被指定操控她的选手”。

E6.8 Taking Evidence and Finding Facts

Add new rule 63.6(e):

(e) When the *protest* concerns an alleged breach of a rule of Part 2, 3 or 4, any witness shall have been in the control area at the time of the incident. If the witness is a competitor who was not acting as an observer, he shall also have been scheduled to race in the relevant heat.

E6.9 Decisions on Redress

Add to rule 64.3:

If a boat is given redress because she was damaged, her redress shall include reasonable time, but not more than 30 minutes, to make repairs before her next heat.

E7 PENALTIES

When a protest committee decides that a boat that is a *party* to a protest hearing has broken a *rule* other than a rule of Part 2, 3 or 4, it shall either

(a) disqualify her or add any number of points (including zero and fractions of points) to her score. The penalty shall be applied, if possible, to the heat or race in which the *rule* was broken; otherwise it shall be applied to the next heat or race for that boat. When points are added, the scores of other boats shall not be changed; or

(b) require her to take one or more One-Turn Penalties that shall be taken as soon as possible after the starting signal of her next heat that is started and not subsequently recalled or *abandoned*.

However, if the boat has broken a rule in Appendix G or rule E8, the protest committee shall act in accordance with rule G4.

E6.8 取证和认定事实

增加新的规则 63. 6（e）：

（e）当*抗议*与涉嫌违反规则第二章、第三章或第四章有关时，任何目击者须在事件发生时位于操控区内。如果目击者是一名不担任观察员的选手，他也须被排入相关组别参加过竞赛。

E6.9 补偿的决定

规则 64. 3 后增加：

如果一条船因为受损获得补偿，其补偿须包括一段合理的时间来进行参加下一组别前的修理工作，但时间不得超过 30 分钟。

E7 惩罚

当抗议委员会认定某条船作为抗议审理的一方违反了除规则第二章、第三章或第四章之外的某条*规则*时，抗议委员会须在以下选项中二选一：

（a）取消其资格或者在其成绩上增加任何数量的分值（包括零和小数分值）。如果可能的话，惩罚须适用于违反*规则*的组别或轮次；否则惩罚须适用于该船的下一个组别或轮次。当增加分值时，其他船的分数不得被更改；或者

（b）要求她在下一组别未发生召回或*放弃*时，须在起航信号发出之后尽快做一个或多个一圈的解脱。

但是，如果该船已经违反了附录 G 的某条规则或者规则 E8，抗议委员会须按照规则 G4 采取措施。

E8 CHANGES TO APPENDIX G, IDENTIFICATION ON SAILS

Rule G1, except the table of National Sail Letters, is changed to:

G1 WORLD SAILING AND IRSA CLASS BOATS

This rule applies to every boat of a class administered or recognised by World Sailing or by the International Radio Sailing Association (IRSA).

G1.1 Identification

(a) A boat of a World Sailing or IRSA Class shall display her class insignia, national letters and sail number as specified in rule G1, unless her class rules state otherwise.

(b) At world and continental championships, sails shall comply with these rules. At other events they shall comply with these rules or the rules applicable at the time of their initial certification.

G1.2 National Letters

At all international events, a boat shall display national letters in accordance with the table of National Sail Letters denoting:

(a) when entered under rule 75(a), the national authority of the nationality, place of residence, or affiliation of the owner or the member.

(b) when entered under rule 75(b), the national authority of the organisation which entered her.

For the purposes of this rule, international events are world and continental championships and events described as international events in their notices of race and sailing instructions.

E8　附录 G 的更改，帆上标识

规则 G1，除国家和地区帆号代码表之外，更改为：

G1　世界帆联和 IRSA 级别的船只

本规则适用于世界帆联或者国际无线电帆船运动协会（IRSA）管理或认证级别的每一条船。

G1.1 识别标志

（a）世界帆联或 IRSA 级别的船只须按照规则 G1 的规定展示其级别标识、国家和地区代码以及帆号，除非其级别规则另有规定。

（b）在世界及洲际锦标赛中，船帆须符合这些规则。在其他赛事中，船帆须符合这些规则或者船只初始认证时适用的规则。

G1.2 国家和地区代码

在所有国际赛事中，一条船须展示与国家和地区帆号代码表相一致的国家和地区代码，用以表明：

（a）当按照规则 75（a）报名时，所属的国家和地区管理机构、居住地，或者船东或成员的隶属关系。

（b）当按照规则 75（b）报名时，给其报名的组织所属的国家和地区管理机构。

本规则所说的国际赛事是指世界和洲际锦标赛，以及在竞赛通知和航行细则中被描述为国际赛事的赛事。

Note: An up-to-date version of the National Sail Letters table is available on the World Sailing website.

G1.3 Sail numbers

(a) The sail number shall be the last two digits of the boat's registration number or the competitor's or owner's personal number, allotted by the relevant issuing authority.

(b) When there is conflict between sail numbers, or when a sail number may be misread, the race committee shall require that the sail numbers of one or more boats be changed to numeric alternatives.

G1.4 Specifications

(a) National letters and sail numbers shall be in capital letters and Arabic numerals, clearly legible and of the same colour. Commercially available typefaces giving the same or better legibility than Helvetica are acceptable.

(b) The height and spacing of letters and numbers shall be as follows:

Dimension	*Minimum*	*Maximum*
Height of sail numbers	100 mm	110 mm
Spacing of adjacent sail numbers	20 mm	30 mm
Height of national letters	60 mm	70 mm
Spacing of adjacent national letters	13 mm	23 mm

G1.5 Positioning

(a) Class insignia, sail numbers and national letters shall be positioned

(1) on both sides of the sail;

注：在世界帆联网站上可获取国家和地区帆号代码表的实时更新版本。

G1.3 帆号

（a）帆号须为船的注册编码或选手或船东的个人编码的最后两位，由相应的管理机构分配。

（b）当帆号间出现冲突，或者帆号可能会被错误识别时，竞赛委员会须要求一条或多条船替换其帆号中的数字。

G1.4 规格

（a）国家和地区代码和帆号须是大写字母和阿拉伯数字，清晰可辨而且颜色相同。可以接受商业上可用的与“Helvetica”字体有同样或更好的清晰度的字体。

（b）字母和数字的高度和间距须如下表所示：

尺寸	*最小*	*最大*
帆号高度	100mm	110mm
帆号数字间距	20mm	30mm
国家和地区代码高度	60mm	70mm
国家和地区代码字母间距	13mm	23mm

G1.5 位置

（a）级别标识、帆号以及国家和地区代码的位置须

（1）在帆的两面；

(2) with those on the starboard side uppermost;

(3) approximately horizontally;

(4) with no less than 40 mm vertical spacing between numbers and letters on opposite sides of the sail;

(5) with no less than 20 mm vertical spacing between class insignia on opposite sides of the sail.

However, symmetrical or reversed class insignia may be positioned back to back.

(b) On a mainsail, sail numbers shall be positioned

(1) below class insignia;

(2) above the line perpendicular to the luff through the quarter leech point;

(3) above national letters;

(4) with sufficient space in front of the sail number for a prefix '1'.

G1.6 Exceptions

(a) Where the size of the sail prevents compliance with rule G1.2, National Letters, then exceptions to rules G1.2, G1.4, and G1.5 shall be made in the following order of precedence. National letters shall

(1) be spaced vertically below sail numbers by less than 30 mm, but no less than 20 mm;

(2) be spaced on opposite sides of the sail by less than 30 mm, but no less than 20 mm;

(3) be reduced in height to less than 45 mm, but no less than 40 mm;

(4) be omitted.

（2）在右舷一侧的位置更高；

（3）近似水平；

（4）与帆上另一面的数字和字母的竖直间距不小于 40 毫米；

（5）与帆上另一面的级别标识的竖直间距不小于 20 毫米。

但是，可对称或反转的级别标识在位置上可以背靠背。

（b）主帆上帆号的位置须

（1）低于级别标识；

（2）高于通过帆后缘 1/4 处且与帆前缘垂直的线；

（3）高于国家和地区代码；

（4）在帆号前为前置字母“1”留有足够的空间。

G1.6 例外

（a）当帆的尺寸无法遵守规则 G1.2，国家和地区代码的要求时，那么规则 G1.2、G1.4 和 G1.5 的例外情形须按下列优先级顺序执行。国家和地区代码须

（1）竖直放置于帆号下方，间距小于 30 毫米，但不小于 20 毫米；

（2）放置于帆的另一侧，间距小于 30 毫米，但不小于 20 毫米；

（3）缩减高度到小于 45 毫米，但不小于 40 毫米；

（4）被省略。

(b) Where the size of the sail prevents compliance with rule G1.3, Sail Numbers, then exceptions to rules G1.4 and G1.5 shall be made in the following order of precedence. Sail numbers shall

(1) extend below the specified line;

(2) be spaced on opposite sides of the sail by less than 30 mm, but no less than 20 mm apart;

(3) be reduced in height to less than 90 mm, but no less than 80 mm;

(4) be omitted on all except the largest sail;

(5) be reduced in height until they do fit on the largest sail.

（b）当帆的尺寸无法遵守规则 G1.3，帆号时，那么规则 G1.4 和 G1.5 的例外情形须按下列优先级顺序执行。帆号须

（1）延伸到指定参考线下方；

（2）放置于帆的另一侧，间距小于 30 毫米，但不小于 20 毫米；

（3）缩减高度到小于 90 毫米，但不小于 80 毫米；

（4）除最大的帆之外，被省略；

（5）缩减高度直到它确实与最大的帆相称。

APPENDIX F KITEBOARDING RACING RULES

Kiteboarding course races shall be sailed under The Racing Rules of Sailing as changed by this appendix. The term 'boat' elsewhere in the racing rules means 'kiteboard' or 'boat' as appropriate.

Note: Rules for other kiteboarding racing formats (such as Short Track, Kitecross, Slalom, Boarder X) or other kiteboarding competitions (such as Freestyle, Wave, Big Air, Speed) are not included in this appendix. Links to current versions of these rules can be found on the World Sailing website.

CHANGES TO THE DEFINITIONS

The definitions Clear *Astern* and *Clear Ahead; Overlap, Finish, Keep Clear, Leeward* and *Windward, Mark-Room, Obstruction, Start, Tack, Starboard* or *Port* and *Zone* are changed to:

Clear Astern and Clear Ahead; Overlap One kiteboard is *clear astern* of another when her hull is behind a line abeam from the aftermost point of the other kiteboard's hull. The other kiteboard is *clear ahead*. They *overlap* when neither is *clear astern*. However, they also *overlap* when a kiteboard between them *overlaps* both. If there is reasonable doubt that two kiteboards are *overlapped*, it shall be presumed that they are not. These terms always apply to kiteboards on the same *tack*. They apply to kiteboards on opposite *tacks* only when both kiteboards are sailing more than ninety degrees from the true wind.

Finish A kiteboard *finishes* when, after *starting*, while the competitor is in contact with the hull, any part of her hull, or

附录F　风筝板竞赛规则

风筝板航线赛须按照本附录更改后的《帆船竞赛规则》执行。竞赛规则中的术语“船”依不同语境表示“风筝板”或者“船”。

注：其他的风筝板竞赛模式（如：短航线、Kitecross［译者注：障碍滑的一种］、障碍滑、BoarderX［译者注：BoarderX是第三届青奥会采用过的一种竞赛模式，航线为带有障碍物的顺风障碍滑］）或其他的风筝板比赛（如：自由式、浪上表演赛、空中特技、竞速）的规则不包含在此附录内。这些规则最新版本的链接可以在世界帆联网站上找到。

定义的更改

*明显在后*和*明显在前*；*相联*、*到达终点*、*避让*、*下风*和*上风*、*绕标空间*、*障碍物*、*起航*、*舷风*、*右舷*或*左舷*、*标区*的定义更改为：

明显在后和明显在前；相联　当一条风筝板的板体处于另一条风筝板板体的最后一点的正横线之后，则该风筝板为*明显在后*，另一条风筝板为*明显在前*。当没有任何一条板为*明显在后*时即为*相联*。但是，当她们中间有一条风筝板与两者均*相联*时，她们仍为*相联*。如果对两条风筝板是否*相联*存在合理质疑，则须假设她们没有*相联*。这些术语总是适用于相同*舷风*的风筝板。除非两条板同真风风向的角度均大于90°，否则这些术语不适用于处于相对*舷风*的风筝板。

到达终点　*起航*后，当选手与板体在接触中，板体或选手的任何部分从航线一侧越过终点线即为*到达终点*。但是，如果

the competitor, crosses the finishing line from the course side. However, she has not *finished* if after crossing the finishing line she

(a) takes a penalty under rule 44.2,

(b) corrects an error in *sailing the course* made at the line, or

(c) continues to *sail the course*.

Keep Clear A kiteboard *keeps clear* of a right-of-way kiteboard

(a) if the right-of-way kiteboard can sail her course with no need to take avoiding action and,

(b) when the kiteboards are *overlapped*, if the right-of-way kiteboard can also change course in both directions or move her kite in any direction without immediately making contact.

Leeward and Windward A kiteboard's *leeward* side is the side that is or, when she is head to wind, was away from the wind. However, when sailing by the lee or directly downwind, her *leeward* side is the side on which her kite lies. The other side is her *windward* side. When two kiteboards on the same *tack overlap*, the one whose hull is on the *leeward* side of the other's hull is the *leeward* kiteboard. The other is the *windward* kiteboard.

Mark-Room *Room* for a kiteboard to sail her *proper course* to round or pass the *mark* on the required side.

Obstruction An object that a kiteboard could not pass without substantially changing her course or the position of her kite, if she were sailing directly towards it and 10 metres from it. An object that can be safely passed on only one side and an object, area or line so designated by the sailing instructions are also *obstructions*. However, a kiteboard *racing* is not an *obstruction* to other kiteboards unless they are required to *keep clear* of her or, if rule 22 applies, avoid her. A vessel under way, including a kiteboard *racing*, is never a continuing *obstruction*.

在越过终点线后她有如下情况，则为没有*到达终点*

(a) 根据规则 44.2 做解脱，

(b) 改正在终点线上犯的*行驶航线*的错误，或者

(c) 继续*行驶航线*。

避让 如果符合下面条件，一条风筝板就*避让*了一条航行权风筝板

(a) 航行权风筝板不需要做出躲避动作就可以行驶在其航线上，同时

(b) 当风筝板*相联*时，航行权风筝板在两个方向上都能改变航线或者可以向任意方向移动她的风筝而不会立即造成接触。

下风和上风 风筝板的*下风*边是离开风的那一边，或当其正顶风行驶时刚刚离开风的那一边。但当背风航行或正顺风航行时，她的*下风*边就是其风筝所在的一边。另外一边为其*上风*边。当两条风筝板同*舷风相联*时，处在一条风筝板板体的*下风*边的是*下风*风筝板，另一条板是*上风*风筝板。

绕标空间 风筝板行驶其*正当航线*从所要求的一侧绕过或通过*标志*的*空间*。

障碍物 当风筝板正直接驶向一个物体并距离其 10 米时，若她不明显改变航线或其风筝的位置就不能通过的物体。只能从一侧安全通过的物体和航行细则中特指的物体、区域或线也可作为*障碍物*。但是，正在*竞赛*的风筝板对其他风筝板不构成*障碍物*，除非她们需要*避让*她或规则 22 适用时，躲避她。正在行驶的船舶，包括正在*竞赛*的风筝板，永远不是连续*障碍物*。

Start A kiteboard *starts* when, her hull and the competitor having been entirely on the pre-start side of the starting line at or after her starting signal, any part of her hull or the competitor crosses the starting line from the prestart side to the course side.

Tack, Starboard or Port A kiteboard is on the *tack, starboard* or *port*, corresponding to the competitor's hand that would be forward if the competitor were in normal riding position (riding heel side with both hands on the control bar and arms not crossed). A kiteboard is on *starboard tack* when the competitor's right hand would be forward and is on the *port tack* when the competitor's left hand would be forward.

Zone The area around a *mark* within a distance of 30 metres. A kiteboard is in the *zone* when any part of her hull is in the *zone*.

Add the following definitions:

Capsized A kiteboard is *capsized* if

(a) her kite is in the water, or

(b) her lines are tangled with another kiteboard's lines.

Jumping A kiteboard is *jumping* when her hull, its appendages and the competitor are clear of the water.

Recovering A kiteboard is *recovering* from the time she loses steerage way until she regains it, unless she is *capsized*.

F1 CHANGES TO THE RULES OF PART 1

[No changes.]

F2 CHANGES TO THE RULES OF PART 2

PART 2 — PREAMBLE

In the second sentence of the preamble, 'injury or serious damage' is changed to 'injury, serious damage or a tangle'.

13 WHILE TACKING

Rule 13 is deleted.

起航　在起航信号发出时或发出后，风筝板的板体和选手已完全位于起航线准备区一侧，板体或选手的任何部分从起航准备区一侧向航线一侧越过起航线即为*起航*。

舷风、右舷或左舷　风筝板的*舷风*边、*右舷*或*左舷*是与选手处于正常操板位置（脚站在切水的一侧，双手都放在控制杆上且手臂没有交叉）时在前的那只手一致的。选手的右手在前，则风筝板为*右舷风*，选手的左手在前，则风筝板为*左舷风*。

标区　距离*标志* 30 米的区域。当板体的任何部分在此*标区*内即为该风筝板在此*标区*内。

增加以下定义：

倾覆　若出现下列情况，则风筝板为*倾覆*

(a) 其风筝处于水中，或者

(b) 其操控绳和其他风筝板的操控绳缠绕在一起。

跳跃　当风筝板的板体、附属物及选手脱离水面即为*跳跃*。

复位　除非风筝板*倾覆*，否则风筝板从失去转向能力那一刻到再次获得转向能力称为*复位*。

F1　对规则第一章的更改

[没有更改。]

F2　对规则第二章的更改

第二章—前言

前言中的第二句，“受伤或严重损坏”更改为“受伤、严重损坏或缠绕”。

13　迎风换舷时

删除规则 13。

16 CHANGING COURSE OR KITE POSITION

Rule 16 is changed to:

16.1 When a right-of-way kiteboard changes course or the position of her kite, she shall give the other kiteboard *room* to continue *keeping clear*.

16.2 In addition, on a beat to windward when a *port-tack* kiteboard is *keeping clear* by sailing to pass to leeward of a *starboard-tack* kiteboard, the *starboard-tack* kiteboard shall not bear away or change the position of her kite if as a result the *port-tack* kiteboard must change course or the position of her kite immediately to continue *keeping clear*.

17 ON THE SAME TACK; PROPER COURSE

Rule 17 is deleted.

18 MARK-ROOM

Rule 18 is changed to:

18.1 When Rule 18 Applies

Rule 18 applies between kiteboards when they are required to leave a *mark* on the same side and at least one of them is in the *zone*. However, it does not apply

(a) between a kiteboard approaching a *mark* and one leaving it, or

(b) between kiteboards on opposite *tacks*.

Rule 18 no longer applies between kiteboards when *mark-room* has been given.

18.2 Giving Mark-Room

(a) When the first kiteboard reaches the *zone*,

(1) if kiteboards are *overlapped*, the outside kiteboard at that moment shall thereafter give the inside kiteboard *mark-room*.

16　改变航线或风筝位置

规则 16 更改为：

16.1 当航行权风筝板改变航线或其风筝的位置时，她须给予另外一条风筝板*空间*去继续*避让*。

16.2 另外，在驶向上风的迎风航段上，一条*左舷*风筝板以从*右舷*风筝板下风通过的方式*避让*时，如果*右舷*风筝板顺风偏转或改变其风筝的位置会造成*左舷*风筝板必须立即改变航线或其风筝的位置继续*避让*，*右舷*风筝板就不得顺风偏转或改变其风筝的位置。

17　同舷风；正当航线

删除规则 17。

18　绕标空间

规则 18 更改为：

18.1 规则 18 适用时

当风筝板被要求以同侧离开*标志*，并且至少其中一条风筝板在*标区*内时，规则 18 在她们之间适用。然而，规则 18 不适用于

(a) 在一条正接近*标志*的风筝板和一条正离开*标志*的风筝板之间，或者

(b) 以相对*舷风*行驶的风筝板之间。

当*绕标空间*已经被给予了，规则 18 不再适用于两条风筝板之间。

18.2 给予绕标空间

(a) 当第一条风筝板到达*标区*时，

(1) 如果风筝板*相联*，此时的外侧风筝板须于此后给予内侧风筝板*绕标空间*。

(2) if kiteboards are not *overlapped*, the kiteboard that has not reached the *zone* shall thereafter give *mark-room*.

(b) If the kiteboard entitled to *mark-room* leaves the *zone*, the entitlement to *mark-room* ceases and rule 18.2(a) is applied again if required based on the relationship of the kiteboards at the time rule 18.2(a) is re-applied.

(c) If a kiteboard obtained an inside *overlap* and, from the time the *overlap* began, the outside kiteboard is unable to give *mark-room*, she is not required to give it.

18.3 Tacking and Gybing

When an inside *overlapped* right-of-way kiteboard must change *tack* at a *mark* to sail her *proper course*, until she changes *tack* she shall sail no farther from the *mark* than needed to sail that course. Rule 18.3 does not apply at a gate *mark* or a finishing *mark* and a kiteboard shall not be penalized for breaking this rule unless the course of another kiteboard was affected by the breach of this rule.

20 ROOM TO TACK AT AN OBSTRUCTION

Rule 20.1(a) is changed to:

(a) she is approaching an *obstruction*, and, to avoid it safely, will soon need to make a substantial change of her course or the position of her kite, and

Add new rule 20.5:

20.5 Arm Signals

The following arm signals are required in addition to the hails

(a) for *room* to tack, repeatedly and clearly circling one hand over the head; and

（2）如果风筝板不*相联*，没有到达*标区*的风筝板须于此后给予*绕标空间*。

（b）如果享有*绕标空间*的风筝板离开了*标区*，则享有的*绕标空间*权终止，并且在规则 18. 2(a)再次适用时，基于风筝板之间的关系，需要的话，规则 18. 2（a）再次适用。

（c）如果一条风筝板获取了内侧*相联*，自*相联*开始的那一刻起，外侧风筝板已经无法给予*绕标空间*，她就无需给予。

18.3 迎风换舷或顺风换舷

当一条内侧*相联*的航行权风筝板必须在*标志*旁换*舷*以行驶其*正当航线*时，到换*舷*前她离*标志*的距离不得远于行驶那个航线所需要的距离。规则 18. 3 不适用于门*标*或终点*标志*，且违反本条规则的风筝板不得被判罚，除非另一条风筝板因其违反规则而受到了影响。

20　障碍物旁迎风换舷的空间

规则 20. 1（a)更改为：

（a）她正接近一个*障碍物*而且很快需要明显改变航线或其风筝的位置来安全地躲避它，和

增加新规则 20. 5：

20.5 手臂信号

呼喊时要求配有如下手臂信号：

（a）呼喊迎风换舷的*空间*时，清楚地重复用一只手在头顶画圈；和

(b) for 'You tack', repeatedly and clearly pointing at the other kiteboard and waving the arm to windward.

SECTION D — PREAMBLE

The preamble to Section D is changed to:

When rule 21 or 22 applies between two kiteboards, Section A and C rules do not.

21 STARTING ERRORS; TAKING PENALTIES; JUMPING

Rule 21.3 is changed and new rule 21.4 is added:

21.3 During the last minute before her starting signal, a kiteboard that stops, slows down significantly, or one that is not making significant forward progress shall *keep clear* of all others unless she is accidentally *capsized*.

21.4 A kiteboard that is *jumping* shall *keep clear* of one that is not.

22 CAPSIZED; RECOVERING; AGROUND; RESCUING

Rule 22 is changed to:

22.1 If possible, a kiteboard shall avoid a kiteboard that is *capsized*, is aground, or is trying to help a person or vessel in danger.

22.2 A kiteboard that is *recovering* shall *keep clear* of a kiteboard that is not.

F3 CHANGES TO THE RULES OF PART 3

26 STARTING RACES

Rule 26 is changed to:

Races shall be started by using the following signals. Times shall be taken from the visual signals; the absence of a sound signal shall be disregarded.

（b）回答“你迎风换舷”时，清楚地重复指向另外一条风筝板并向上风挥动手臂。

D 节——前言

D 节的前言更改为：

当规则 21 或 22 在两条风筝板之间适用时，A 节和 C 节规则不适用。

21　起航失误；解脱；跳跃

更改规则 21.3 并增加新规则 21.4：

21.3 在起航信号前的最后 1 分钟，除意外*倾覆*，停下、明显减速或没有明显向前推进的风筝板须*避让*其他所有风筝板。

21.4 *跳跃*的风筝板须*避让*没有在这样做的风筝板。

22　倾覆；复位；搁浅；救援

规则 22 更改为：

22.1 如有可能，一条风筝板须躲避*倾覆*的风筝板，搁浅的风筝板，或正在帮助处于危险中的人或船舶的风筝板。

22.2 正在*复位*的风筝板须*避让*没有在这样做的风筝板。

F3　对规则第三章的更改

26　竞赛起航

规则 26 更改为：

竞赛起航须使用下列信号。计时须以视觉信号为准；音响信号的缺失不必理会。

Minutes before starting signal	*Visual signal*	*Sound signal*	*Means*
3	Class flag	One	Warning signal
2	U or black flag	One	Preparatory signal
1	U or black flag removed	One long	One minute
0	Class flag removed	One	Starting signal

29 RECALLS

Rule 29.1 is deleted.

30 STARTING PENALTIES

Rules 30.1 and 30.2 are deleted.

In rules 30.3 and 30.4, 'hull' is changed to 'hull or competitor'. In rule 30.4, 'sail number' is changed to 'competitor number'.

31 TOUCHING A MARK

Rule 31 is changed to:

While *racing*, a kiteboard shall not touch a windward *mark*.

36 RACES RESTARTED OR RESAILED

Rule 36(b) is changed to:

(b) cause a kiteboard to be penalized except under rule 2, 30.4 or 69 or under rule 14 when she has caused injury, serious damage or a tangle.

F4 CHANGES TO THE RULES OF PART 4

41 OUTSIDE HELP

Add new rules 41(e) and 41(f):

起航信号前的时间	*视觉信号*	*音响信号*	*含义*
3	级别旗	一声	预告信号
2	U 旗或黑旗	一声	准备信号
1	移除 U 旗或黑旗	一长声	1 分钟
0	移除级别旗	一声	起航信号

29　召回

删除规则 29. 1。

30　起航惩罚

删除规则 30. 1 和 30. 2。

规则 30. 3 和 30. 4 中的“船体”更改为“板体或选手”。

规则 30. 4 中的“帆号”更改为“选手号码”。

31　碰标

规则 31 更改为：

*竞赛*时，风筝板不得触碰上风标。

36　重新起航或重新竞赛

规则 36（b）更改为：

（b）导致一条风筝板被判罚，除非是根据规则 2、30. 4 或 69，或是违反了规则 14 并造成了受伤、严重损坏或缠绕时。

F4　对规则第四章的更改

41　外部援助

增加新规则 41（e）和 41（f）：

(e) help from another competitor in the same race to assist a relaunch;

(f) help to change equipment, but only in the launching area.

42 PROPULSION

Rule 42 is changed to:

42.1 Basic Rule

Except when permitted in rule 42.2, a kiteboard shall compete by using only the wind and water to increase, maintain or decrease her speed.

42.2 Exceptions

(a) A kiteboard may be propelled by unassisted actions of the competitor on the kiteboard.

(b) A competitor may swim, walk or paddle while *capsized* or *recovering*, provided that the kiteboard does not gain a significant advantage in the race.

(c) Any means of propulsion may be used to help a person or another vessel in danger.

43 EXONERATION

Rule 43.1(c) is changed to:

(c) A right-of-way kiteboard, or one sailing within the *room* or *mark-room* to which she is entitled, is exonerated for breaking rule 14 if the contact does not cause damage, injury or a tangle.

Add new rule 43.1(d):

(d) When a kiteboard breaks rule 15 and there is no contact, she is exonerated for her breach.

44 PENALTIES AT THE TIME OF AN INCIDENT

Rules 44.1 and 44.2 are changed to:

（e）来自于参加同一轮竞赛的其他选手的重新水起的帮助；

（f）帮助更换器材，但仅限于在水起的区域。

42 推进

规则 42 更改为：

42.1 基本规则

除规则 42.2 允许的情况外，一条风筝板在竞赛中须仅利用风和水来增加、保持或降低风筝板的速度。

42.2 例外

（a）可以通过板上选手的独立动作来推进风筝板。

（b）*倾覆*或*复位*时，选手可以游泳、行走或划桨，前提是该板在本轮竞赛中没有明显获益。

（c）为帮助处于危险中的人或船舶，可以使用任何形式的推进手段。

43 免责

规则 43.1（c）更改为：

（c）一条航行权风筝板或航行在所享有的*空间*或*绕标空间*内的风筝板违反了规则 14，若接触没有造成损坏、受伤或缠绕，则该违规被免责。

增加新规则 43.1（d）：

（d）当一条风筝板违反了规则 15 且没有发生接触时，该违规被免责。

44 事件发生时的惩罚

规则 44.1 和 44.2 更改为：

44.1 Taking a Penalty

A kiteboard may take a One-Turn Penalty when she may have broken one or more rules of Part 2 or rule 31 in an incident while *racing*. Alternatively, the notice of race or sailing instructions may specify the use of the Scoring Penalty or some other penalty, in which case the specified penalty shall replace the One-Turn Penalty. However,

(a) when a kiteboard may have broken a rule of Part 2 and rule 31 in the same incident she need not take the penalty for breaking rule 31; and

(b) if the kiteboard caused injury, serious damage or a tangle or, despite taking a penalty, gained a significant advantage or caused significant disadvantage to the other kiteboard in the race or series by her breach, her penalty shall be to retire.

44.2 One-Turn Penalty

After getting well clear of other kiteboards as soon after the incident as possible, a kiteboard takes a One-Turn Penalty by promptly making one turn with her hull appendage in the water. The turn shall include one completed tack and one completed gybe. When a kiteboard takes the penalty at or near the finishing line, her hull and competitor shall be completely on the course side of the line before she *finishes*.

50 COMPETITOR CLOTHING AND EQUIPMENT

Rule 50.1(a) is changed to:

(a) Competitors shall not wear or carry clothing or equipment for the purpose of increasing their weight. However, a competitor may wear a drinking container that shall have a capacity of at least one litre and weigh no more than 1.5 kilograms when full.

44.1 解脱

在竞赛中，当风筝板在事件中违反了第二章的一条或多条规则或规则 31 时，她可以做一个一圈解脱。或者，竞赛通知或航行细则可规定分数惩罚和其他惩罚的用法，在这种情况下，该特定的惩罚须替换一圈解脱。但是，

（a）当一条风筝板在同一事件中违反了规则第二章和规则 31 时，她无需因违反规则 31 做解脱；同时

（b）如果风筝板造成了受伤、严重损坏或缠绕，或尽管做了解脱，但由于犯规而在该轮竞赛或系列赛中获得了明显优势，或使另一条板处于明显失利，对她的惩罚须是退出竞赛。

44.2 一圈解脱

风筝板在事件发生后尽快完全避让其他风筝板后，保持板体附属物在水中时，迅即转一圈来做一个一圈解脱。这一圈须包括一个完整的迎风换舷和一个完整的顺风换舷。当风筝板在终点线或终点线附近做解脱时，其板体和选手在*到达终点*前须完全位于终点线的航线一侧。

50 选手的服装与器材

规则 50. 1（a）更改为：

（a）选手不得穿着或携带意在增加自己体重的服装或器材。然而，选手可以穿戴容量至少 1 升，装满后重量不超过 1. 5 千克的饮水容器。

PART 4 RULES DELETED

Rules 45, 48, 49, 50.2, 51, 52, 54, 55 and 56.1 are deleted.

F5 CHANGES TO THE RULES OF PART 5

61 PROTEST REQUIREMENTS

Rule 61.1(a) is changed to:

(a) The protesting kiteboard shall inform the other kiteboard at the first reasonable opportunity. When her *protest* will concern an incident in the racing area, she shall hail 'Protest' at the first reasonable opportunity. However,

(1) if the other kiteboard is beyond hailing distance, the protesting kiteboard need not hail but she shall inform the other kiteboard at the first reasonable opportunity;

(2) no red flag need be displayed;

(3) if the incident was an error by the other kiteboard in *sailing* the *course*, she need not hail but she shall inform the other kiteboard before that kiteboard *finishes* or at the first reasonable opportunity after she *finishes*;

(4) if at the time of the incident it is obvious to the protesting kiteboard that either competitor is in danger, or that injury, serious damage or a tangle resulted, the requirements of this rule do not apply to her, but she shall attempt to inform the other boat within the time limit of rule 61.3.

63 HEARINGS

For a race of an elimination series that will qualify a kiteboard to compete in a later stage of an event, rules 61.2 and 65.2 are deleted and rule 63.6 is changed to:

第四章删除的规则

删除规则 45、48、49、50. 2、51、52、54、55 和 56. 1。

F5 对规则第五章的更改

61 对抗议的要求

规则 61. 1 (a)更改为:

(a) 提出抗议的风筝板须在第一合理时机通知另外一条风筝板。当她的*抗议*涉及竞赛区域中的事件时,她须在第一合理时机呼喊"抗议"。但是,

(1) 如果另一条风筝板远于可呼喊距离,抗议的风筝板无需呼喊,但她须在第一合理时机通知这条风筝板;

(2) 无需展示红旗;

(3) 如果该事件是另一条风筝板*行驶航线*的错误,她无需呼喊,但须在*到达终点*前或*到达终点*后的第一合理时机通知这条风筝板;

(4) 如果事件发生时,任一选手明显处于危险中,或提出抗议的风筝板有明显的受伤、严重损坏或缠绕,那么此条规则的要求对她不适用,但是她须尽力在规则 63. 1 规定的时限内通知另外那条风筝板。

63 审理

对于将决出参加下一阶段赛事的风筝板的淘汰系列赛,删除规则 61. 2 和 65. 2,规则 63. 6 更改为:

63.6 *Protests* and requests for redress need not be in writing; they shall be made orally to a member of the protest committee as soon as reasonably possible following the race. The protest committee may take evidence in any way it considers appropriate and may communicate its decision orally.

64 DECISIONS

Add new rule 64.2(c):

(c) if a kiteboard has broken a *rule* and, as a result, caused a tangle for the second or subsequent time during the event, her penalty shall be a disqualification that is not excludable.

Rules 64.4(a) and 64.4(b) are changed to:

(a) When the protest committee finds that deviations in excess of acceptable manufacturing tolerances were caused by damage or normal wear and do not improve the performance of the kiteboard, it shall not penalize her. However, the kiteboard shall not *race* again until the deviations have been corrected, except when the protest committee decides there is or has been no reasonable opportunity to do so.

(b) When the protest committee is in doubt about any matter concerning the measurement of a kiteboard, the interpretation of a class rule, or a matter involving damage to a kiteboard, it shall refer its questions, together with the relevant facts, to an authority responsible for interpreting the rule. In making its decision, the committee shall be bound by the reply of the authority.

70 APPEALS AND REQUESTS TO A NATIONAL AUTHORITY

Add new rule 70.7:

63.6 *抗议*和补偿要求无需以书面形式提交；须在该轮竞赛后尽可能快地口头告知抗议委员会的一名成员。抗议委员会可以按照其认为适当的任何方式取证，并可以口头传达其裁决结果。

64　裁决

增加新规则 64. 2（c）：

（c）当一条风筝板违反了*规则*，并因此导致赛事期间的第二次或后续缠绕，则对她的惩罚须为不能去掉的取消资格。

规则 64. 4（a）和 64. 4（b）更改为：

（a）当抗议委员会发现由于受损或正常磨损而使误差超过可接受的建造公差，但并不会提高该风筝板的性能时，不得对她做出惩罚。但是，该风筝板在修正误差之前不得再参加*竞赛*，除非抗议委员会认为该风筝板没有或已经没有合理的机会进行修正。

（b）当抗议委员会对一条风筝板的丈量相关事项、级别规则的解释或有关风筝板损坏的相关问题存有疑问时，须将问题连同有关事实一起提交给负责解释规则的一个管理机构。抗议委员会须依据管理机构的回复进行裁决。

70　上诉和对国家和地区管理机构的请求

增加新规则 70. 7：

70.7 Appeals are not permitted in disciplines and formats with elimination series.

F6 CHANGES TO THE RULES OF PART 6

[No changes.]

F7 CHANGES TO THE RULES OF PART 7

90 RACE COMMITTEE; SAILING INSTRUCTIONS; SCORING

The last sentence of rule 90.2(c) is changed to: 'Oral instructions may be given only if the procedure is stated in the sailing instructions.'

F8 CHANGES TO APPENDIX A

A1 NUMBER OF RACES; OVERALL SCORES

Rule A1 is changed to:

The number of races scheduled and the number required to be completed to constitute a series shall be stated in the notice of race or sailing instructions. If an event includes more than one discipline or format, the notice of race or sailing instructions shall state how the overall scores are to be calculated.

A5 SCORES DETERMINED BY THE RACE COMMITTEE

Rule A5.2 is changed to:

A5.2 A kiteboard that did not *start*, did not *sail the course*, did not *finish*, retired or was disqualified shall be scored points for the finishing place one more than the number of kiteboards entered in the series or, in a race of an elimination series, the number of kiteboards in that heat.

A10 SCORING ABBREVIATIONS

Add to Rule A10:

DCT Disqualified after causing a tangle in an incident

F9 CHANGES TO APPENDIX G

Appendix G is changed to:

70.7 在竞赛项目与模式中有淘汰赛时，不允许上诉。

F6 对规则第六章的更改

[没有更改。]

F7 对规则第七章的更改

90 竞赛委员会；航行细则；计分

规则 90. 2（c）的最后一句更改为："只有在航行细则中有关于此程序的描述时才可以给予口头通知。"

F8 对附录 A 的更改

A1 竞赛轮次；总分

规则 A1 更改为：

竞赛通知或航行细则中须注明所排定的竞赛轮次及组成完整的系列赛所要求的轮次数目。如果一场赛事包含一种以上的竞赛项目或模式，竞赛通知或航行细则须注明总分的计算方式。

A5 竞赛委员会决定的计分

规则 A5. 2 更改为：

A5.2 一条风筝板没有*起航*、没有*行驶航线*、没有*到达终点*、退出竞赛或被取消资格，其终点名次分数须计为参加该系列赛的风筝板总数加 1 分，或者，在淘汰赛的一轮竞赛中，分数须为那一轮预赛的风筝板总数加 1 分。

A10 计分缩写

规则 A10 后增加：

DCT 因在事件中造成缠绕而被取消资格

F9 对附录 G 的更改

附录 G 更改为：

Appendix G — Identification

G1 Every kiteboard shall be identified as follows:

(a) Each competitor shall be provided with and wear a bib with a personal competition number of no more than three digits. The bib shall be worn as intended with the competition number clearly displayed.

(b) The numbers shall be displayed as high as possible on the front, back and sleeves of the bib. They should be at least 20 cm tall on the back and at least 6 cm tall on the front and the sleeves.

(c) The numbers shall be Arabic numerals, all of the same solid colour, clearly legible and in a commercially available typeface giving the same or better legibility as Helvetica. The colour of the numbers shall contrast with the colour of the bib.

附录 G——标识

G1 每条风筝板都须按照如下要求标识：

（a）每位选手都须被提供并穿着带有不多于三位数的个人比赛号码背心。背心须以清晰展示比赛号码为目的进行穿着。

（b）这些号码须在背心的前面、后面和袖子的尽可能高的位置上展示。背面的号码高度应至少为 20 厘米，前面和袖子上的号码高度应至少为 6 厘米。

（c）这些号码须为阿拉伯数字，颜色相同，清晰可辨，可以接受商业上可用的与“Helvetica”字体有同样或更好的清晰度的字体。号码的颜色须为背心颜色的反差色。

APPENDIX G IDENTIFICATION ON SAILS

See rule 77.

G1 WORLD SAILING CLASS BOATS

G1.1 Identification

Every boat of a World Sailing Class shall carry on her mainsail and, as provided in rule G1.3(c) for letters and numbers only, on her spinnaker and headsail

(a) the insignia denoting her class;

(b) at all international events, except when the boats are provided to all competitors, national letters denoting her national authority from the table below. For the purposes of this rule, international events are World Sailing events, world and continental championships, and events described as international events in their notices of race and sailing instructions; and

(c) a sail number of no more than four digits allotted by her national authority or, when so required by the class rules, by the class association. The four-digit limitation does not apply to classes whose World Sailing membership or recognition took effect before 1 April 1997. Alternatively, if permitted in the class rules, an owner may be allotted a personal sail number by the relevant issuing authority, which may be used on all his boats in that class.

Sails measured before 31 March 1999 shall comply with rule G1.1 or with the rules applicable at the time of measurement.

Note: An up-to-date version of the table below is available on the World Sailing website.

附录 G　帆上标识

参见规则 77。

G1　世界帆联级别的帆船

G1.1 识别标记

世界帆联级别的每条帆船须在其主帆上携有，并仅按照规则 G1.3（c）的字母和号码规定在球帆和前帆上携有：

（a）代表该级别的标识；

（b）在所有国际赛事中，除了向所有选手提供帆船外，下表中的代表国家和地区管理机构的国家和地区代码。针对本规则而言，国际赛事是指世界帆联赛事、世界和洲际锦标赛，以及在竞赛通知和航行细则中描述为国际赛事的赛事；以及

（c）由国家和地区管理机构分配的，或者级别规则或级别协会这样要求的不多于四位数字的帆号。这四位数字的限制不适用于在 1997 年 4 月 1 日前获得世界帆联成员资格或承认的级别。或者，如果级别规则允许，船东可以由相应的认证机构分配一个个人帆号，可以用于该级别中他所有的帆船。

1999 年 3 月 31 日前丈量的帆须符合规则 G1.1 或符合其丈量时所适用的规则。

注：世界帆联网站上可以查询到下表的实时更新版本。

NATIONAL SAIL LETTERS

National authority	Letters
Algeria	ALG
American Samoa	ASA
Andorra	AND
Angola	ANG
Antigua	ANT
Argentina	ARG
Armenia	ARM
Aruba	ARU
Australia	AUS
Austria	AUT
Azerbaijan	AZE
Bahamas	BAH
Bahrain	BRN
Barbados	BAR
Belarus	BLR
Belgium	BEL
Belize	BIZ
Bermuda	BER
Botswana	BOT
Brazil	BRA
British Virgin Islands	IVB
Brunei Darussalam	BRU
Bulgaria	BUL
Cambodia	CAM
Canada	CAN

National authority	Letters
Cayman Islands	CAY
Chile	CHI
China, PR	CHN
Chinese Taipei	TPE
Colombia	COL
Cook Islands	COK
Croatia	CRO
Cuba	CUB
Cyprus	CYP
Czech Republic	CZE
Denmark	DEN
Djibouti	DJI
Dominican Republic	DOM
Ecuador	ECU
Egypt	EGY
El Salvador	ESA
Estonia	EST
Fiji	FIJ
Finland	FIN
France	FRA
Georgia	GEO
Germany	GER
Great Britain	GBR
Greece	GRE
Grenada	GRN

国家和地区帆上代码

国家和地区管理机构	字母代码
阿尔及利亚	ALG
美属萨摩亚	ASA
安道尔	AND
安哥拉	ANG
安提瓜	ANT
阿根廷	ARG
亚美尼亚	ARM
阿鲁巴岛	ARU
澳大利亚	AUS
奥地利	AUT
阿塞拜疆	AZE
巴哈马	BAH
巴林	BRN
巴巴多斯	BAR
白俄罗斯	BLR
比利时	BEL
伯利兹	BIZ
百慕大	BER
博茨瓦纳	BOT
巴西	BRA
英属维尔京群岛	IVB
文莱达鲁萨兰国	BRU
保加利亚	BUL
柬埔寨	CAM
加拿大	CAN

国家和地区管理机构	字母代码
开曼群岛	CAY
智利	CHI
中华人民共和国	CHN
中国台北	TPE
哥伦比亚	COL
库克群岛	COK
克罗地亚	CRO
古巴	CUB
塞浦路斯	CYP
捷克共和国	CZE
丹麦	DEN
吉布提	DJI
多米尼加共和国	DOM
厄瓜多尔	ECU
埃及	EGY
艾萨瓦尔多	ESA
爱沙尼亚	EST
斐济	FIJ
芬兰	FIN
法国	FRA
格鲁吉亚	GEO
德国	GER
英国	GBR
希腊	GRE
格林纳达	GRN

National authority	*Letters*
Guam	GUM
Guatemala	GUA
Hong Kong, China	HKG
Hungary	HUN
Iceland	ISL
India	IND
Indonesia	INA
Iran	IRN
Iraq	IRQ
Ireland	IRL
Israel	ISR
Italy	ITA
Jamaica	JAM
Japan	JPN
Kazakhstan	KAZ
Kenya	KEN
Korea, DPR	PRK
Korea, Republic of	KOR
Kosovo	KOS
Kuwait	KUW
Kyrgyzstan	KGZ
Latvia	LAT
Lebanon	LIB
Libya	LBA
Liechtenstein	LIE
Lithuania	LTU

National authority	*Letters*
Luxembourg	LUX
Macau, China	MAC
Madagascar	MAD
Malaysia	MAS
Malta	MLT
Mauritius	MRI
Mexico	MEX
Moldova	MDA
Monaco	MON
Montenegro	MNE
Montserrat	MNT
Morocco	MAR
Mozambique	MOZ
Myanmar	MYA
Namibia	NAM
Netherlands	NED
Netherlands Antilles	AHO
New Zealand	NZL
Nigeria	NGR
North Macedonia	MKD
Norway	NOR
Oman	OMA
Pakistan	PAK
Palestine	PLE
Panama	PAN
Papua New Guinea	PNG

国家和地区管理机构	字母代码
关岛	GUM
危地马拉	GUA
中国香港	HKG
匈牙利	HUN
冰岛	ISL
印度	IND
印度尼西亚	INA
伊拉克	IRQ
爱尔兰	IRL
以色列	ISR
意大利	ITA
牙买加	JAM
日本	JPN
哈萨克斯坦	KAZ
肯尼亚	KEN
朝鲜	PRK
韩国	KOR
科索沃	KOS
科威特	KUW
吉尔吉斯斯坦	KGZ
拉脱维亚	LAT
黎巴嫩	LIB
利比亚	LBA
列支敦士登	LIE
立陶宛	LTU
卢森堡	LUX

国家和地区管理机构	字母代码
中国澳门	MAC
马达加斯加	MAD
马来西亚	MAS
马耳他	MLT
毛里求斯	MRI
墨西哥	MEX
摩尔多瓦	MDA
摩纳哥	MON
黑山共和国	MNE
摩洛哥	MAR
莫桑比克	MOZ
缅甸	MYA
纳米比亚	NAM
荷兰	NED
荷属安的列斯	AHO
新西兰	NZL
尼日利亚	NGR
北马其顿	MKD
挪威	NOR
阿曼	OMA
巴基斯坦	PAK
巴勒斯坦	PLE
巴拿马	PAN
巴布亚新几内亚	PNG
巴拉圭	PAR
秘鲁	PER

National authority	*Letters*
Paraguay	PAR
Peru	PER
Philippines	PHI
Poland	POL
Portugal	POR
Puerto Rico	PUR
Qatar	QAT
Romania	ROU
Russia	RUS
Samoa	SAM
San Marino	SMR
Senegal	SEN
Serbia	SRB
Seychelles	SEY
Singapore	SGP
Slovak Republic	SVK
Slovenia	SLO
South Africa	RSA
Spain	ESP
Sri Lanka	SRI
St Kitts & Nevis	SKN
St Lucia	LCA

National authority	*Letters*
Sudan	SUD
Sweden	SWE
Switzerland	SUI
Tahiti	TAH
Tanzania	TAN
Thailand	THA
Timor Leste	TLS
Trinidad & Tobago	TTO
Tunisia	TUN
Turkey	TUR
Turks & Caicos	TKS
Uganda	UGA
Ukraine	UKR
United Arab Emirates	UAE
United States of America	USA
Uruguay	URU
US Virgin Islands	ISV
Vanuatu	VAN
Venezuela	VEN
Vietnam	VIE
Zimbabwe	ZIM

国家和地区管理机构	*字母代码*
菲律宾	PHI
波兰	POL
葡萄牙	POR
波多黎各	PUR
卡塔尔	QAT
罗马尼亚	ROU
俄罗斯	RUS
萨摩亚	SAM
圣马力诺	SMR
塞内加尔	SEN
塞尔维亚	SRB
塞舌尔	SEY
新加坡	SGP
斯洛伐克共和国	SVK
斯洛文尼亚	SLO
南非	RSA
西班牙	ESP
斯里兰卡	SRI
圣基茨和尼维斯	SKN
圣卢西亚	LCA
苏丹	SUD

国家和地区管理机构	*字母代码*
瑞典	SWE
瑞士	SUI
法属波利尼西亚	TAH
坦桑尼亚	TAN
泰国	THA
帝汶岛	TLS
特立尼达和多巴哥	TTO
突尼斯	TUN
土耳其	TUR
英属特科斯和开科斯	TKS
乌干达	UGA
乌克兰	UKR
阿拉伯联合酋长国	UAE
美利坚合众国	USA
乌拉圭	URU
美属维尔京群岛	ISV
瓦努阿图	VAN
委内瑞拉	VEN
越南	VIE
津巴布韦	ZIM

G1.2 Specifications

(a) National letters and sail numbers shall be:

(1) in capital letters and Arabic numerals,

(2) of the same colour,

(3) of a contrasting colour to the body of the sail, and

(4) of a sans-serif typeface.

In addition, the letters and numbers identifying the boat shall be clearly legible when the sail is set.

(b) The height of characters and space between adjoining characters on the same and opposite sides of the sail shall be related to the boat's overall length as follows:

Overall length	*Minimum height*	*Minimum space between characters and from edge of sail*
Under 3.5 m	230 mm	45 mm
3.5 m – 8.5 m	300 mm	60 mm
8.5 m – 11 m	375 mm	75 mm
Over 11 m	450 mm	90 mm

G1.3 Positioning

Class insignia, national letters and sail numbers shall be positioned as follows:

(a) General

(1) Class insignia, national letters and sail numbers, where applicable, shall be place on both sides and such that those on the starboard side are uppermost.

(2) National letters shall be placed above the sail numbers on each side of the sail.

G1.2 规格

（a）国家和地区代码和帆号须符合以下要求：

（1）大写字母和阿拉伯数字，

（2）颜色相同，

（3）与帆的主体颜色呈对比色，以及

（4）无衬线字体。

此外，在帆升起时，识别该船的字母和数字须清晰可辨。

（b）字符的高度和在帆的同一面或反面相邻字符的距离与船的总长关系如下：

总长	*最小高度*	*字符之间与帆边的最小间隔*
3. 5m 以下	230mm	45mm
3. 5m ～ 8. 5m	300mm	60mm
8. 5m ～ 11m	375mm	75mm
11m 以上	450mm	90mm

G1.3 位置

级别标识、国家和地区代码和帆号的位置须符合以下要求：

（a）总体

（1）若适用，级别标识、国家和地区代码和帆号须放置在帆的两面，且右舷一面的较高。

（2）国家和地区代码须在帆的每一面上高于帆号放置。

(b) Mainsails

(1) The class insignia, national letters and sail numbers shall, if possible, be wholly above an arc whose centre is the head point and whose radius is 60% of the leech length.

(2) The class insignia shall be placed above the national letters. If the class insignia is of a design that it may be placed back to back, then it may be so placed.

(c) Headsails and Spinnakers

(1) National letters and sail numbers are only required on a headsail whose foot length is greater than 1.3 x foretriangle base.

(2) The national letters and sail numbers of headsails shall be displayed wholly below an arc whose centre is the head point and whose radius is 50% of the luff length and, if possible, wholly above an arc whose radius is 75% of the luff length.

(3) The national letters and sail number shall be displayed on the front side of a spinnaker but may be placed on both sides. They shall be displayed wholly below an arc whose centre is the head point and whose radius is 40% of the foot median and, if possible, wholly above an arc whose radius is 60% of the foot median.

G2 OTHER BOATS

Other boats shall comply with the rules of their national authority or class association in regard to the allotment, carrying and size of insignia, letters and numbers. Such rules shall, when practicable, conform to the above requirements.

G3 CHARTERED OR LOANED BOATS

When so stated in the notice of race or sailing instructions, a boat chartered or loaned for an event may carry national letters or a sail number in contravention of her class rules.

（b）主帆

（1）在可能的情况下，级别标识、国家和地区代码和帆号须完全位于以帆顶为圆心、以帆后缘长度的60%为半径画出的圆弧线的上方。

（2）级别标识须位于国家和地区代码之上。如果级别标识的设计背靠背放置于帆的两面时是重合的，就可以这样放置。

（c）前帆和球帆

（1）仅要求在底边长度大于前三角底边长度1.3倍以上的前帆上展示国家和地区代码和帆号。

（2）前帆上的国家和地区代码和帆号须完全位于以帆顶为圆心、以前缘长度的50%为半径画出的弧线的下方；如果可能的话，完全位于以前缘长度的75%为半径画出的弧线的上方。

（3）国家和地区代码和帆号须放置在球帆的前面一侧，但也可以放置在球帆的两面。它们须完全位于以帆顶为圆心、以底边中线的40%为半径画出的弧线的下方，如果可能的话，完全位于以底边中线60%为半径画出的弧线的上方。

G2　其他帆船

其他帆船在标志、字母和数字的分配、携有和尺寸方面须遵守其国家和地区管理机构或级别协会的规则。这些规则在实施时须与上述要求一致。

G3　租借的船

当竞赛通知或航行细则中有规定时，为参加某一赛事租借的帆船可以携有违背其级别规则的国家和地区代码或帆号。

G4 WARNINGS AND PENALTIES

When a protest committee finds that a boat has broken a rule of this appendix, it shall either warn her and give her time to comply or penalize her.

G5 CHANGES BY CLASS RULES

World Sailing Classes may change the rules of this appendix provided the changes have first been approved by World Sailing.

G4 警告和惩罚

当抗议委员会认定一条船已经违反了本附录的规则时，须警告该船并给其时间改正或对其进行惩罚。

G5 级别规则所做的更改

世界帆联级别组织可以更改本附录的规则，前提是首先要得到世界帆联的批准。

APPENDIX H WEIGHING CLOTHING AND EQUIPMENT

See rule 50. This appendix shall not be changed by the notice of race, sailing instructions or prescriptions of national authorities.

H1 Items of clothing and equipment to be weighed shall be arranged on a rack. After being saturated in water the items shall be allowed to drain freely for one minute before being weighed. The rack must allow the items to hang as they would hang from clothes hangers, so as to allow the water to drain freely. Pockets that have drain-holes that cannot be closed shall be empty, but pockets or items that can hold water shall be full.

H2 When the weight recorded exceeds the amount permitted, the competitor may rearrange the items on the rack and the member of the technical committee in charge shall again soak and weigh them. This procedure may be repeated a second time if the weight still exceeds the amount permitted.

H3 A competitor wearing a dry suit may choose an alternative means of weighing the items.

(a) The dry suit and items of clothing and equipment that are worn outside the dry suit shall be weighed as described above.

(b) Clothing worn underneath the dry suit shall be weighed as worn while *racing*, without draining.

(c) The two weights shall be added together.

附录 H　服装和器材的称重

参见规则 50。本附录不得因竞赛通知、航行细则或国家和地区管理机构的规定而更改。

H1　需要被称重的服装和器材须放置在架子上。在水中浸过的物品在称重前须得到 1 分钟的时间去排干水分。架子必须可以悬挂物品，如同晾晒衣服的衣架，这样有利于衣物排水。有排水孔但无法关闭的口袋须是空的，但是可以盛水的口袋或物品须装满水。

H2　若称重记录超过允许的数值，选手可以重新在架子上摆放物品，然后主管的技术委员会成员须再次将其浸湿并称重。如果重量依然超过允许的数值，那么可以再重复一次该过程。

H3　身着干式保温服的选手可以选择其他方法称重物品。

（a）干式保温服和穿在其外面的服装以及器材物品均须按上述规定称重。

（b）穿在干式保温服里面的衣服须像在*竞赛*时的穿着一样，在不经过控干的情况下称重。

（c）这两项重量须相加。

APPENDIX J NOTICE OF RACE AND SAILING SAILING INSTRUCTIONS

See rules 89.2 and 90.2. In this appendix, the term 'event' includes a race or series of races.

A rule in the notice of race need not be repeated in the sailing instructions.

Care should be taken to ensure that there is no conflict between rules in the notice of race, the sailing instructions or any other document that governs the event.

J1 NOTICE OF RACE CONTENTS

J1.1 The notice of race shall include the following:

(1) the title, place and dates of the event and name of the organizing authority;

(2) that the event will be governed by the *rules* as defined in *The Racing Rules of Sailing*;

(3) a list of any other documents that will govern the event (for example, *The Equipment Rules of Sailing*, to the extent that they apply), stating where or how each document or an electronic copy of it may be obtained;

(4) the classes to race, any handicap or rating system that will be used, and the classes to which it will apply; conditions of entry and any restrictions on entries;

(5) the procedures and times for registration or entry, including fees and any closing dates;

(6) the times of warning signals for the practice race, if one is scheduled, and the first race, and succeeding races if known.

J1.2 The notice of race shall include any of the following that will apply:

附录 J　竞赛通知和航行细则

参见规则 89.2 和 90.2。本附录中，术语“赛事”包括一轮竞赛或数轮竞赛的系列赛。

竞赛通知中的规则无需再在航行细则中重复。

应仔细确保竞赛通知和航行细则或赛事执行的其他文件中的规则间没有冲突。

J1　竞赛通知的内容

J1.1 竞赛通知须包括以下信息：

(1) 赛事的名称、地点和时间，以及组织机构的名称；

(2) 赛事将执行*《帆船竞赛规则》*所定义的*规则*；

(3) 赛事将执行的其他文件的清单（比如*《帆船器材规则》*，它们所适用的范围），指明哪里可以得到或怎样可以获取每个文件或其电子副本；

(4) 竞赛的级别、使用的让分系数或评级方法及其所适用的级别；报名条件和报名的限制；

(5) 注册或报名的程序和时间，包括费用和报名截止日期；

(6) 练习赛（如果已安排）和第一轮竞赛以及随后竞赛（如果已知）的预告信号时间。

J1.2 竞赛通知须包括适用的以下内容：

(1) times or procedures for equipment inspection or event measurement, or requirements for measurement or rating certificates;

(2) changes to the racing rules authorized by World Sailing under rule 86.2, referring specifically to each rule and stating the change (also include the statement from World Sailing authorizing the change);

(3) changes to class rules, as permitted under rule 87, referring specifically to each rule and stating the change;

(4) categorization or classification requirements that some or all competitors must satisfy;

  (a) for sailor categorization (see rule 79 and the World Sailing Sailor Categorization Code), or

  (b) for functional classification for Para World Sailing events (see World Sailing Para Classification Rules);

(5) that boats will be required to display advertising chosen and supplied by the organizing authority (see rule 6 and the World Sailing Advertising Code) and other information related to advertising;

(6) when entries from other countries are expected, any national prescriptions that may require advance preparation (see rule 88);

(7) prescriptions that will apply if boats will pass through the waters of more than one national authority while *racing*, and when they will apply (see rule 88.1);

(8) alternative communication required in place of hails under rule 20 (see rule 20.4(b));

(9) any change in the weight limit for a competitor's clothing and equipment permitted by rule 50.1(b);

（1）器材检查或赛事丈量的时间或程序，或者对丈量证书和评分证书的要求；

（2）根据规则 86. 2，经世界帆联授权更改的竞赛规则，指明具体的每条规则并说明更改的内容（还要包括世界帆联授权此更改的声明）；

（3）规则 87 所允许的对级别规则的更改，指明具体的每条规则并说明更改的内容；

（4）部分或全体选手必须符合的分类或分级要求；

（a）对于选手分类（参见规则 79 和世界帆联选手分类法规），或

（b）对于世界帆联残疾人赛事的功能分级（参见世界帆联残疾人选手分级规则）；

（5）组织机构要求参赛船展示其挑选和提供的广告（参见规则 6 和世界帆联广告守则），以及其他与广告相关的信息；

（6）当预计有其他国家和地区报名时，可能需要提前准备的任何国家和地区规定（参见规则 88）；

（7）*竞赛*时，当参赛船将航越一个以上国家和地区管理机构的水域时，适用的国家和地区规定及何时适用（参见规则 88. 1）；

（8）根据规则20，替代呼喊所要求的其他沟通方式［参见规则20. 4（b）］；

（9）规则 50. 1（b）允许的选手服装和器材的重量限制的更改；

(10) any requirements necessary for compliance with data protection legislation that applies in the venue of the event;

(11) an entry form, to be signed by the boat's owner or owner's representative, containing words such as 'I agree to be bound by *The Racing Rules of Sailing* and by all other *rules* that govern this event.';

(12) replacement of the rules of Part 2 with the right-of-way rules of the *International Regulations for Preventing Collisions at Sea* or other government right-of-way rules, the time(s) or place(s) they will apply, and any night signals to be used by the race committee.

J1.3 The notice of race shall include any of the following that will apply and that would help competitors decide whether to attend the event or that conveys other information they will need before the sailing instructions become available:

(1) changes to the racing rules permitted by rule 86, referring specifically to each rule and stating the change;

(2) changes to the national prescriptions (see rule 88.2);

(3) the time and place at which the sailing instructions will be available;

(4) a general description of the course, or type of courses, to be sailed;

(5) the scoring system, if different from the system in Appendix A, included by reference to class rules or other *rules* governing the event, or stated in full. State the number of races scheduled and the minimum number that must be completed to constitute a series. If appropriate, for a series where the number of starters may vary substantially, state that rule A5.3 applies;

（10）遵守赛事场馆适用的数据保护法规所必需的要求；

（11）由船东或船东代表签字的报名表，包括类似“我同意遵守*《帆船竞赛规则》*和其他所有该赛事执行的*规则*”这样的词句；

（12）替换规则第二章的*《国际海上避碰规则》*的航行权规则或其他的政府航行权规则，其适用的时间或地点，以及竞赛委员会使用的任何夜间信号。

J1.3 竞赛通知须包括适用的以下内容和可以帮助选手决定是否参赛或在拿到航行细则前所需要的其他信息：

（1）规则 86 允许更改的竞赛规则，指明具体的每条规则并说明更改的内容；

（2）对国家和地区规定的更改（参见规则 88. 2）；

（3）可以得到航行细则的时间和地点；

（4）行驶的航线的大致描述或航线类型；

（5）若不同于附录 A，说明其计分方法，包括参考级别规则或其他赛事执行的*规则*，或者完整说明。说明排定的轮次数目及构成系列赛所必须完成的最少轮数。适当时，对于起航船数可能变化很大的系列赛，说明规则 A5. 3 适用；

(6) the penalty for breaking a rule of Part 2, other than the Two-Turns Penalty;

(7) the time after which no warning signal will be made on the last scheduled day of racing;

(8) denial of the right of appeal, subject to rule 70.5;

(9) for chartered or loaned boats, whether rule G3 applies;

(10) prizes.

J2 SAILING INSTRUCTION CONTENTS

J2.1 Unless included in the notice of race, the sailing instructions shall include the following:

(1) the information in rules J1.3(1), (2) and (5) and, when applicable, rules J1.3(6), (7), (8), (9) and (10);

(2) the schedule of races and the times of warning signals for each class;

(3) a complete description of the course(s) to be sailed, or a list of *marks* from which the course will be selected and, if relevant, how courses will be signalled;

(4) descriptions of *marks*, including starting and finishing *marks*, stating the order in which *marks* are to be passed and the side on which each is to be left and identifying all rounding *marks* (see the definition *Sail the Course*);

(5) descriptions of the starting and finishing lines, class flags and any special signals to be used;

(6) the race time limit, if any, for the first boat to *finish* (see rule 35);

(7) location(s) of official notice board(s) or address of online notice board; location of the race office.

J2.2 Unless included in the notice of race, the sailing instructions shall include those of the following that will apply:

(1) whether Appendix P will apply;

（6）当不采用两圈解脱时，违反第二章规则的惩罚方法；

（7）在排定的最后一个竞赛日不再发出预告信号的时间；

（8）根据规则 70. 5 对上诉权的驳回；

（9）对于租船或借船，规则 G3 是否适用；

（10）奖励。

J2　航行细则的内容

J2.1 除非竞赛通知中有包含，否则航行细则须包括以下内容：

（1）规则 J1. 3（1）、（2）和（5）中的信息，若适用，还有规则 J1. 3（6）、（7）、（8）、（9）和（10）中的信息；

（2）竞赛日程和每个级别预告信号发出的时间；

（3）一份详细的竞赛航线描述或一份*标志*清单，可以从中选取航线，以及对应的航线如何用信号通知；

（4）*标志*的描述，包括起航和终点*标志*，说明绕行*标志*的顺序和从每个*标志*哪一侧离开并说明所有要绕行的*标志*（参见定义*行驶航线*）；

（5）起航线和终点线、级别旗以及任何将会使用的特殊信号的描述；

（6）竞赛时限，如果有，第一条船*到达终点*的时限（参见规则 35）；

（7）官方公告栏的地点或者在线公告栏的地址；竞赛办公室的位置。

J2.2 除非竞赛通知中有包含，否则航行细则须包括下列适用的内容：

（1）附录 P 是否适用；

(2) when appropriate, at an event where entries from other countries are expected, a copy in English of the national prescriptions that will apply;

(3) procedure for changing the sailing instructions;

(4) procedure for giving oral changes to the sailing instructions on the water (see rule 90.2(c));

(5) safety requirements, such as requirements and signals for personal flotation devices, check-in at the starting area, and check-out and check-in ashore;

(6) signals to be made ashore and location of signal station(s);

(7) restrictions controlling changes to boats when supplied by the organizing authority;

(8) when and under what circumstances propulsion is permitted under rule 42.3(i);

(9) restrictions on use of *support person* vessels, plastic pools, radios, etc.; on trash disposal; on hauling out; and on outside assistance provided to a boat that is not *racing*;

(10) the racing area (a chart is recommended);

(11) location of the starting area and any restrictions on entering it;

(12) any special procedures or signals for individual or general recall;

(13) approximate course length and approximate length of windward legs;

(14) any special procedures or signals for changing a leg of the course (see rule 33);

(15) description of any object, area or line designated by the race committee to be an *obstruction* (see the definition *Obstruction*), and any restriction on entering such an area or crossing such a line;

（2）适当时，在预计有其他国家和地区报名的赛事中，所适用的国家和地区规定的英文版复印件；

（3）更改航行细则的程序；

（4）在水上给予航行细则口头更改的程序［参见规则90.2（c)］；

（5）安全要求，例如个人助浮装置的要求和信号，起航区的检录和上下水签到；

（6）岸上信号及岸上信号台的位置；

（7）当由组织机构提供船时，限制对船只改动的条款；

（8）何时以及何种情况下允许根据规则 42.3（i)推进；

（9）使用*后援人员*船舶、塑料池、无线电等的限制；垃圾处理的限制；拖船上岸的限制；对不在*竞赛*中的船提供外部援助的限制；

（10）竞赛区域（建议用海图形式呈现）；

（11）起航区的位置以及任何进入起航区的限制；

（12）任何单召或全召的特殊程序或信号；

（13）航线大致长度和迎风航段的大致长度；

（14）改变航线中某一航段的任何特殊程序或信号（参见规则 33）；

（15）描述竞赛委员会指明的作为*障碍物*的任何物体、区域或线（参见定义*障碍物*），以及进入这样的区域或越过这样的线的限制；

(16) boats identifying *mark* locations;

(17) any special procedures for shortening the course or for *finishing* a shortened course;

(18) the time limit, if any, for boats other than the first boat to *finish* and any other time limits or target times that apply while boats are *racing*;

(19) declaration requirements;

(20) time allowances;

(21) time limits, place of hearings, and special procedures for *protests*, requests for redress or requests for reopening;

(22) the national authority's approval of the appointment of an international jury, when required under rule 91(b);

(23) the time limit for requesting a hearing under rule N1.4(b), if not 30 minutes;

(24) when required by rule 70.3, the national authority to which appeals and requests are required to be sent;

(25) substitution of competitors;

(26) the minimum number of boats appearing in the starting area required for a race to be started;

(27) when and where races *postponed* or *abandoned* for the day will be sailed;

(28) tides and currents;

(29) other commitments of the race committee and obligations of boats.

（16）展示*标志*位置的船只；

（17）任何缩短航线或在缩短航线时*到达终点*的特殊程序；

（18）时间限制（如果有的话），除了第一条船*到达终点*的时限，帆船*竞赛*时适用的其他针对船的时间限制和目标时间；

（19）声明要求；

（20）时限宽限；

（21）*抗议*、要求补偿或要求重审的时间限制、审理地点和特殊程序；

（22）根据规则 91（b）的要求，国家和地区管理机构对国际仲裁委员会的任命的批准；

（23）若不是 30 分钟，根据规则 N1.4（b）要求审理的时间限制；

（24）根据规则 70.3 的要求，上诉和请求要递交到的国家和地区管理机构；

（25）选手的替换；

（26）一轮竞赛起航所需的在起航区域出现的最少船数；

（27）当天*推迟*或*放弃*的竞赛何时何地再次起航；

（28）潮汐和水流；

（29）竞赛委员会的其他承诺和船的义务。

NOTICE OF RACE GUIDE Previously Appendix K

SAILING INSTRUCTIONS GUIDE Previously Appendix L

These guides, updated to conform to the rules in this edition of The Racing Rules of Sailing, *are available, in various formats, at the World Sailing website at sailing.*org/racingrules/documents. *National authorities are encouraged to translate the guides, and World Sailing will make translated versions available at that website.*

The guides, which will have a two-letter designation starting with 'K' or 'L', may be downloaded either as PDF documents or as Word documents. This will enable users to easily and quickly create, using the tested wording in the guides, either the notice of race or the sailing instructions, or both, for a particular event.

*Suggestions for improving these guides are welcome and should be sent to rules@*sailing.org.

竞赛通知指南　之前的附录 K

航行细则指南　之前的附录 L

这些指南已经根据此版本的《帆船竞赛规则》中的规则进行了更新，可以在世界帆联网站 sailing. org/racingrules/documents 上获取不同格式的文件。鼓励各国家和地区管理机构对指南进行翻译，世界帆联将在网站上提供翻译版本。

指南的名称以“K”或“L”开头的两个字母表示，可以以 PDF 文档或 Word 文档的形式下载。这可以让使用者使用指南中测试过的措辞，简单且快速地针对某一特定赛事撰写竞赛通知或航行细则，或同时撰写这两者。

欢迎对这些指南提出改进建议，建议应发送至 rules@sailing. org。

APPENDIX M RECOMMENDATIONS FOR PROTEST COMMITTEES

This appendix is advisory only; in some circumstances changing these procedures may be advisable. It is addressed primarily to protest committee chairmen but may also help judges, protest committee secretaries, race committees and others connected with protest and redress hearings.

In a protest or redress hearing, the protest committee should weigh all testimony with equal care; should recognize that honest testimony can vary, and even be in conflict, as a result of different observations and recollections; should resolve such differences as best it can; should recognize that no boat or competitor is guilty until a breach of a *rule* has been established to the satisfaction of the protest committee; and should keep an open mind until all the evidence has been heard as to whether a boat or competitor has broken a *rule*.

M1 PRELIMINARIES (may be performed by race office staff)

- Receive the *protest* or request for redress.
- Note on the form the time the *protest* or request is delivered and the protest time limit.
- Inform each *party*, and the race committee when necessary, when and where the hearing will be held.

M2 BEFORE THE HEARING

M2.1 Make sure that

- each *party* has a copy of or the opportunity to read the *protest*, request for redress or allegation and has had reasonable time to prepare for the hearing.

附录 M　对抗议委员会的建议

本附录只作建议性使用；在一些情况下，更改这些步骤或许是明智的。本附录主要针对抗议委员会主席，但也能帮助到仲裁、抗议委员会秘书、竞赛委员会和其他与抗议和补偿审理相关的人员。

在抗议或补偿审理中，抗议委员会应以相同标准对待所有证词；应意识到，由于不同的观察角度和回忆，即便是诚实的证词也可能存在差异和矛盾之处；应尽可能地解决好这些差异；应认可在抗议委员会认定某船或选手确实违反了某一*规则*前，其应是无辜的；应在没有审完某船或选手是否违反了*规则*的全部证据前不抱成见。

M1　前期工作(可由竞赛办公室工作人员办理)

- 接收*抗议*或补偿请求。
- 在表上注明*抗议*或请求所递交的时间以及抗议时限。
- 将审理于何时何地举行通知到*各方*，必要时还包括竞赛委员会。

M2　审理前

M2.1 确保

- *各方*都有一份或有机会能够看到*抗议*或补偿申请的复印件，并有合理的时间为审理做准备。

- only one person from each boat (or *party*) is present unless an interpreter is needed.
- all boats and people involved are represented. If they are not, however, the committee may proceed under rule 63.3(b).
- boats' representatives were on board when required (rule 63.3(a)). When the *parties* were in different events, both organizing authorities must accept the composition of the protest committee (rule 63.8). In a *protest* concerning class rules, obtain the current class rules and identify the authority responsible for interpreting them (rule 64.4(b)).

M2.2 Determine if any members of the protest committee saw the incident. If so, require each of them to state that fact in the presence of the *parties* (rule 63.6(b)).

M2.3 Assess *conflicts of interest*.

- Ensure that all protest committee members declare any possible *conflicts of interest*. At major events this will often be a formal written declaration made before the event starts that will be kept with the protest committee records.
- At the start of any hearing, ensure that the *parties* are aware of any *conflicts of interest* of protest committee members. Ask the *parties* if they consent to the members. If a *party* does not object as soon as possible after a *conflict of interest* has been declared, the protest committee may take this as consent to proceed and should record it.
- If a *party* objects to a member, the remainder of the protest committee members need to assess whether the *conflict of interest* is significant. The assessment will consider the level of the event, the level of the conflict and the perception of fairness. It may be acceptable to balance conflicts between protest committee members. Guidance may be found on the World Sailing website. Record the decision and the grounds for that decision.

• 每条船（或一方）仅 1 人出席，除非需要翻译。

• 涉及审理的所有船和人员都有代表出席。但是，如果做不到，委员会可按照规则 63.3（b）继续进行。

• 有要求时［规则63.3（a）］，代表需要是在船上的人。当*各方*是来自不同的赛事时，双方的组织机构必须接受抗议委员会的构成（规则63.8）。涉及级别规则的*抗议*中，要拿到现行的级别规则并确定负责解释规则的机构［规则64.4（b）］。

M2.2 确定是否有抗议委员会的成员看到了事件的发生。如果有人看到，他们中的每个人都要在*各方*面前陈述事件发生的事实［规则63.6（b）］。

M2.3 评估*利益冲突*。

• 确保所有抗议委员会的成员就任何有可能的*利益冲突*都做了声明。在重大赛事中，通常会在开赛前以正式书面声明的形式进行并保存在抗议委员会的记录里。

• 在任何审理开始时，确保*各方*都了解抗议委员会成员的*利益冲突*。询问*各方*是否同意委员会成员的构成。如果一*方*在声明*利益冲突*后没有尽快提出反对，抗议委员会可以视其为同意并应记录在案。

• 如果一方反对委员会的一名成员，委员会的其他成员需要评估这个*利益冲突*是否显著。评估将会考虑赛事的等级、冲突的程度和对公平的认知。在抗议委员会成员之间平衡冲突是可以接受的。关于这方面的指南可以参见世界帆联的官网。记录该决定及其依据。

- In cases of doubt it may be preferable to proceed with a smaller protest committee. Except for hearings under rule 69, there is no minimum number of protest committee members required.
- When a request for redress is made under rule 62.1(a) and is based on an improper action or omission of a body other than the protest committee, a member of that body should not be a member of the protest committee.

M3 THE HEARING

M3.1 Check the validity of the *protest* or request for redress.

- Are the contents adequate (rule 61.2 or 62)?
- Was it delivered in time? If not, is there good reason to extend the time limit (rule 61.3 or 62.2)?
- When required, was the protestor involved in or a witness to the incident (rule 60.1(a))?
- When necessary, was 'Protest' hailed and, if required, a red flag displayed correctly (rule 61.1(a))?
- When the flag or hail was not necessary, was the protestee informed?
- Decide whether the *protest* or request for redress is valid (rule 63.5).
- Once the validity of the *protest* or request has been determined, do not let the subject be introduced again unless truly new evidence is available.

M3.2 Take the evidence (rule 63.6).

- Ask the protestor and then the protestee to tell their stories. Then allow them to question one another. In a redress matter, ask the *party* to state the request.
- Make sure you know what facts each *party* is alleging before calling any witnesses. Their stories may be different.

- 如果有疑虑，最好是以更少成员的抗议委员会继续开展工作。除了根据规则 69 召集的审理，对抗议委员会成员的最少人数没有要求。
- 根据规则 62. 1（a）提出补偿要求时，如果补偿是由于除抗议委员会外的其他机构的不恰当行为或疏忽而造成，该机构的成员不应作为抗议委员会的成员。

M3 审理

M3.1 核查*抗议*或补偿请求的有效性。

- 内容是否充分（规则 61. 2 或 62）？
- 是否按时递交？若没有，是否有延长时限的充分理由（规则 61. 3 或 62. 2）？
- 有要求时，抗议者是事件的当事人或目击者吗［规则60. 1（a）］？
- 必要时，是否呼喊了“抗议”？以及有要求时，是否正确地展示了红旗［规则61. 1（a）］？
- 当无需出旗和呼喊时，是否通知了被抗议人？
- 决定*抗议*或补偿请求是否有效（规则 63. 5）。
- 一旦确定了*抗议*或请求的有效性，除非有真正的新证据，否则不要再次探讨该问题。

M3.2 取证（规则 63. 6）。

- 请抗议人和被抗议人先后陈述经过。然后允许他们相互提问。在补偿事件中，请一方陈述请求。
- 在传召证人前，确定你已知晓*各方*所宣称的事实。他们的陈述会有所不同。

- Allow anyone, including a boat's crew, to give evidence. It is the *party* who normally decides which witnesses to call, although the protest committee may also call witnesses (rule 63.6(a)). The question asked by a *party* 'Would you like to hear N?' is best answered by 'It is your choice.'
- Call each *party's* witnesses (and the protest committee's if any) one by one. Limit *parties* to questioning the witness(es). (They may wander into general statements.)
- Invite the protestee to question the protestor's witness first (and vice versa). This prevents the protestor from leading his witness from the beginning.
- Allow members of the protest committee who saw the incident to give evidence (rule 63.6(b)), but only while the *parties* are present. Members who give evidence may be questioned, should take care to relate all they know about the incident that could affect the decision, and may remain on the protest committee (rule 63.3(a)).
- Try to prevent leading questions, but if that is impossible discount the evidence so obtained.
- The protest committee chairman should advise a *party* or a witness giving hearsay, repetitive or irrelevant evidence that the protest committee must give such evidence appropriate weight, which may be little or no weight at all.
- Accept written evidence from a witness who is not available to be questioned only if all *parties* agree. In doing so they forego their rights to question that witness (rule 63.6(c)).
- Ask one member of the committee to note down evidence, particularly times, distances, speeds, etc.
- Invite questions from protest committee members.

- 允许包括船员在内的任何人提供证据。虽然抗议委员会也可以传召证人，但通常是由一方决定要传召的证人人选［规则63.6（a）］。一方提出的问题“你是否想听N的证词？”的最好答案是“这是你的选择”。
- 逐一传召各方的证人（以及抗议委员会的证人，如果有的话）。限制各方对证人的提问。（他们可能会陷入一般性的说明中。）
- 先请被抗议人提问抗议人的证人（然后反过来）。这样可以防止抗议人从一开始就引导证人。
- 允许目睹了该事件的抗议委员会成员作证［规则63.6（b）］，但是只能在各方都在场的情况下。作证的成员可能会被提问，对他们所知晓的事件过程确认时要十分小心，这可能会影响到裁决结果。他们可以留在抗议委员会内［规则63.3（a）］。
- 尽力防止引导性提问，但若无法避免，所获证据的可靠性需打折扣。
- 抗议委员会主席应就一方或证人提供的传闻证据、重复或不相关的证据提出警告，以表明抗议委员会必须给予此类证据适当的分量权衡，分量可能很小或根本没有分量。
- 只有在各方都同意的前提下，才可以接受不能到场接受提问的证人的书面证词。这样做他们就放弃了提问证人的权利［规则63.6（c）］。
- 请委员会的一人记录证词，特别是时间、距离、速度等。
- 请抗议委员会成员提问。

- Invite first the protestor and then the protestee to make a final statement of her case, particularly on any application or interpretation of the *rules*.

M3.3 Find the facts (rule 63.6(d)).

- Write down the facts; resolve doubts one way or the other.
- Call back *parties* for more questions if necessary.
- When appropriate, draw a diagram of the incident using the facts you have found.

M3.4 Decide the case (rule 64).

- Base the decision on the facts found. (If you cannot, find some more facts.)
- In redress cases, make sure that no further evidence is needed from boats that will be affected by the decision.

M3.5 Inform the *parties* (rule 65).

- Recall the *parties* and read them the facts found, conclusions and *rules* that apply, and the decision. When time presses it is permissible to read the decision and give the details later.
- Give any *party* a copy of the decision on request. File the *protest* or request for redress with the committee records.

M4 REOPENING A HEARING (rule 66)

M4.1 When a *party*, within the time limit, has asked for a hearing to be reopened, hear the *party* making the request, look at any video, etc., and decide whether there is any significant new evidence that might lead you to change your decision. Decide whether your interpretation of the *rules* may have been wrong; be open-minded as to whether you have made a mistake. If none of these applies refuse to reopen; otherwise schedule a hearing.

- 先请抗议人再请被抗议人对自身情况做最后陈述，特别是对*规则*的任何适用和解释。

M3.3 认定事实［规则63. 6（d）］。

- 写下事实；不管怎样，要把疑问解决掉。
- 若必要，召回*各方*进行更多提问。
- 若可行，根据认定的事实画出事件示意图。

M3.4 裁决案件（规则 64）。

- 基于认定的事实。（如果不行，寻求更多事实。）
- 在补偿事件中，确保无需从会受到裁决结果影响的船那里寻求更多证据。

M3.5 通知*各方*（规则 65）。

- 召回*各方*，宣读认定的事实、结论、适用的*规则*和裁决。时间紧张时，允许先宣布裁决，稍后再给出细节。
- 任何一方有要求时提供裁决的复印件。将*抗议*或补偿请求连同委员会记录一并归档。

M4　重新审理(规则 66)

M4.1 如果一方在时限内提出重新审理，听取提出要求的一方的陈述及查看录像等，然后决定是否有能导致你改变裁决结果的任何显著的新证据。确定对于*规则*的解释是否出现错误；要正确对待自己是否犯了错误。如果均不符合上述情况，则拒绝重审，否则安排审理。

M4.2 Evidence is 'new'

- if it was not reasonably possible for the *party* asking for the reopening to have discovered the evidence before the original hearing,
- if the protest committee is satisfied that before the original hearing the evidence was diligently but unsuccessfully sought by the *party* asking for the reopening, or
- if the protest committee learns from any source that the evidence was not available to the *parties* at the time of the original hearing.

M5 MISCONDUCT (rule 69)

M5.1 An action under this rule is not a *protest*, but the protest committee gives its allegations in writing to the competitor before the hearing. The hearing is conducted under rules similar to those governing a protest hearing but the protest committee must have at least three members (rule 69.2(a)). Use the greatest care to protect the competitor's rights.

M5.2 A competitor or a boat cannot protest under rule 69, but the hearing request form of a competitor who tries to do so may be accepted as a report to the protest committee, which can then decide whether or not to call a hearing.

M5.3 Unless World Sailing has appointed a person for the role, the protest committee may appoint a person to present the allegation. This person might be a race official, the person making the allegation or other appropriate person. When no reasonable alternative person is available, a person who was appointed as a member of the protest committee may present the allegation.

M4.2 如果符合下列条件，则证据是“新的”：

- 是要求重新审理的一方在最初审理前无法发现的证据，
- 抗议委员会认定要求重新审理的一方在最初审理前虽无果但已努力寻找过的证据，或者
- 抗议委员会从任何渠道得到的证据在最初审理时对各方不可用。

M5　品行不端(规则 69)

M5.1 依照此规则采取的行动不是*抗议*，但是抗议委员会要在审理前将书面形式的指控交给选手。违反此规则的审理将和审理其他*抗议*的程序类似，但是抗议委员会必须至少有3名成员［规则69. 2（a）］。尽最大努力保护选手的权益。

M5.2 选手或船不能根据规则 69 提出抗议，但是力图这样做的选手的审理要求表可以作为给抗议委员会的报告被接收，之后抗议委员会可以决定是否召集审理。

M5.3 抗议委员会可以指定一人提出指控，除非世界帆联已经委派他人。这个人可以是竞赛官、提出指控的人或其他合适人选。在没有合适备用人选的情况下，被任命为抗议委员会成员的一个人可以提出指控。

M5.4 When it is desirable to call a hearing under rule 69 as a result of a Part 2 incident, it is important to hear any boat-vs.-boat *protest* in the normal way, deciding which boat, if any, broke which *rule*, before proceeding against the competitor under rule 69.

M5.5 Although action under rule 69 is taken against a competitor, boat owner or *support person*, and not a boat, a boat may also be penalized (rules 69.2(h)(2) and 64.5).

M5.6 When a protest committee upholds a rule 69 allegation it will need to consider if it is appropriate to report to either a national authority or World Sailing. Guidance on when to report may be found in the World Sailing Case Book. When the protest committee does make a report it may recommend whether or not further action should be taken.

M5.7 Unless the right of appeal is denied in accordance with rule 70.5, a *party* to a rule 69 hearing may appeal the decision of the protest committee.

M5.8 Further guidance for protest committees about misconduct may be found on the World Sailing website.

M6 APPEALS (rule 70 and Appendix R)

When decisions can be appealed,

- retain the papers relevant to the hearing so that the information can easily be used for an appeal. Is there a diagram endorsed or prepared by the protest committee? Are the facts found sufficient? (Example: Was there an *overlap*? Yes or No. 'Perhaps' is not a fact found.) Are the names of the protest committee members and other important information on the form?

M5.4 当由于规则第二章的事件需要根据规则 69 召集审理时，在指控选手违反规则 69 前以常态方式听取任何船对船的*抗议*是非常重要的，如果有船违反*规则*，要裁决出是哪条船违反了哪条*规则*。

M5.5 虽然根据规则 69 采取的行动是针对选手、船东或*后援人员*的，而不是针对某条船，但是该船可能也会被惩罚［规则 69.2（h）(2)和 64.5］。

M5.6 当抗议委员会支持规则 69 的指控时，需要考虑其是否适合报告给国家和地区管理机构或世界帆联。世界帆联案例书里有关于何时报告的指导。当抗议委员会确实做出报告时，可以给出是否应采取进一步行动的建议。

M5.7 除非根据规则 70.5 否决了上诉权，否则规则 69 审理的一*方*可以对抗议委员会的裁决提出上诉。

M5.8 关于抗议委员会处理品行不端的进一步指导可参见世界帆联网站。

M6 上诉(规则 70 和附录 R)

当裁决可以被上诉时，

- 要保留与审理相关的纸质文件，这样方便在上诉中使用这些信息。是否有抗议委员会批注或准备的示意图？认定的事实是否充分？（如：是否有*相联*？是或否。“可能”不能作为认定的事实。)抗议委员会成员的姓名和其他重要信息是否都在表上？

- comments by the protest committee on any appeal should enable the appeals committee to picture the whole incident clearly; the appeals committee knows nothing about the situation.

M7 PHOTOGRAPHIC EVIDENCE

Photographs and videos can sometimes provide useful evidence but protest committees should recognize their limitations and note the following points:

- The *party* producing the photographic evidence is responsible for arranging the viewing.
- View the video several times to extract all the information from it.
- The depth perception of any single-lens camera is very poor; with a telephoto lens it is non-existent. When the camera views two *overlapped* boats at right angles to their course, it is impossible to assess the distance between them. When the camera views them head on, it is impossible to see whether an *overlap* exists unless it is substantial.
- Ask the following questions:
- Where was the camera in relation to the boats?
- Was the camera's platform moving? If so in what direction and how fast?
- Is the angle changing as the boats approach the critical point? Fast panning causes radical change.
- Did the camera have an unrestricted view throughout?

- 抗议委员会对任何上诉的评述应能使上诉委员会清楚地勾画出整个事件;上诉委员会对当时情况一无所知。

M7 图像证据

照片和视频有时可以提供有用的证据,但抗议委员会应认识到其局限性并注意以下几点:

- 提供图像证据的一方有责任安排观看。
- 多看几遍视频以从中提取所有信息。
- 任何单镜头相机的景深感都很差;使用长焦镜头时则不存在景深感。当相机的取景点与两条*相联*的船的航线成直角时,是无法估算她们之间的距离的。当相机的取景点与她们正面相对时,除非是重叠的情况,否则是无法看到*相联*是否存在的。
- 询问以下问题:
- 相机与船的相对位置?
- 相机的底座是否移动?如果移动,移动的方向和速度如何?
- 当船接近关键点时角度是否发生变化?快速平移会导致彻底改变。
- 相机镜头是否全程不受取景限制?

APPENDIX N INTERNATIONAL JURIES

See rules 70.5 and 91(b). This appendix shall not be changed by the notice of race, sailing instructions or national prescriptions.

N1 COMPOSITION, APPOINTMENT AND ORGANIZATION

N1.1 An international jury shall be composed of experienced sailors with excellent knowledge of the racing rules and extensive protest committee experience. It shall be independent of and have no members from the race committee or the technical committee, and it shall be appointed by the organizing authority, subject to approval by the national authority if required (see rule 91(b)), or by World Sailing under rule 89.2(c).

N1.2 The jury shall consist of a chairman, a vice chairman if desired, and other members for a total of at least five. A majority shall be International Judges.

N1.3 No more than two members (three, in Groups M, N and Q) shall be from the same national authority.

N1.4

(a) The chairman of a jury may appoint one or more panels composed in compliance with rules N1.1, N1.2 and N1.3. This can be done even if the full jury is not composed in compliance with these rules.

(b) The chairman of a jury may appoint panels of at least three members each, of which the majority shall be International Judges. Members of each panel shall be from at least three different national authorities except in Groups M, N and Q, where they shall be from at least two different national authorities. If dissatisfied with a panel's decision, a *party*

附录 N　国际仲裁委员会

参见规则 70.5 和 91（b）。竞赛通知、航行细则或国家和地区规定不得更改本附录。

N1　构成、任命和组织

N1.1 国际仲裁委员会成员须为具有丰富竞赛规则知识和资深抗议委员会经验的帆船水手。国际仲裁委员会须独立于竞赛委员会和技术委员会且没有来自竞赛委员会和技术委员会的成员，其须是由组织机构任命的，如有要求，须得到国家和地区管理机构的批准［参见规则91（b）］，或根据规则89.2（c）由世界帆联任命。

N1.2 该仲裁委员会须包括一名主席，如需要可以包括一名副主席，以及其他成员，总人数最少 5 名。其中大多数须为国际仲裁。

N1.3 来自同一国家和地区管理机构的成员不得超过 2 名（在 M、N 和 Q 组中为 3 名）。

N1.4

（a）仲裁委员会主席可以根据规则 N1.1、N1.2 和 N1.3 任命一个或多个小组。即使整个仲裁委员会没有按照这些规则完整建制也可以执行这一点。

（b）仲裁委员会主席可以任命每组至少 3 人的小组，每组中的大多数成员须为国际仲裁。每组成员须至少来自 3 个不同的国家和地区管理机构；除非是在 M、N 和 Q 组里，其成员须至少来自于 2 个不同的国家和地区管理机构。如果对小组的裁决不满，对所认定事实的考虑除外，

is entitled to a hearing by a panel composed in compliance with rules N1.1, N1.2 and N1.3, except concerning the facts found, if requested within 30 minutes or the time limit specified in the sailing instructions.

N1.5 When a full jury, or a panel, has fewer than five members, because of illness or emergency, and no qualified replacements are available, it remains properly constituted if it consists of at least three members and if at least two of them are International Judges. When there are three or four members they shall be from at least three different national authorities except in Groups M, N and Q, where they shall be from at least two different national authorities.

N1.6 When it is considered desirable that some members not participate in discussing and deciding a *protest* or request for redress, and no qualified replacements are available, the jury or panel remains properly constituted if at least three members remain and at least two of them are International Judges.

N1.7 In exception to rules N1.1 and N1.2, World Sailing may in limited circumstances (see World Sailing Regulation 25.8.13) authorize an international jury consisting of a total of only three members. All members shall be International Judges. The members shall be from three different national authorities (two, in Groups M, N and Q). The authorization shall be stated in a letter of approval to the organizing authority and in the notice of race or sailing instructions, and the letter shall be posted on the official notice board.

N1.8 When the national authority's approval is required for the appointment of an international jury (see rule 91(b)), notice of its approval shall be included in the sailing instructions or be posted on the official notice board.

如果是在 30 分钟内或航行细则规定的时限内提出，审理的一方有权要求一个按照规则 N1. 1、N1. 2 和 N1. 3 组成的仲裁小组进行审理。

N1.5 当整个仲裁委员会或小组因病或紧急事件导致不足 5 人且没有具备资质的替补人员时，只要还有至少 3 名成员并且其中至少有 2 名是国际仲裁时，那么其仍是正常建制。当有 3 或 4 名成员时，他们须至少来自 3 个不同的国家和地区管理机构，除非是在 M、N 和 Q 组里，成员须至少来自于 2 个不同的国家和地区管理机构。

N1.6 当考虑到一些成员不适合参加某一*抗议*或补偿要求的讨论和决策，且没有具备资质的替补人员在场时，若仲裁委员会或小组有至少 3 名成员且其中至少 2 名为国际仲裁时，其仍为正常建制。

N1.7 除了规则 N1. 1 和 N1. 2，世界帆联在有限的情况下可以授权总共由 3 人构成的国际仲裁委员会（参见世界帆联规章 25. 8. 13）。所有的成员须为国际仲裁。成员须来自于 3 个（在 M、N 和 Q 组里为 2 个）不同的国家和地区管理机构。授权须以批准函件的形式发送给国家和地区管理机构，且体现在竞赛通知或航行细则中，并须张贴在赛事官方公告栏上。

N1.8 当对国际仲裁委员会的任命需要得到国家和地区管理机构的批准时［参见规则91（b）］，批准的通知须包含在航行细则里或张贴于官方公告栏上。

N1.9 If the jury or a panel acts while not properly constituted, its decisions may be appealed.

N2 RESPONSIBILITIES

N2.1 An international jury is responsible for hearing and deciding all *protests*, requests for redress and other matters arising under the rules of Part 5. When asked by the organizing authority, the race committee or the technical committee, it shall advise and assist them on any matter directly affecting the fairness of the competition.

N2.2 Unless the organizing authority directs otherwise, the jury shall decide

(a) questions of eligibility, measurement or rating certificates; and

(b) whether to authorize the substitution of competitors, boats or equipment when a *rule* requires such a decision.

N2.3 The jury shall also decide matters referred to it by the organizing authority, the race committee or the technical committee.

N3 PROCEDURES

N3.1 Members shall not be regarded as having a significant *conflict of interest* (see rule 63.4) by reason of their nationality, club membership or similar. When otherwise considering a significant *conflict of interest* as required by rule 63.4, considerable weight must be given to the fact that decisions of an international jury cannot be appealed and this may affect the perception of fairness and lower the level of conflict that is significant. In case of doubt, the hearing should proceed as permitted by rule N1.6.

N1.9 如果仲裁委员会或一个小组在没有正常建制的情况下行事，可以对其裁决提出上诉。

N2 责任

N2.1 国际仲裁委员会对审理和裁决所有*抗议*、补偿请求和其他根据第五章规则所产生的事件负责。当组织机构、竞赛委员会或技术委员会提出要求时，国际仲裁委员会须在任何直接影响到比赛公正性的事件中给予建议和帮助。

N2.2 除非组织机构另有指示，否则仲裁委员会须裁决：

(a) 资格、丈量或评分证书的问题；和

(b) 当*规则*要求做这样的裁决时，裁决是否批准选手、船或器材的替换。

N2.3 仲裁委员会还须对组织机构、竞赛委员会或技术委员会向其提出的事件做出裁决。

N3 程序

N3.1 成员不得因为国籍、俱乐部会员或者相似的因素被认为有显著*利益冲突*（参见规则 63. 4）。当根据规则 63. 4 要求以其他方式考虑显著*利益冲突*时，必须慎重考虑不能对国际仲裁委员会的裁决进行上诉这一事实，因为这可能会影响对公平的认知和降低显著*利益冲突*的等级。如有异议，应根据规则 N1. 6 召集审理。

N3.2 If a panel fails to agree on a decision it may adjourn, in which case the chairman shall refer the matter to a properly constituted panel with as many members as possible, which may be the full jury.

N4 MISCONDUCT (Rule 69)

N4.1 The World Sailing Disciplinary Code contains procedures that apply to specific international events with regard to the appointment of a person to conduct any investigation. These procedures override any conflicting provision of this appendix.

N4.2 A person shall be responsible for presenting to the hearing panel any allegations of misconduct under rule 69. This person shall not be a member of the hearing panel but may be a member of the jury. Such a person shall be required to make full disclosure of all material that may come into his possession in the course of his investigation to the person subject to allegations of a breach of rule 69.

N4.3 Prior to a hearing, the hearing panel, to the extent practically possible, shall not act as an investigator of any allegations made under rule 69. However, during the hearing the panel shall be entitled to ask any investigative questions it may see fit.

N4.4 If the panel decides to call a hearing, all material disclosed to the panel in order for them to make that decision must be disclosed to the person subject to the allegations before the hearing begins.

N3.2 如果一个小组没有对裁决达成一致，它可以休会；在这种情况下，仲裁委员会主席须将此事件转交给一个正常建制的小组，其成员越多越好，甚至可以是完整的仲裁委员会。

N4 品行不端（规则 69）

N4.1 世界帆联纪律守则包含了适用于特定国际赛事中任命某人执行调查的程序。这些程序可推翻该附录中任何冲突的条款。

N4.2 根据规则 69，须有一人承担向审理小组陈述任何品行不端指控的责任。这个人不得为审理小组的成员，但可以是仲裁委员会的成员。这个人须被要求向违反规则 69 的被指控人充分披露调查过程中自己获得的所有材料。

N4.3 审理前，审理小组在可能的条件下不得充当涉嫌规则 69 指控的调查员角色。但是，在审理过程中，审理小组须有权询问任何其认为适宜的调查性问题。

N4.4 如果小组决定召集审理，所有为了帮助小组做决策而披露给小组的材料必须在审理前同样披露给受指控的当事人。

APPENDIX P SPECIAL PROCEDURES FOR RULE 42

All or part of this appendix applies only if the notice of race or sailing instructions so state.

P1 OBSERVERS AND PROCEDURE

P1.1 The protest committee may appoint observers, including protest committee members, to act in accordance with rule P1.2. A person with a significant *conflict of interest* shall not be appointed as an observer.

P1.2 An observer appointed under rule P1.1 who sees a boat breaking rule 42 may penalize her by, as soon as reasonably possible, making a sound signal, pointing a yellow flag at her and hailing her sail number, even if she is no longer *racing*. A boat so penalized shall not be penalized a second time under rule 42 for the same incident.

P2 PENALTIES

P2.1 First Penalty

When a boat is first penalized under rule P1.2 her penalty shall be a Two-Turns Penalty under rule 44.2. If she fails to take it she shall be disqualified without a hearing.

P2.2 Second Penalty

When a boat is penalized a second time during the event, she shall promptly retire. If she fails to do so she shall be disqualified without a hearing and her score shall not be excluded.

附录 P　规则 42 的特殊程序

只有竞赛通知或航行细则中有此说明时，本附录的全部或部分才适用。

P1　观察员和程序

P1.1 抗议委员会可以任命包括抗议委员会成员在内的人担任观察员，来执行规则 P1. 2 的规定。有显著*利益冲突*的人不得被任命为观察员。

P1.2 根据规则 P1. 1 任命的观察员看到有船违反规则 42 时，可以尽快发出音响信号，用黄旗指向该船并呼喊其帆号来判罚她，即使她已经不再*竞赛*。在同一事件中，已经被如此判罚的船不得再次被判罚。

P2　判罚

P2.1 第一次判罚

当一条船根据规则 P1. 2 第一次被判罚时，对她的惩罚须为符合规则 44. 2 的一个两圈解脱。如果她没有做解脱，无需审理，她须被取消资格。

P2.2 第二次判罚

当一条船在一场赛事中第二次被判罚时，她须迅即退出当轮竞赛。如果她没有这样做，无需审理，她须被取消资格且该分数不得被去掉。

P2.3 Third and Subsequent Penalties

When a boat is penalized a third or subsequent time during the event, she shall promptly retire. If she does so her penalty shall be disqualification without a hearing and her score shall not be excluded. If she fails to do so her penalty shall be disqualification without a hearing from all races in the event, with no score excluded, and the protest committee shall consider calling a hearing under rule 69.2.

P2.4 Penalties Near the Finishing Line

If a boat is penalized under rule P2.2 or P2.3 and it was not reasonably possible for her to retire before *finishing*, she shall be scored as if she had retired promptly.

P3 POSTPONEMENT, GENERAL RECALL OR ABANDONMENT

If a boat has been penalized under rule P1.2 and the race committee signals a *postponement*, general recall or *abandonment*, the penalty is cancelled, but it is still counted to determine the number of times she has been penalized during the event.

P4 REDRESS LIMITATION

A boat shall not be given redress for an action by a member of the protest committee or its designated observer under rule P1.2 unless the action was improper due to a failure to take into account a race committee signal or a class rule.

P5 FLAGS O AND R

P5.1 When Rule P5 Applies

Rule P5 applies if the class rules permit pumping, rocking and ooching when the wind speed exceeds a specified limit.

P2.3 第三次及其后的判罚

当一条船在一场赛事中第三次或更多次被判罚时，她须迅即退出竞赛。如果她这样做了，无需审理，她须被取消资格且该分数不得被去掉。如果她没有这样做，无需审理，对她的惩罚须为取消其在该赛事中所有轮次的资格，分数均不得去掉，而且抗议委员会须考虑根据规则 69. 2 召集审理。

P2.4 靠近终点线处的判罚

如果一条船根据规则 P2. 2 或者 P2. 3 被判罚，且在其*到达终点*之前没有合理的可能来退出竞赛，她须按照她迅即退出了竞赛那样被计分。

P3　推迟、全召或放弃

如果一条船已经根据规则 P1. 2 被判罚，之后竞赛委员会发出*推迟*、全召或*放弃*信号，那么对她的判罚将被取消，但是她在此赛事中被判罚的次数将被累计。

P4　补偿的限制

只有当抗议委员会成员或者其任命的观察员因为没有考虑到竞赛委员会信号或级别规则时，根据规则 P1. 2 做出的错误行动才可以被给予补偿。

P5　O 旗和 R 旗

P5.1 当规则 P5 适用时

如果级别规则在风速超过某一限定值时允许摇帆、摇船和前冲，那么规则 P5 适用。

P5.2 Before the Starting Signal

(a) The race committee may signal that pumping, rocking and ooching are permitted, as specified in the class rules, by displaying flag O before or with the warning signal.

(b) If the wind speed becomes less than the specified limit after flag O has been displayed, the race committee may *postpone* the race. Then, before or with a new warning signal, the committee shall display either flag R, to signal that rule 42 as changed by the class rules applies, or flag O, as provided in rule P5.2(a).

(c) If flag O or flag R is displayed before or with the warning signal, it shall be displayed until the starting signal.

P5.3 After the Starting Signal

After the starting signal,

(a) if the wind speed exceeds the specified limit, the race committee may display flag O with repetitive sounds at a *mark* to signal that pumping, rocking and ooching are permitted, as specified in the class rules, after passing the *mark*;

(b) if flag O has been displayed and the wind speed becomes less than the specified limit, the race committee may display flag R with repetitive sounds at a *mark* to signal that rule 42, as changed by the class rules, applies after passing the *mark*.

P5.2 在起航信号发出前

(a) 竞赛委员会可按级别规则的规定，通过在预告信号之前或与预告信号一起展示 O 旗来发出信号，表明允许摇帆、摇船和前冲。

(b) 如果风速在展示 O 旗后变得比规定的风速限制小，竞赛委员会可以*推迟*竞赛。接下来，在新的预告信号发出前或发出时，竞赛委员会须展示 R 旗表示被级别规则更改的规则 42 适用，或者根据规则 P5. 2 (a)的规定展示 O 旗。

(c) 如果 O 旗或 R 旗在预告信号之前或与预告信号一起展示，它须被一直展示至起航信号发出。

P5.3 在起航信号发出后

在起航信号发出后，

(a) 如果风速超过了规定的限制，竞赛委员会可以在*标志*旁展示 O 旗同时伴随重复音响，表示根据级别规则，船通过该*标志*后可以摇帆、摇船和前冲；

(b) 当 O 旗已经被展示但是风力变得小于规定的限制时，竞赛委员会可以在*标志*旁展示 R 旗同时伴随重复音响，表示船通过该*标志*后，根据级别规则更改的规则 42 适用。

APPENDIX R PROCEDURES FOR APPEALS AND REQUESTS

See rule 70. A national authority may change this appendix by prescription, but it shall not be changed by the notice of race or sailing instructions.

R1 APPEALS AND REQUESTS

Appeals, requests by protest committees for confirmation or correction of their decisions, and requests for interpretations of the *rules* shall be made in compliance with this appendix.

R2 SUBMISSION OF DOCUMENTS

R2.1 To make an appeal,

(a) no later than 15 days after receiving the protest committee's written decision or its decision not to reopen a hearing, the appellant shall send an appeal and a copy of the protest committee's decision to the national authority. The appeal shall state why the appellant believes the protest committee's decision or its procedures were incorrect;

(b) when the hearing required by rule 63.1 has not been held within 30 days after a *protest* or request for redress was delivered, the appellant shall, within a further 15 days, send an appeal with a copy of the *protest* or request and any relevant correspondence. The national authority shall extend the time if there is good reason to do so;

(c) when the protest committee fails to comply with rule 65, the appellant shall, within a reasonable time after the hearing, send an appeal with a copy of the *protest* or request and any relevant correspondence.

附录 R　上诉和申请程序

参见规则 70。国家和地区管理机构可以根据其规定来更改本附录，但是不得根据竞赛通知或航行细则来更改本附录。

R1　上诉和申请

上诉、抗议委员会就其裁决提出的确认或更正的申请，以及要求对*规则*进行解释的申请须按本附录执行。

R2　文件的递交

R2.1 提请一个上诉时：

(a) 在收到抗议委员会书面裁决或其不重新审理的决定之后的 15 日内，申诉人须向国家和地区管理机构递交一份上诉申请和抗议委员会的裁决复印件。该上诉须写明申诉人认为抗议委员会的裁决或其程序不正确的原因；

(b) 如果按照规则 63. 1 要求的审理没有在*抗议*或者要求补偿的申请递交后的 30 日内召集的话，申诉人须在此后的 15 日内，连同*抗议*或者补偿请求以及任何与此有关的文件的复印件一起，递交一份上诉申请。如果理由充分，国家和地区管理机构须延长这个时限；

(c) 当抗议委员会未能遵守规则 65 时，申诉人须在审理后适当的时间内，连同*抗议*或补偿请求以及任何与此有关联的文件的复印件一起，递交一份上诉申请。

If a copy of the *protest* or request is not available, the appellant shall instead send a statement of its substance.

R2.2 The appellant shall also send, with the appeal or as soon as possible thereafter, all of the following documents that are available to her:

(a) the written *protest(s)* or request(s) for redress;

(b) a diagram, prepared or endorsed by the protest committee, showing the positions and tracks of all boats involved, the course to the next *mark* and the required side, the force and direction of the wind, and, if relevant, the depth of water and direction and speed of any current;

(c) the notice of race, the sailing instructions, any other documents governing the event, and any changes to them;

(d) any additional relevant documents; and

(e) the names, postal and email addresses, and telephone numbers of all *parties* to the hearing and the protest committee chairman.

R2.3 A request from a protest committee for confirmation or correction of its decision shall be sent no later than 15 days after the decision and shall include the decision and the documents listed in rule R2.2. A request for an interpretation of the *rules* shall include assumed facts.

R3 RESPONSIBILITIES OF NATIONAL AUTHORITY AND PROTEST COMMITTEE

Upon receipt of an appeal or a request for confirmation or correction, the national authority shall send to the *parties* and protest committee copies of the appeal or request and the protest committee's decision. It shall ask the protest committee for any relevant documents listed in rule R2.2 not sent by the appellant or the protest committee, and the protest committee shall promptly send them to the national authority. When the national authority has received them it shall send copies to the *parties*.

如果无法获得*抗议*或者补偿请求的复印件，申诉人须递交一份相关事实陈述作为替代。

R2.2 申诉人还须在提交上诉时或提交上诉后尽快递交下列其所拥有的材料：

(a) 书面*抗议*或补偿申请；

(b) 由抗议委员会准备或认可的示意图，其展示了所有涉及该事件的船只的位置和轨迹、到下一*标志*的航线和规定的一侧、风力和风向，如果相关的话，还有水深及水流的方向与速度；

(c) 竞赛通知、航行细则、赛事执行的其他文件及对它们的更改；

(d) 任何其他相关的文件；以及

(e) 审理*各方*和抗议委员会主席的姓名、邮政编码、电子邮箱地址和电话号码。

R2.3 来自抗议委员会的对其裁决的确认和更正的请求须在做出裁决后的 15 日内提请，且须包括裁决内容和规则 R2. 2 列出的文件。对*规则*解释的请求须包括假定的事实。

R3 国家和地区管理机构和抗议委员会的责任

当收到上诉或者要求确认或更正的请求时，国家和地区管理机构须向*各方*和抗议委员会发送该上诉或请求以及抗议委员会裁决的复印件。国家和地区管理机构须要求抗议委员会提交规则 R2. 2 列出的申诉人和抗议委员会没有递交的任何相关材料，抗议委员会须迅即向国家和地区管理机构递交这些材料。国家和地区管理机构收到这些材料后须将其复印件发送给*各方*。

R4 COMMENTS AND CLARIFICATIONS

R4.1 The *parties* and protest committee may make comments on the appeal or request or on any of the documents listed in rule R2.2 by sending them in writing to the national authority.

R4.2 The national authority may seek clarifications of *rules* governing the event from organizations that are not *parties* to the hearing.

R4.3 The national authority shall send copies of comments and clarifications received to the *parties* and protest committee as appropriate.

R4.4 Comments on any document shall be made no later than 15 days after receiving it from the national authority.

R5 INADEQUATE FACTS; REOPENING

The national authority shall accept the protest committee's finding of facts except when it decides they are inadequate. In that case it shall require the committee to provide additional facts or other information, or to reopen the hearing and report any new finding of facts, and the committee shall promptly do so.

R6 WITHDRAWING AN APPEAL

An appellant may withdraw an appeal before it is decided by accepting the protest committee's decision.

R4 意见与说明

R4.1 *各方*和抗议委员会可以通过向国家和地区管理机构递交书面报告的形式，对上诉或请求，或规则 R2.2 中列出的任何文件提出意见。

R4.2 国家和地区管理机构可以向不作为审理*各方*的组织机构寻求对赛事执行的*规则*的说明。

R4.3 国家和地区管理机构须视情况向*各方*和抗议委员会发送其收到的意见和说明的复印件。

R4.4 对任何文件的意见须在不晚于收到国家和地区管理机构发出的文件后 15 日内提出。

R5 事实不足；重新审理

国家和地区管理机构须接受抗议委员会认定的事实，除非其认为这些事实不充分。在这种情况下，国家和地区管理机构须要求抗议委员会提交事实补充材料或其他信息，或重新审理并报告任何新认定的事实，抗议委员会须迅即按此执行。

R6 撤销上诉

申诉人可以接受抗议委员会的裁决，在上诉被裁决前将其撤销。

APPENDIX S STANDARD SAILING INSTRUCTIONS

This appendix applies only if the notice of race so states.

These Standard Sailing Instructions may be used at an event in place of printed sailing instructions made available to each boat. To use them, state in the notice of race that 'The sailing instructions will consist of the instructions in RRS Appendix S, Standard Sailing Instructions, and supplementary sailing instructions that will be posted on the official notice board located at ______.'

The supplementary sailing instructions will include:

1. *The location of the race office and of the flag pole on which signals made ashore will be displayed (see SI 4.1 below).*
2. *A table showing the schedule of races, including the day and date of each scheduled day of racing, the number of races scheduled each day, the scheduled time of the first warning signal each day, and the latest time for a warning signal on the last scheduled day of racing (SI 5).*
3. *A list of the marks that will be used and a description of each one (SI 8). How new marks will differ from original marks (SI 10).*
4. *The time limits, if any, that are listed in SI 12.*
5. *Any changes or additions to the instructions in this appendix.*

A copy of the supplementary sailing instructions will be available to competitors on request.

SAILING INSTRUCTIONS

1 RULES

1.1 The event will be governed by the rules as defined in *The Racing Rules of Sailing*.

附录 S　标准航行细则

本附录只有在竞赛通知中有如此说明时才适用。

这些标准航行细则可以在一场赛事中替代纸质版航行细则提供给各参赛船。使用时，在竞赛通知中写明“航行细则将由《帆船竞赛规则》附录 S，标准航行细则中的细则，以及将张贴在位于__________的官方公告栏上的补充的航行细则构成。”

补充的航行细则将包括：

1. *竞赛办公室和展示岸上信号的旗杆的位置(见下述 SI4. 1)。*
2. *一个写明竞赛日程的表格，包括每个排定的竞赛日是哪一天和哪一日(译者注：星期 X)、每个竞赛日排定的竞赛轮数、每个竞赛日第一次预告信号的排定时间，以及排定的最后一个竞赛日发出预告信号的最晚时间(SI 5)。*
3. *将使用的标志的清单以及每个标志的描述(SI 8)。新标志与原标志如何区分(SI 10)。*
4. *若有时间限制，在 SI 12 中列明。*
5. *对本附录中细则的所有更改或添加。*

选手索要时向其提供补充航行细则的复印件。

航行细则

1　规则

1.1 赛事将执行*《帆船竞赛规则》*所定义的规则。

2 NOTICES TO COMPETITORS

2.1 Notices to competitors will be posted on the official notice board.

2.2 Supplementary sailing instructions (called 'the supplement' below) will be posted on the official notice board.

3 CHANGES TO SAILING INSTRUCTIONS

3.1 Any change to the sailing instructions will be posted before 0800 on the day it will take effect, unless this time is changed in the supplement. Any change to the schedule of races will be posted by 2000 on the day before it will take effect.

4 SIGNALS MADE ASHORE

4.1 Signals made ashore will be displayed from the flag pole. The supplement will state its location.

5 SCHEDULE OF RACES

5.1 The supplement will include a table showing the days, dates, number of races scheduled, the scheduled times of the first warning signal each day, and the latest time for a warning signal on the last scheduled day of racing.

5.2 To alert boats that a race or sequence of races will begin soon, the orange starting line flag will be displayed with one sound at least five minutes before a warning signal is made.

6 CLASS FLAGS

6.1 Each class flag will be the class insignia on a plain background or as stated in the supplement.

7 THE COURSES

7.1 No later than the warning signal, the race committee will designate the course, and it may also display the approximate compass bearing of the first leg.

7.2 The course diagrams are on the pages following SI 13. They show the courses, the order in which marks are to be passed, and the side on which each mark is to be left. The supplement may include additional courses.

2 选手通知

2.1 选手通知将张贴于官方公告栏上。

2.2 补充的航行细则（以下简称“补充”）将张贴于官方公告栏上。

3 航行细则更改

3.1 航行细则的任何更改将在生效当天的0800之前公布，除非补充更改了这个时间。对竞赛日程的更改将在其生效的前一天2000之前公布。

4 岸上信号

4.1 岸上信号将在旗杆上展示。补充将注明其位置。

5 竞赛日程

5.1 补充中将包括一个表格，写明天数、日期、排定的竞赛轮数、每个竞赛日第一次预告信号的排定时间，以及排定的最后一个竞赛日预告信号发出的最晚时间。

5.2 为了提示参赛船即将开始一轮竞赛或一系列竞赛，在发出预告信号前至少5分钟，将展示橙色起航线旗并伴随一声音响。

6 级别旗

6.1 每面级别旗将为简单背景上印有级别标志或如补充中所述。

7 航线

7.1 竞赛委员会将不晚于预告信号指明航线，并且可能还会展示第一航段的大致罗经方位。

7.2 航线示意图在后续SI 13的下一页。它们展示了航线、绕标顺序以及离开每个标志的要求一侧。补充可能包括其他航线。

8 MARKS

8.1 A list of the marks that will be used, including a description of each one, will be included in the supplement.

9 THE START

9.1 Races will be started by using RRS 26.

9.2 The starting line will be between a staff displaying an orange flag on the race committee vessel and the course side of the starting mark.

10 CHANGE OF THE NEXT LEG OF THE COURSE

10.1 To change the next leg of the course, the race committee will lay a new mark (or move the finishing line) and remove the original mark as soon as practicable. When in a subsequent change a new mark is replaced, it will be replaced by an original mark.

11 THE FINISH

11.1 The finishing line will be between a staff displaying a blue flag on the race committee vessel and the course side of the finishing mark.

12 TIME LIMITS

12.1 The supplement will state which of the following time limits, if any, will apply and, for each, the time limit.

- Mark 1 Time Limit — Time limit for the first boat to pass Mark 1.
- Race Time Limit — Time limit for the first boat to start, sail the course and finish.
- Finishing Window — Time limit for boats to finish after the first boat starts, sails the course and finishes.

12.2 If no boat has passed Mark 1 within the Mark 1 Time Limit, the race shall be abandoned.

12.3 Boats failing to finish within the Finishing Window shall be scored Did Not Finish without a hearing. This changes RRS 35, A5.1 and A5.2.

8 标志

8.1 补充中将包括要使用的标志清单，包括每个标志的描述。

9 起航

9.1 竞赛将按规则 26 起航。

9.2 起航线为竞赛委员会船上展示橙色旗的旗杆与起航标志航线一侧之间的连线。

10 航线下一航段的改变

10.1 如果改变航线的下一航段，竞赛委员会将布设新的标志（或移动终点线）并尽快地移走原标志。在连续的改变中要替换新标志时，将由原标志替代。

11 终点

11.1 终点线为竞赛委员会船上展示蓝色旗的旗杆与终点标志航线一侧之间的连线。

12 时间限制

12.1 补充将说明以下哪个时间限制适用，如果适用，列出每个时间限制。

• 1 标时限	第一条船通过 1 标的时间限制。
• 竞赛时限	第一条船起航、行驶航线并到达终点的时间限制。
• 终点封闭时间	第一条船起航、行驶航线并到达终点后其他船到达终点的时间限制。

12.2 若在 1 标时限内没有船通过 1 标，则该轮竞赛须被放弃。

12.3 没有在封闭时间内到达终点的船须被记为 DNF 而无需审理。此条更改规则 35、A5. 1 和 A5. 2。

13 PROTESTS AND REQUESTS FOR REDRESS

13.1 Hearing request forms are available at the race office. Protests and requests for redress or reopening shall be delivered there within the appropriate time limit.

13.2 For each class, the protest time limit is 60 minutes after the last boat has finished the last race of the day or the race committee signals no more racing today, whichever is later.

13.3 Notices will be posted no later than 30 minutes after the protest time limit to inform competitors of hearings in which they are parties or named as witnesses and where the hearings will be held.

13.4 Notices of protests by the race committee, technical committee or protest committee will be posted to inform boats under RRS 61.1(b).

COURSE DIAGRAMS

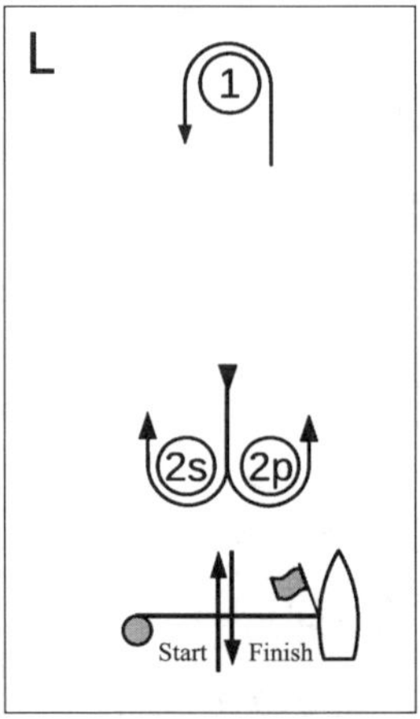

Course L – Windward/Leeward, Leeward Finish	
Signal	*Mark Rounding Order*
L2	Start – 1 – 2s/2p – 1 – Finish
L3	Start – 1 – 2s/2p – 1 – 2s/2p – 1 – Finish
L4	Start – 1 – 2s/2p – 1 – 2s/2p – 1 – 2s/2p – 1 – Finish

13　抗议和补偿要求

13.1 审理申请表可在竞赛办公室领取。抗议表、要求补偿表或重新审理表须在适当时限内递交至竞赛办公室。

13.2 抗议时限为各级别最后一条船在当天最后一轮竞赛达到终点后或竞赛委员会发出今天再没有竞赛的信号后 60 分钟内，以这两个时刻中较晚的那个为准。

13.3 将于抗议时限结束后不晚于 30 分钟张贴通知以告知审理各方或被点名的证人以及审理的地点。

13.4 竞赛委员会、技术委员会或抗议委员会根据规则 61. 1（b）提出的抗议通知将被张贴以通知相关各船。

航线示意图

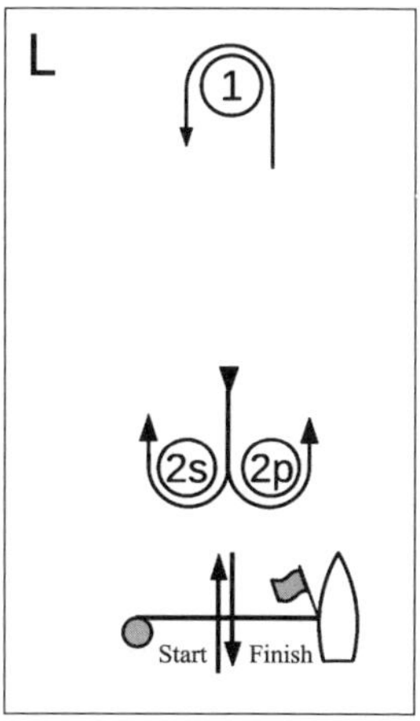

L 航线——迎尾风航线，顺风冲终点	
信号	*绕标顺序*
L2	起点 - 1 - 2s/2p - 1 - 终点
L3	起点 - 1 - 2s/2p - 1 - 2s/2p - 1- 终点
L4	起点 - 1 - 2s/2p - 1 - 2s/2p - 1 - 2s/2p - 1 - 终点

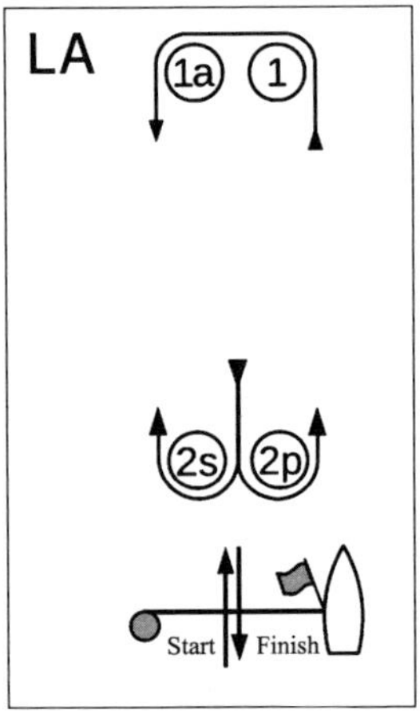

Course LA – Windward/Leeward with Offset Mark, Leeward Finish	
Signal	*Mark Rounding Order*
LA2	Start – 1 – 1a – 2s/2p – 1 – 1a – Finish
LA3	Start – 1 – 1a – 2s/2p – 1 – 1a – 2s/2p – 1 – 1a – Finish
LA4	Start – 1 – 1a – 2s/2p – 1 – 1a – 2s/2p – 1 – 1a – 2s/2p – 1 – 1a – Finish

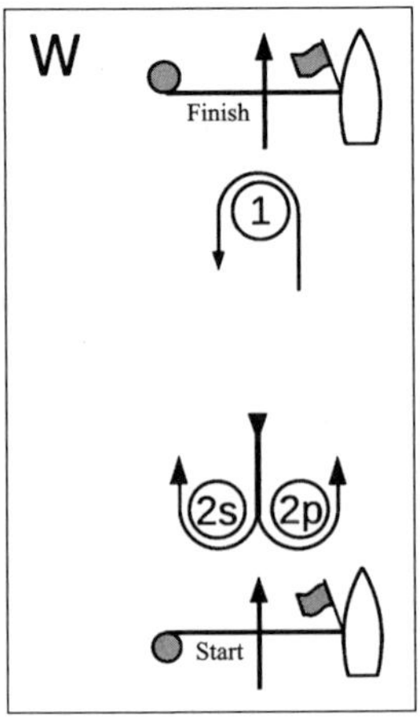

Course W – Windward/Leeward, Windward Finish	
Signal	*Mark Rounding Order*
W2	Start – 1 – 2s/2p – Finish
W3	Start – 1 – 2s/2p – 1 – 2s/2p – Finish
W4	Start – 1 – 2s/2p – 1 – 2s/2p – 1 – 2s/2p – Finish

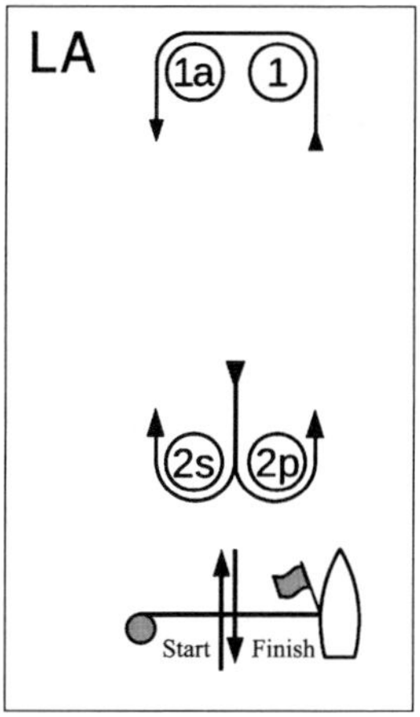

LA 航线——有外设标的迎尾风航线，顺风冲终点	
信号	*绕标顺序*
LA2	起点 - 1 - 1a - 2s/2p - 1 - 1a - 终点
LA3	起点 - 1 - 1a - 2s/2p - 1 - 1a - 2s/2p - 1 - 1a - 终点
LA4	起点 - 1 - 1a - 2s/2p - 1 - 1a - 2s/2p - 1 - 1a - 2s/2p - 1 - 1a - 终点

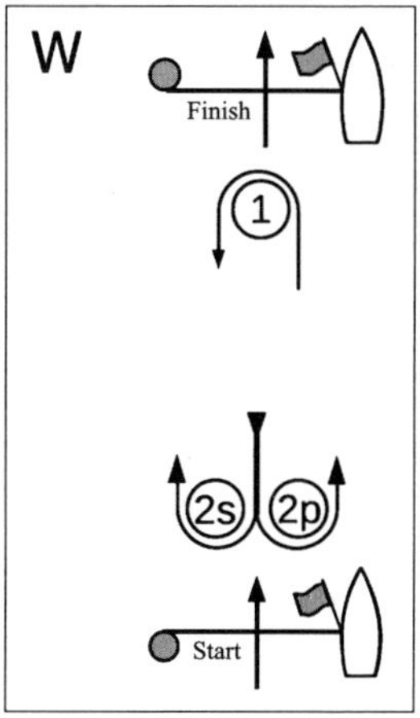

W 航线——迎尾风航线，迎风冲终点	
信号	*绕标顺序*
W2	起点 - 1 - 2s/2p - 终点
W3	起点 - 1 - 2s/2p - 1 - 2s/2p - 终点
W4	起点 - 1 - 2s/2p - 1 - 2s/2p - 1 - 2s/2p - 终点

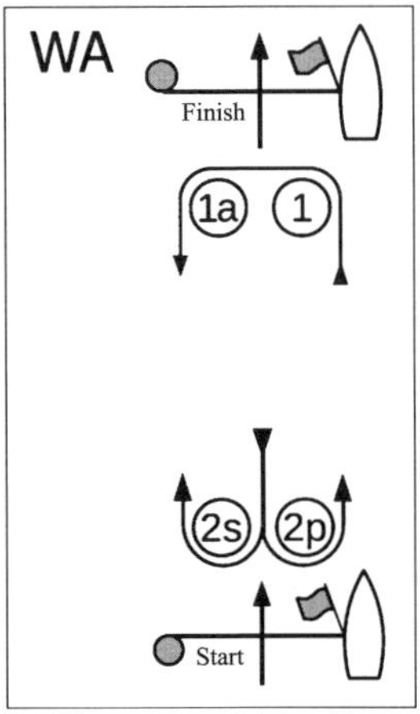

Course WA – Windward/Leeward with Offset Mark, Windward Finish	
Signal	*Mark Rounding Order*
WA2	Start – 1 – 1a – 2s/2p – Finish
WA3	Start – 1 – 1a – 2s/2p – 1 – 1a – 2s/2p – Finish
WA4	Start – 1 – 1a – 2s/2p – 1 – 1a – 2s/2p – 1 – 1a – 2s/2p – Finish

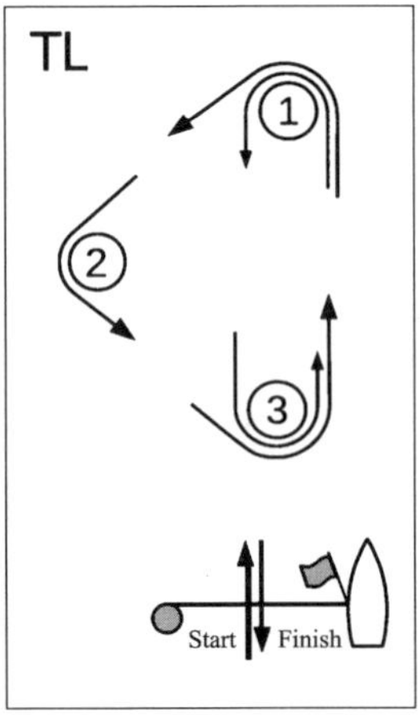

Course TL – Triangle, Leeward Finish	
Signal	*Mark Rounding Order*
TL2	Start – 1 – 2 – 3 – 1 – Finish
TL3	Start – 1 – 2 – 3 – 1 – 3 – 1 – Finish
TL4	Start – 1 – 2 – 3 – 1 – 3 – 1 – 3 – 1 – Finish

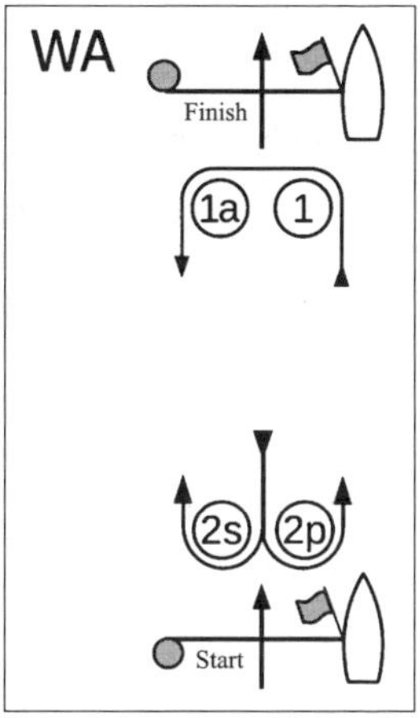

WA 航线——有外设标的迎尾风航线，迎风冲终点	
信号	绕标顺序
WA2	起点 - 1 - 1a-2s/2p - 终点
WA3	起点 - 1 - 1a - 2s/2p - 1 - 1a-2s/2p - 终点
WA4	起点 - 1 - 1a - 2s/2p - 1 - 1a - 2s/2p - 1 - 1a - 2s/2p - 终点

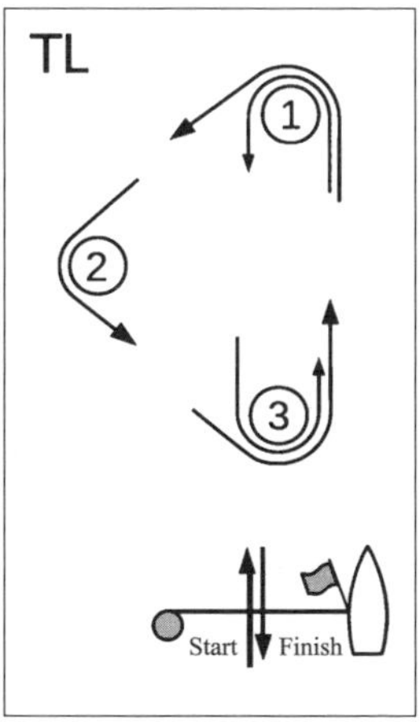

TL 航线——三角形航线，顺风冲终点	
信号	绕标顺序
TL2	起点 - 1 - 2 - 3 - 1 - 终点
TL3	起点 - 1 - 2 - 3 - 1 - 3 - 1 - 终点
TL4	起点 - 1 - 2 - 3 - 1 - 3 - 1 - 3 - 1 - 终点

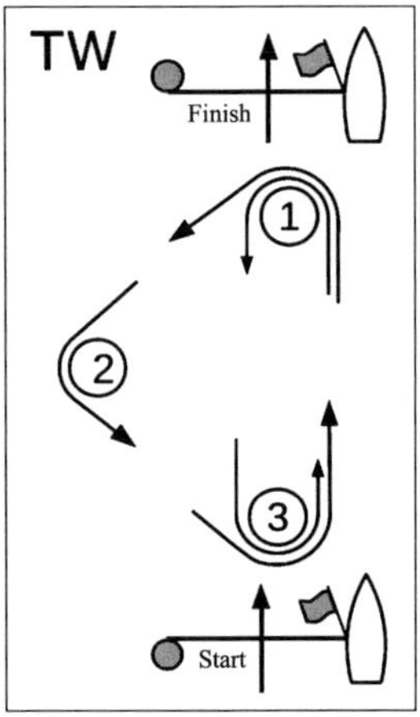

Course TW – Triangle, Windward Finish	
Signal	*Mark Rounding Order*
TW2	Start – 1 – 2 – 3 – Finish
TW3	Start – 1 – 2 – 3 – 1 – 3 – Finish
TW4	Start – 1 – 2 – 3 – 1 – 3 – 1 – 3 – Finish

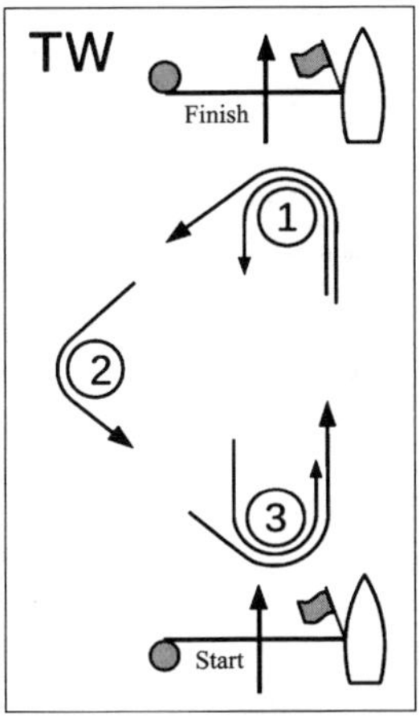

TW 航线——三角形航线，迎风冲终点	
信号	*绕标顺序*
TW2	起点 -1-2-3- 终点
TW3	起点 -1-2-3-1-3- 终点
TW4	起点 -1-2-3-1-3-1-3- 终点

APPENDIX T ARBITRATION

This appendix applies only if the notice of race or sailing instructions so state.

Arbitration adds an extra step to the protest resolution process but can eliminate the need for some protest hearings, thus speeding up the process for events in which many protests are expected. Arbitration may not be appropriate for all events as it requires an additional knowledgeable person to act as the arbitrator. Further guidance on arbitration can be found in the World Sailing Judges Manual, *which can be downloaded from the World Sailing website.*

T1 POST-RACE PENALTIES

(a) Provided that rule 44.1(b) does not apply, a boat that may have broken one or more rules of Part 2 or rule 31 in an incident may take a Post-Race Penalty at any time after the race until the beginning of a protest hearing involving the incident.

(b) A Post-Race Penalty is a 30% Scoring Penalty calculated as stated in rule 44.3(c). However, rule 44.1(a) applies.

(c) A boat takes a Post-Race Penalty by delivering to the arbitrator or a member of the protest committee a written statement that she accepts the penalty and that identifies the race number and where and when the incident occurred.

附录 T　仲裁调解

只有在竞赛通知或航行细则中有如此说明时，本附录才适用。仲裁调解给抗议决策过程添加了额外步骤，但是能够减少一些抗议审理的必要，因此加速了预期会有很多抗议的赛事的进程。仲裁调解可能不适合所有赛事，因为其需要一个额外的具有相关知识的人担任调解仲裁一职。可以从世界帆联网站上下载《世界帆联仲裁手册》来进一步了解仲裁调解指南。

T1　赛后惩罚

（a）如果规则 44.1（b）不适用，一条在一次事件中违反了一条或多条第二章规则或规则 31 的船，直至涉及该事件的抗议审理开始前，可以在赛后的任一时间接受赛后惩罚。

（b）赛后惩罚是根据规则 44.3（c）的规定计算的 30% 的分数惩罚。但是，规则 44.1（a）适用。

（c）接受赛后惩罚的船要通过向调解仲裁或一名抗议委员会成员递交一份书面声明来表明她接受了惩罚，并确认轮次和事件发生的时间与地点。

T2 ARBITRATION MEETING

An arbitration meeting will be held prior to a protest hearing for each incident resulting in a *protest* by a boat involving one or more rules of Part 2 or rule 31, but only if each *party* is represented by a person who was on board at the time of the incident. No witnesses will be permitted. However, if the arbitrator decides that rule 44.1(b) may apply or that arbitration is not appropriate, the meeting will not be held, and if a meeting is in progress, it will be closed.

T3 ARBITRATOR'S OPINION

Based on the evidence given by the representatives, the arbitrator will offer an opinion as to what the protest committee is likely to decide:

(a) the *protest* is invalid,

(b) no boat will be penalized for breaking a *rule*, or

(c) one or more boats will be penalized for breaking a *rule*, identifying the boats and the penalties.

T4 ARBITRATION MEETING OUTCOMES

After the arbitrator offers an opinion,

(a) a boat may take a Post-Race Penalty, and

(b) a boat may ask to withdraw her *protest*. The arbitrator may then act on behalf of the protest committee in accordance with rule 63.1 to allow the withdrawal.

Unless all *protests* involving the incident are withdrawn, a protest hearing will be held.

T2　调解仲裁会议

每一个涉及一条船因违反一条或多条第二章规则或规则 31 而导致*抗议*的事件，将在抗议审理前召开仲裁调解会议，但前提是*各方*的代表在事件发生时都在船上。不允许有证人。但是，如果调解仲裁认定规则 44.1（b）可能适用或仲裁调解不适用，将不会进行会议，如果会议正在进行中，则将关停此会议。

T3　调解仲裁的意见

根据代表们提供的证据，调解仲裁将就抗议委员会可能做出的裁决提出意见：

（a）*抗议*无效，

（b）没有船因违反*规则*而被判罚，或

（c）一条或多条船将因违反*规则*而被判罚，确定被判罚的船和惩罚。

T4　调解仲裁会议的结果

在调解仲裁提出意见后，

（a）一条船可能受到赛后惩罚，以及

（b）一条船可能要求撤销*抗议*。之后调解仲裁可以根据规则 63.1 采取行动，允许其撤回。

除非涉及该事件的所有*抗议*都撤销，否则将举行抗议审理。

图书在版编目（CIP）数据

2021—2024帆船竞赛规则：汉英对照 / 世界帆船运动联合会编著. —青岛：中国海洋大学出版社，2020.11（2022.7重印）

书名原文：Racing Rules of Sailing：2021-2024

ISBN 978-7-5670-2662-9

Ⅰ. ①2…　Ⅱ. ①世…　Ⅲ. ①帆船运动—竞赛规则—世界—2021—2024—汉、英　Ⅳ. ①G861.44

中国版本图书馆CIP数据核字（2020）第230724号

出版发行	中国海洋大学出版社		
社　　址	青岛市香港东路23号	**邮政编码**	266071
网　　址	http://pub.ouc.edu.cn		
出 版 人	杨立敏		
责任编辑	矫恒鹏	**电　　话**	0532-85902349
电子信箱	2586345806@qq.com		
印　　制	青岛海蓝印刷有限责任公司		
版　　次	2021年1月第1版		
印　　次	2022年7月第3次印刷		
成品尺寸	140 mm × 210 mm		
印　　张	11.25		
字　　数	244千		
印　　数	2801 ~ 4300		
定　　价	98.00元		
订购电话	0532-82032573（传真）		

发现印装质量问题，请致电0532-88786655，由印刷厂负责调换。